Cuba:

Castroism and Communism,

1959-1966

CENTER FOR INTERNATIONAL STUDIES
MASSACHUSETTS INSTITUTE OF TECHNOLOGY

Studies in International Communism

Cuba:
Castroism and Communism, 1959-1966

Andrés Suárez

with a foreword by Ernst Halperin

translated by Joel Carmichael and Ernst Halperin

THE M.I.T. PRESS

Massachusetts Institute of Technology
Cambridge, Massachusetts, and London, England

PREFATORY NOTE

Books on Castro's Cuba have too often shed more heat than light. The Center for International Studies is therefore the more pleased to sponsor this scholarly study by Dr. Andrés Suárez of the University of Florida. Delays in translation and editing — for which Dr. Suárez was in no way responsible — have postponed its publication longer than we would have wished, but they have also given the author an opportunity to analyze more recent developments as well. I should like to record my gratitude to my colleague, Dr. Ernst Halperin, and to my research assistant, Dr. Robin A. Remington, for the great time and effort they have given to editing the study. Its publication has been made possible by The Ford Foundation's generous grant to M.I.T. for research and teaching in international affairs.

Munich, Germany
April 19, 1967

WILLIAM E. GRIFFITH
Director,
International Communism Project

FOREWORD

Was the Cuban revolution unique? Was it the result of special circumstances that will not recur elsewhere? And if this is not the case, what measures are required to prevent, or on the other hand to ensure, its repetition? Today these questions are being debated assiduously by Communists and non-Communists alike.[1]

In order to answer them, one must of course first settle the underlying historical problem: How and why did the Cuban revolution become Communist? It is my belief that Dr. Andrés Suárez' study of the relations between Fidel Castro and the Communists provides the correct and definitive answer to this question.

Dr. Suárez is not the first to point out that the old, established Communist party, the PSP (Partido Socialista Popular), played only a minor role in the Cuban revolution. But he is the first to document this so thoroughly and extensively. His documentation shows that all the measures that were decisive in transforming Cuba's capitalist, free-enterprise system into a Communist command economy — agrarian reform, urban reform, nationalization of foreign and domestic enterprises — were taken without consulting or even informing the PSP; that in each case the PSP leadership was caught by surprise and hurriedly had to adjust its policy to the new situation. If the PSP played any role in these events it was that of attempting — most ineffectively, it is true — to slow down the revolution. And even in the brief period from July 1961 to March 1962, when the PSP leaders were entrusted with the task of organizing a ruling party in order to adapt the regime to the pattern of the Soviet camp countries, they were mere instruments to be pushed aside as soon as they were no longer needed.

[1] For a Communist treatment of the problem see the important article by J. M. Fortuny, "Has the Revolution Become More Difficult in Latin America?" in *World Marxist Review*, Vol. 8, No. 8 (August 1965); also Régis Debray, "América Latina: algunos problemas de estrategia revolucionaria," *Casa de las Américas* (Havana), July–August 1965.

What, then, was the driving force of the revolution? Was the communization of Cuba the result of powerful pressures from below, of forces that had been unleashed in the struggle against Batista and were now to strong to be contained? Dr. Suárez denies this. He points to what he aptly calls the "administrative character" of the Cuban revolution: The decisive measures were invariably decreed from above, with little or no preparation or warning and no indication of popular pressure. Castro's own supporters were caught unawares; and although they happily applauded them, they did so as mere followers not as revolutionaries who had demanded the measures and brought them about.

These findings run counter to the modern sociological interpretation of history, according to which the course of events is determined not by the decisions of individuals but by the clash of powerful social forces. This theory, which is espoused by Marxists and non-Marxists alike, appears to me to be dubious even when applied to the French and Russian revolutions, in which "the masses" undoubtedly took an active part. It is inapplicable to Cuba. There is not a shred of evidence that Fidel Castro's march to communism was impelled by pressure from below. Such uncontrolled, spontaneous demonstrations as have occurred in the course of Cuba's transformation to communism were invariably "counter-revolutionary," that is, they were protests against the radical policies of the revolutionary government. No such uncontrolled demonstrations, meetings, or even committee resolutions in favor of further, more drastic, revolutionary measures have been reported at any stage of the transformation.[2]

One man alone, Fidel Castro, is responsible for the course of events in Cuba. Dr. Suárez does not hide his dislike of Castro. One may disagree with some of his opinions (such as his statement that Castro is a "consummate opportunist"), but one is never tempted to place his book in the familiar category of polemical *émigré*

[2] One exponent of the theory that the Cuban leaders were instruments of the "revolutionary will of the masses" is Adolfo Gilly. In his book *Inside the Cuban Revolution* (New York: Monthly Review Press, 1964), Gilly explained the pro-Chinese trend of the Cuban revolution in 1963 and 1964 as being determined by these "revolutionary masses" and claimed that because of this the leadership could not turn against China even if it wanted to do so. Since then, the man who implemented the pro-Chinese line in Cuba, "Che" Guevara, has quietly disappeared, his policies have been reversed, and Castro has savagely attacked Peking without eliciting the slightest protest from the "revolutionary masses."

literature. He does not portray Castro as a fool, a coward, a traitor, or a Soviet stooge, as so many *émigré* writers have done. The sheer political genius of the man comes out very clearly in Suárez' account.

Castro is not, of course, a constructive genius; otherwise the Cuban economy would not be the shambles that it is today. Nor is he a genius at strategic planning. Castro's basic assumption, the assessment of the world situation that caused him to join the Soviet camp, has turned out to be completely wrong. His genius is that of an inspired tactician. Through sheer skill he has managed both to give his small and economically bankrupt country a political importance out of all proportion to its size and to maintain a remarkable freedom of maneuver in spite of his complete military and economic dependence on the Soviet Union.

Dr. Suárez sees Castro as possessed by a love of power so total that he is averse to delegating any part of it to even the most loyal subordinate. Suárez substantiates this by pointing to what he terms Castro's "allergy to organization." To establish any permanent form of organization would mean that he would have to delegate power to others, thus diminishing his own. That is why the situation in Cuba is still so fluid and the process of institutionalization so slow. Castro is constantly shifting the apparent basis of his power: from army to militia to defense committees to party to army. And even in the army, an organization that has been forced upon him by pressures from abroad, he incessantly shifts the men who are at the levers of command. Meanwhile his one real power base, his charismatic faculty for inspiring devotion, remains unchanged and impervious to all the organizational transformations.

Although highly critical of Washington's Cuban policy, or rather the lack of such a policy, Dr. Suárez does not share the opinion that Castro was unwillingly pushed into the Soviet camp by American blunders or malevolence. He regards Castro's aversion to organization and institutionalization, which is so clearly manifested in his subsequent policies, as the reason for his failure to restore democracy after he came to power on January 1, 1959. Castro could easily have had himself elected the constitutional President of Cuba, but in that case he would have had to respect institutions, to delegate and share power. Instead, he chose to carry the revolution further, internally by a drastic agrarian reform, externally by promoting the expedition to Santo Domingo that landed and was defeated on June 14, 1959. His decision led to serious tension with the United States, a development that in turn caused the Soviet Union to take an interest in Cuba.

To Castro, Soviet support opened the perspective of spreading the revolution to the Latin American mainland and becoming a new Bolívar, the leader of a continental liberation struggle against American imperialism while under the protection of the Soviet nuclear umbrella. Immediately after Khrushchev had made his first "figurative" promise of nuclear protection, Castro called upon the peoples of Latin America to follow the Cuban example by making the Andes mountain range into the Sierra Maestra of the entire continent.[3]

As long as Castro remained a mere "national democratic" ally he could not, however, be reasonably sure of Soviet support. He therefore resolved to force his way into the Soviet bloc by obtaining recognition of Cuba as a member of the "socialist camp." The Soviets hesitated to permit this; they would have preferred to let him remain an expendable ally. This reluctance was faithfully reflected in the PSP's persistent though ineffective efforts to slow down the revolution.

By the time Castro obtained membership in the "socialist camp" the missile crisis had shown that his whole foreign policy was based on a serious underestimation of American and overestimation of Soviet strength. But at that stage it was already far too late for him to turn back. Going beyond Suárez, I would add that the bombing of North Vietnam makes the protection afforded by membership in the "socialist camp" even more dubious: hence Castro's repeated call for a more massive Soviet military engagement in that country.[4]

The sequence of events clearly shows that foreign policy considerations determined Castro's conversion to communism and the transformation of Cuba into a Communist state. To have demonstrated this is Dr. Suárez' most important achievement. He thus provides the answer to the question of how and why Cuba became Communist: not because of pressures from the people, nor because of the machinations of the old-guard Communists of the PSP, nor

[3] In his speech of July 26, 1960.

[4] See, for instance, Castro's government statement on the quarrel with Peking on February 6, 1966, the speech by the Cuban guest delegate Armando Hart at the Twenty-Third Congress of the CPSU on March 31, 1966, and Castro's speech of July 26, 1966.

because of any infatuation with Marxism-Leninism on Castro's part but because of Soviet nuclear power.

Thus this study also enables us to answer a further question: Yes, the Cuban experience can be repeated elsewhere in Latin America; but only if the Soviet Union recovers from the setback of the missile crisis and again appears able and willing to challenge U.S. hegemony in the Western Hemisphere. In that case a new Castro might well arise—and this time perhaps not on a Caribbean island but in a mainland country stronger and less vulnerable to invasion or blockade. The new Castro need not be a Communist—Fidel himself did not start out as a Communist—but possibly a demagogic dictator of the type of Perón, or even a constitutionally elected president.

The pro-United States sentiment of the Latin American armies is usually regarded as a safeguard against such a development. But since military men respect military power, their pro-American feelings might rapidly evaporate if the United States showed itself weak and unwilling to face a Soviet challenge. It was the appearance of U.S. weakness which led to the upsurge of Castroite and pro-Soviet trends that swept Latin America in the years preceding the missile crisis. It did not take American military intervention in Cuba to make the tide recede; what happened was simply that an American President addressed himself directly to the real author of the threat, whose seat was in Moscow and not in Havana, or, for that matter, in Guatemala City or Santo Domingo.

Dr. Suárez' study also has something to say to those whose interests lie in a more theoretical field of political science. Castro's regime is indubitably totalitarian. Rigidly centralized, all-encompassing organization is usually regarded as the essence of totalitarianism. How, then, can one account for Castro's "allergy to organization," his habit of shifting his organizational base, his extreme reluctance to allow the institutionalization of the revolution?

Castro's example shows that organizational forms are of secondary importance in totalitarian regimes. These regimes really depend on the ability of the leader to inspire blind devotion in a large enough number of followers to control the country—10 per cent or even 5 per cent of the population may suffice. Goerdeler was not captured by the Gestapo but by a simple *Luftwaffenhelferin*. "The Secret Police themselves are pretty inefficient," a Yugoslav once told me during his country's grim Stalinist period after the war. "It is only through their thousands of unpaid voluntary helpers that they are so dangerous."

Institutionalization is a threat to totalitarian rule because it means delegation of power and hence the creation of separate power centers. Stalin, an organization man par excellence, left the organizational machine intact and sought a solution by wiping out and replacing its entire personnel in the Great Purge of the 1930's. From then on he maintained control by balancing the various organizations against each other, never allowing one to become too strong. But already in 1949 he instituted a new, minor purge, and at the time of his fortunate demise, in 1953, he was preparing another, all-encompassing one. And now Mao Tse-tung is combating the institutionalization of the Chinese revolution by means of the Red Guards, who are sacking party offices from one end of his realm to the other.

Castro, the dictator of a mere Caribbean island, has nothing to learn from these two Red emperors. In the art of maintaining totalitarian control he is a master in his own right.

Cambridge, Massachusetts   ERNST HALPERIN
September 1966

PREFACE

The research project for this book was finished in May 1963. Seven chapters were written in 1964; the last two in 1965 and 1966, respectively; the Epilogue was written when the book was already in the galley proof stage. It will be useful to keep those dates in mind, because, although the manuscript has undergone a final revision, its thesis has not changed. This implies that in a few cases the circumstances that existed at the time of writing may have altered, but the analysis of Castroism and its meaning for Cuba and for Cubans has not.

The book is based on some assumptions arising out of my experiences in Cuba and constant reflection about it. The assumptions can be summarized briefly. First, I was never able to verify the close correlation pointed out by some observers between the strains of Cuba's socioeconomic structure and popular rebelliousness. On the contrary, even under the miserable conditions of 1932 and 1933, the most widespread attitude among the people was the rejection of any rebel action that could bring repressive measures down upon them. Only after the machinery of the state had lost its effectiveness did a revolutionary wave arise. But even that wave had a short life span. Furthermore, during that brief interval, habits inherited from the traditional political culture made the revolutionary masses extraordinarily unamenable to measures that might have proved useful for alleviating their obvious distresses.

Only at times of social disorganization, when the army and the police had disappeared from the streets leaving the field to the masses, did the question of the social structure — or the lack of it — arise. It remains to be proved that there were, strictly speaking, classes, pressure groups, or relevant differences of political behavior between the rural and the urban sectors of the population in Cuba. But there is no doubt that the success of the revolution wiped out whatever elements might have existed in any measure of such social structure. The inevitable consequence was a situation in which there existed only the masses and the revolutionary leaders, giving the leaders a maximum degree of maneuverability.

It is naïve to assume that the success of these leaders was entirely the result of their identification with the aspirations of the people: first, because the masses were confused, and second, because the qualities of the leaders would not support such an assumption. Our revolutions were always led by insignificant minorities. These minorities had no major ideological motivations; furthermore, the political situation was such that they were under the constant threat of torture and death, and they were forced into terrorism, armed fight, or military conspiracy. Under such conditions, the few pure souls (present in every revolution) who were genuinely concerned with the people rarely survived. But even if they did, their accession to positions of leadership after victory was highly improbable — first, because of the confusion and backwardness of the masses and second, because their own revolutionary ardor was apt to be as evanescent as it was exalted; in a very short time they would consume their energies and revert again to their usual passivity.

It was starting from these assumptions, as I have said, that this book was undertaken. Therefore, the analysis and description of the sociological milieu has been reduced to the strictly necessary, while major emphasis is placed on the events, both external and internal, of the development of the revolution. The Fidel Castro visible in the following pages is not only the virtuous leader dedicated to easing the sufferings of the humble but the survivor of many years of relentless struggle—the skillful operator who unyieldingly defends the decisive political power that he won in the first months of 1959. Finally, since this book is not intended in any way to be a history of the Cuban revolution (its objectives are more limited and they are clearly set forth in the title), I hope I shall not be reproached for, among other things, failing to acknowledge the accomplishments of the Castro regime. According to the majority of observers, these accomplishments are centered on education, public health, racial relations, and national sovereignty—if national sovereignty is identified with the will of Fidel Castro.

I want to express here my deep gratitude to the many generous people who helped in the preparation of this book. Dr. William E. Griffith proposed the research topic and, at Mr. Theodore Draper's suggestion, entrusted the work to me. His encouragement was invaluable when delays in the publication increased my anxieties. There are several reasons for my gratitude to Dr. Ernst Halperin.

Lengthy conversations with him were priceless for the clarification of many points. Moreover, he helped to translate the manuscript, did a prodigious amount of editing, and contributed a Foreword that I deeply appreciate. Dr. Robin A. Remington, who also edited extensively, not only displayed an inexhaustible patience but has shown a workmanship that deserves my deepest thanks. Of course, the shortcomings are all mine. The manuscript was typed by Lila T. Fernandez.

I am also grateful to Mrs. Rose Spitz, Professor David A. Dudley, and Dr. Justo Carrillo, all of whom helped in some way to make this book feasible. The debt to my wife Hortensia and to my children, Teresita and Carlos Andrés, cannot be expressed in mere words. It can only be guessed at, knowing that the first chapters of this book were written in the kitchen of our tiny apartment in Miami. The very different surroundings at the University of Florida have not diminished at all our gratitude for that precious assistance or our full devotion to Cuba.

Gainesville, Florida   ANDRÉS SUÁREZ
April 1967

CONTENTS

Cuba:
Castroism and Communism,
1959-1966

CHAPTER ONE

FIDEL CASTRO AND THE CUBAN COMMUNIST PARTY (UP TO THE VICTORY OF JANUARY 1959)

The Cuban Communist Party

The Cuban section of the Third International (Partido Comunista de Cuba — PCC) was founded on August 16, 1925, three months after President Machado took office, by delegates of various Cuban Communist groups and with the participation of a delegate of the Mexican Communist Party, Enrique Flores Magón.[1] Only two of the founders require comment: Carlos Baliño, who was of some importance both because of his participation in the Cuban Revolutionary Party organized by José Martí in 1892 to undertake the War of Independence (1895–1898) and because of his role in the social struggles of the republic that was instituted on May 20, 1902; and Julio Antonio Mella, an exceptionally gifted and influential student leader.

Because it had no legal standing, the party was soon subjected to police action. Its first secretary-general, José Miguel Pérez, was arrested and deported. Mella, who was also imprisoned and forced to leave Cuba, went to Mexico, where he was assassinated in 1929. Baliño died in 1926. These losses created a highly critical situation[2] for the PCC; but it gained new strength and prestige when in 1927 Rubén Martínez Villena, the most attractive personality in the new generation of intellectuals, joined the party ranks.

1 See Jacques Arnault, *Cuba et le marxisme* (Paris: Editions Sociales, 1962), p. 34, for what appears to be part of the act of constitution of the PCC.

2 For the early years of the PCC see Fabio Grobart (probably one of the party's founders), "Recuerdos sobre Rubén" [Memories of Rubén], *Hoy*, January 16, 1964, and Nicolás Guillén, "Recuerdos de Joaquín Ordoqui" [Memories of Joaquín Ordoqui], *ibid.*, August 14, 1960. According to Ordoqui, who joined the party in 1927, in that year "the whole party, including officials and ordinary members, could fit in one room."

In 1928 President Machado, after violating the constitution by extending the presidential term to six years, had himself re-elected in an uncontested election, thereby arousing the first stirrings of resistance among the students. Soon after this the Great Depression began to make itself felt: The living standard of the Cuban masses sank to a level of poverty unprecedented in the republican era. These factors created a climate favorable to the Communists, who obtained control of the clandestine Cuban National Confederation of Workers (Confederación Nacional Obrera de Cuba — CNOC), expanded and strengthened the party's organization, and, above all, succeeded in creating a determined and dedicated leadership, for the most part made up of young intellectuals.[3]

The struggle against Machado reached its peak in August 1933. Early in the month a transport strike rapidly turned into a general strike and took on a political character. The party leadership, headed by Martínez Villena, advised the workers not to join the other, "bourgeois" opposition groups in insisting that the strike go on until the dictatorship was overthrown; and Martínez Villena also urged that the workers return to work as soon as Machado promised to satisfy their economic demands. The workers disregarded this advice, the strike went on, and on August 11, with the encouragement of the U.S. ambassador, a military uprising took place that forced the President to flee the following day.

The action of the Communist party leadership was attacked as a betrayal by the other revolutionary organizations, but the general situation at the time prevented this accusation from having its full effect. The fall of the Machado regime started the collapse of the whole governmental structure, which became total on September 4 when the so-called "Sergeants' Revolt" of noncommissioned officers and soldiers deposed both the army officers and the new government, replacing the latter first with a revolutionary junta and then, on September 10, with the presidency of Ramón Grau San Martín.

All this created an ideal atmosphere for Communist activity. Party membership rose to 6,000;[4] the party gained legal recognition

---

[3] In 1935 a Foreign Policy Association report on Cuba gave this evaluation of the PCC leadership: "The Party, generally speaking, has had the good fortune to have, in many cases, leaders who are intelligent, dynamic, and honest." (See Foreign Policy Association, *Problema de la nueva Cuba* [New York, 1935], p. 217).

[4] Concerning the growth and influence of Cuban communism in late 1933 and early 1934 see *ibid.*, pp. 200–219. On p. 215 of this work the PCC is said to have had 6,000 members in April 1934.

for the National Confereration of Workers, and, taking advantage of the discontent among the workers, launched a wave of strikes and occupied many work sites, including thirty-six sugar mills, in some of which it even set up "soviets," revolutionary workers' councils. Apparently these accomplishments were not enough to satisfy the Executive Committee of the Comintern. While Martínez Villena was dying of tuberculosis in January 1934, the Comintern sent representatives to Cuba to carry out a purge. The party was "Stalinized." Francisco Calderío, a self-educated cobbler known by the name of Blas Roca, replaced Martínez Villena, the sophisticated author of the poem "La Pupila Insomne" (The Sleepless Eye); and the group of young intellectuals drawn into the party by the noble enterprise of redeeming the humble, captivated by the apparent logic of Marxist ideology, and seduced by the fascinating personality of Villena, was eliminated from the Central Committee, and in the end left the party altogether.[5]

In 1935 Blas Roca attended the Seventh Congress of the Third International, at which the new popular front policy was approved. The Cuban Communist Party accordingly began to abandon its extremism and to adopt an increasingly moderate position in order to create the popular front alliance recommended by the Congress.

The attempt failed. A military leader, Fulgencio Batista, had come up out of the "Sergeants' Revolt" of September 4, 1933 and by January 15 of the following year had become sufficiently powerful to replace Grau with Carlos Mendieta; and from this time until 1940 Batista, as head of the army, was strong enough to appoint and dismiss presidents. The democratic forces indispensable for the formation of the popular front sought by the Communists were opposed to Batista. They had united in the Cuban Revolutionary Party (Partido Revolucionario Cubano — PRC), also known as Auténtico, organized by Grau after his removal from office;[6] and Grau had not forgiven the Communists for their subversive activities, the occupation of factories, and setting up of "soviets" during

[5] The visit of the Comintern delegates and the subsequent purge of the Central Committee were described to me by a member of the committee, who was a victim of the purge and whose name cannot be revealed. It is probable that no one who was a member of the Central Committee before 1934 was still a member of the party in 1952.

[6] Up to 1935 another organization was in existence, Jóven Cuba (Young Cuba), founded by Antonio Guiteras, Secretary of Internal Affairs in the Grau administration. Guiteras, however, was killed in a fight with the police on May 8, 1935, and from then on the organization was of no importance.

his brief rule. Moreover, whereas the Auténticos believed in a revolutionary coup as the only effective method of removing Batista, the Communists preferred "mass struggle," a formula that in practice meant nothing more drastic than calling for mass demonstrations and strikes. Hence, the efforts of the Cuban Communist Party to form a popular front, that is, an alliance with the democratic forces, came to nothing.

About 1938 Grau realized that he could not gain power by violent revolution, while Batista by that stage had realized that he needed to legitimize his position by assuming the presidency himself. The two soon reached agreement that the convocation of a constituent assembly would be the correct way to return to political normalcy. As soon as the necessary arrangements had been made, the election of delegates to the assembly took place, in April 1939.

It was the popularity and nationalist tendency of Grau's brief government in 1933, combined with the incompetence and corruption of the governments that succeeded him, that had made the Cuban Revolutionary Party a powerful popular force. Since Batista could depend on the electoral expertise of the traditional bureaucratized parties alone, he needed a new force that would be capable of counteracting the dynamism of the Auténticos; consequently he made an agreement with the Communists (which lasted until 1944) by virtue of which they could publish a daily newspaper, *Noticias de Hoy* (Today's News), which first appeared on May 15, 1938. They also obtained legal recognition for the party, took over control of the new organization of trade unions, the Cuban Workers' Confederation (Confederación de Trabajadores de Cuba — CTC), and later received two ministries without portfolio (one of which went to the same Carlos Rafael Rodríguez who was to become president of Fidel Castro's National Institute of Agrarian Reform [Instituto Nacional de Reforma Agraria — INRA]). In exchange, Batista received Communist support in the 1940 presidential election and was able to take advantage of the parades and demonstrations organized by the Communist Party to give the appearance of popularity to a victory obtained only through an electoral deal.[7]

[7] The constitution that was approved in July 1940 provided for free and direct voting in presidential elections. A final clause, however, provided that the new constitution was not to go into effect until the elected President took office on October 10 of that year. Thus the electoral system that operated in Batista's favor went on.

In the next presidential elections in 1944 the Communists, under the new name of "People's Socialist Party" (Partido Socialista Popular — PSP),[8] again supported Batista's governmental coalition, which, however, was defeated by Grau. But Grau, after assuming office as President, had to wait for two years, until he obtained a majority in Congress, to settle accounts with the Communists. Then, in 1947, the Minister of Labor, Carlos Prío Socarrás, swung the full weight of governmental influence to the side of the Auténtico element in the trade unions — which then pushed out the Communists. Since the Communists' hold over the trade-union leadership had been the decisive factor enabling them to secure and maintain control of the labor movement, once they lost this hold they also lost their basic instrument for the collection of funds and the organization of demonstrations, in short, their ability to create the impression that the Communist movement in Cuba constituted an important power.

The following year, 1948, none of the other parties running for office would accept an alliance with the Communists (PSP), whose presidential candidate obtained 157,000 votes; the winner by a substantial majority was the Auténtico candidate Prío Socarrás. The Communists were still in this position of isolation four years later, in February 1952, when their Seventh Party Congress passed the following resolution on the forthcoming presidential election: "to vote for the candidate of the Ortodoxo party [Cuban People's Party (Partido del Pueblo Cubano), founded in 1946 by Senator Eduardo Chibás as a breakaway group from the Auténticos], even in the absence of an electoral agreement."[9]

According to Carlos Rafael Rodríguez, a member of the party's Politburo, the PSP presented 61,000 names of supporters in order to qualify for participation in the 1952 general elections.[10] But on March 10, 1952, three months before the elections that were to designate President Carlos Prío Socarrás' successor, Batista engineered another *coup d'état* and took over the presidency himself.

Since the Batista coup marks the beginning of the period that

[8] In 1937 the Communists formed a legal party, the Revolutionary Union (Unión Revolucionaria), to help bring about the popular front. In the 1940 elections a coalition of both organizations ran under the name of Revolutionary Communist Union (Unión Revolucionaria Comunista).

[9] Blas Roca, *The Cuban Revolution: Report to the Eighth National Congress of the People's Socialist Party of Cuba* (New York: New Century Publishers, 1961), p. 7.

[10] Arnault, *Cuba et le marxisme, op cit.*, p. 92.

was to give the PSP such a decisive role in Cuban history, it is advisable to give a brief review of the state of the party in the initial stages of this period.

No data are available on the membership of the PSP during its peak period, 1939–1944. In 1946, however, it is credited with 37,000 members, though this figure was substantially reduced six years later. Carlos Rafael Rodríguez maintains that when the party was declared illegal in July 1953 it had 20,000 members. Other sources disagree. In 1957 the CIA in Havana estimated the membership of the PSP at 10,000, while in January 1959 the French Communist Arnault gave a figure of only 7,000. It seems incredible that during the period 1953–1959, when the Cuban party was being treated with much indulgence, even though it was illegal, it should have lost more than half its members. Nor is it clear why Arnault should have minimized the number of his Cuban comrades. Hence we conclude that Rodríguez' figure for 1953 was greatly inflated.[11]

As in every Communist party, the Cuban party consisted of a Central Committee (referred to in Cuba as the National Committee, or National Directorate) directed by a Politburo (which in the PSP was also called the Executive Committee). This was made up almost completely of veterans of the fight against Machado, and was composed of two distinct age groups: those over fifty years old in 1952 — Blas Roca, Aníbal Escalante, Manuel Luzardo, Joaquín Ordoqui, Lázaro Peña, and Juan Marinello — and those approximately ten years younger — Carlos Rafael Rodríguez, César Escalante, Flavio Bravo, and Ursinio Rojas.[12] There is no need to discuss the social origin of these leaders because they had all spent at least a decade in the party machine and were thus consummate *apparatchiki.*

The PSP was a strictly Stalinist and monolithic party under the undisputed direction of Blas Roca, who had been secretary-general since 1934. Its theoretical level was very low; not one of its members

---

[11] A figure of 37,000 members in 1946, attributed to "a Party spokesman," appears in Wyatt MacGaffey, Clifford R. Barnett, and others, *Cuba: Its People, Its Society, Its Culture* (New Haven, Conn.: Human Resources Area Files, 1962), p. 131. The figures cited by Carlos Rafael Rodríguez and Arnault appear in Arnault, *Cuba et le marxisme, op. cit.,* pp. 92 and 154. For the CIA estimates see Earl E. T. Smith, *The Fourth Floor* (New York: Random House, 1962), p. 33.

[12] These are the persons appearing as members of the Politburo in the Eighth National Congress of the PSP (see *Hoy,* August 17, 1960). Given the stability of the leadership of the PSP, it is almost certain that these were the same ones who made up the Politburo in 1952.

ever made a contribution worthy of mention in any Marxist bibliography. It had never been a force imbued with authentic revolutionary initiative; and the fact that for a long period it had been legal had the effect also of depriving it of the spirit of self-sacrifice that had characterized Cuban communism until 1933. Later, Carlos Rafael Rodríguez himself was to admit that "the rank and file of the party was penetrated by 'electoralism' . . . [and] it lost part of its 'bite.' "[13]

The PSP's lack of influence in those circles most susceptible to Communist penetration can be judged from the following data: Within the working class, of the 4,500 delegates to the last congress held by the CTC, before the coup of March 10, 1952, only 11 were Communists. And at the Tenth Congress of this same organization, which took place in November 1959, eleven months after the victory of Castro's revolution, out of 3,240 delegates the number of Communists had risen to 170.[14]

In student circles it had been many years since a Communist had been elected as a students' representative in any school at the University of Havana. It is true that in 1949 and 1950 two members of the PSP, Alfredo Guevara and Lionel Soto, were in turn elected president of the School of Philosophy, but this was only because they took pains to conceal their membership. It was not until 1955 that a Communist woman, Amparo Chaple, was elected openly as a Communist. Her election, however, cannot be ascribed to any growth of the Communist youth group at the university, for two years later, when the group had seven cells in the university, its total membership was only 26.[15]

The situation was the same with respect to the intellectuals. As a result of the Stalinization of the party in 1934, the agreement with Batista, and the general disappearance of ideological content from Cuban politics (by virtue of a process that will be described later), the influence of Marxist ideas dwindled as rapidly as it had begun to spread in 1925. After 1940 it is impossible to point to a single one of the young literary reviews — few in number to be

13 Arnault, Cuba et le marxisme, op. cit., p. 92.

14 On the congress that took place prior to the coup d'état see Robert J. Alexander, Communism in Latin America (New Brunswick, N.J.: Rutgers University Press, 1957), p. 292.

15 The evidence of Raúl Valdés Vivó and César Gómez at the trial of Marcos Rodríguez, session of March 24, 1964 (see Bohemia, April 3, 1964). Valdés Vivó was secretary of the Socialist Youth at the University of Havana in 1955; Gómez held the same post in 1957.

sure — that was Marxist or even commented on Marxist ideology. This gives some idea of Marxism's lack of influence at that time. Even up to 1960 it was very difficult to find any disciple of Marx among the new intellectual generation. One should not be misled by the fact that the writer Juan Marinello was president of the PSP. Marinello was chosen for this position because of his flexibility, and from the time he became the figurehead of Cuban communism his literary output declined so much that his influence on recent literature is imperceptible.

Finally, among the peasants there was some Communist influence from 1933 to 1935 in a number of rural centers of Oriente province, but there is no indication that this influence had been maintained into the 1950's. The Communists had thus become a very minor factor in Cuban politics by the time Fidel Castro picked them to serve as his instrument in the political, economic, and social transformation of the country.

The Political Milieu

At the time of Fidel Castro's birth on August 13, 1926, a new generation had begun to rebel against what they called "Cuban decadence"[16] with the primary aim of reviving the national spirit and of radically renovating public life. This group, under the in-

[16] This is the title of a pamphlet published by Fernando Ortiz in 1924 (*La decadencia cubana* [Havana: Imprenta La Universal, 1924]). The year before, Carlos M. Trelles had published another, entitled *El progreso (1902–1906) y el retroceso (1906–1922) de la República de Cuba* [The Progress (1902–1906) and Decline (1906–1922) of the Cuban Republic] (Matanzas, Cuba: Imp. de T. González, 1923), 26 pp. The problems confronting this generation and its reaction to them, all briefly described in the text, are in accord with the sources cited and with others, such as Jorge Mañach, *La crisis de la alta cultura* [The Crisis of High Culture] (Havana: Imprenta y Papelería La Universal, 1925), and Ramiro Guerra, *Azúcar y población en las Antillas* [Sugar and Population in the Antilles] (3rd ed.; Havana: Cultural S.A., 1944), originally published in 1927. (For an English translation of Guerra's book see *Sugar and Society in the Caribbean* [New Haven, Conn.: Yale University Press, 1964].) The political position of the non-Marxist majority of this generation is summarized in Partido ABC, *Manifiesto-Programa del ABC* [Manifesto and Program of the ABC] of 1932 (Havana: Editorial Cenit, 1942). For the group's intellectual background, of decisive importance for the whole evolution of the process, see the excellent work of one of its members, Francisco Ichaso, *Ideas y aspiraciones de la primera generación republicana* [Ideas and Aspirations of the First Generation of the Republic], Vol. VIII of Ramiro Guerra *et al.*, eds., *Historia de la nación cubana* [History of the Cuban Nation] (Havana: Editorial Historia de la Nación Cubana, 1952). On the influence of Marxist thought during these years see José Antonio Portuondo, "Mella y los intelectuales" [Mella and the Intellectuals], *Hoy*, January 5, 1964.

fluence of ideas taken over from the aftermath of World War I and from the Russian Revolution, became nationalist and anti-imperialist; though it must be admitted that from the very beginning its ideological efforts were rather feeble.

From 1928 to 1930, when Machado ruled in violation of the Constitution and the economic slump became still deeper, these young people took to the road of revolution. In August 1931, when the failure of an uprising led by two veterans of the War of Independence definitively discredited both the "traditional politicians" and the customary procedure of "taking to the hills," it was these young people who directed the fight against Machado, concentrating their activity in the cities and making use of a combat technique without precedent in Cuban history — terrorism.

After 1925 the unity of this "generational movement" was shaken by the emergence of Marxist ideas. Nevertheless the majority rejected the formulas presented by the Marxists, and after the failure of the August 1931 revolt concentrated in only two organizations: the University Student Directorate (Directorio Estudiantil Universitario — DEU), and the secret ABC organization. At that time the differences between these two organizations were minimal: a question mainly of greater political realism and ideological preoccupation in the ABC and of pure revolutionary romanticism in the DEU. Unfortunately, however, the events of 1933 made these differences unbridgeable.

In the summer of that year U.S. Ambassador Sumner Welles tried to set up some form of mediation between the regime and the opposition. The ABC joined in, the DEU rejected it. On August 12, 1933 the ABC joined the government that succeeded Machado; the DEU criticized the ABC for participating in a regime that was so obviously the product of compromise. On September 4 the DEU identified itself with the uprising of the noncommissioned officers and soldiers, enthusiastically supporting the government that was formed on September 10 with Grau as president. The ABC, on the other hand, went over to the opposition and finally, after organizing rebellions and conspiracies against Grau, joined the administration of the new President, Carlos Mendieta, a few months after the coup of January 15, 1934. Meanwhile Grau and the DEU, after founding the Auténtico party, concentrated on the task of organizing the uprising that they hoped would return them to power.

This internal conflict within the new generation proved to be disastrous for the revolutionary movement that it had been leading.

In the first place, the ABC, alarmed by the extent of the social unrest that had broken out on September 4, shifted from realism to outright conservatism, began to be attracted by Italian fascism, moved away from the masses completely, and finally lost all influence.

Second, the "Sergeants' Revolt" of September 4 had produced a leader, Batista, who was the decisive figure within the government from the time of his coup of January 15, 1934. The only reason that Batista, a sergeant-stenographer with absolutely no revolutionary merits, could gain such power was that he was able to arouse and satisfy the ambitions of the noncommissioned officers and the rank and file of the professional army that had served Machado unwaveringly until August 12. No particular perspicacity was needed for Batista to realize what would help him win these men over; most of them were from rural areas, had a negligible education, had never fought in any campaign, and had been drawn into military service by anything but a military vocation. Their principal ambition was to supplant the officers, quickly amass a fortune for themselves, and find posts for their relatives and friends in public administration. Batista made them generals like himself and then showed them the way to get everything else. Consequently one of the central themes of Cuban politics, superseding the original aims of the revolutionary movement initiated in the twenties, now became the defense of (or the attack against) the vested interests of this *Lumpenproletariat* in uniform.

Grau, Batista's victim of January 15, acquired great popularity by continuing to oppose him. Grau was a professor of physiology with only the most tangential relationship to the ideological preoccupations of the younger generation, but he soon displayed a sense of vocation that no one had ever suspected him of having. The moment he felt wanted by the masses of the people he became convinced that Providence had singled him out as the nation's savior, which he would of course become by being made President once again. From this time on he would neither listen to advice nor tolerate disagreement. Within the ranks of the Auténticos a negative selection took place. The best members of the Directorate finally left it, while the rest grew accustomed to concealing that they were followers of such a strange and unpredictable person — whom his adversaries were later to call, quite justifiably, the "divine gibberer."

Both Batista and Grau were estranged from the younger generation; and Batista, moreover, represented the vested interests that had sprung from the Sergeants' Revolt. The emergence of these men as the two main political leaders of the Cuban people initiated a development that, after reaching its peak in 1944, had the following effects:

In the first place, the moral and ideological preoccupations that had produced the movement against Machado disappeared altogether from political life or became mere rhetorical expressions recalled only during campaign speeches and in the formulation of political programs. Second, the violence that accompanies all revolutionary movements became independent of the political content that had originally justified it and established its own organs of expression, for example, the "action groups" or "revolutionary groups." It was in one of these that Fidel Castro started his political apprenticeship.

CASTRO AND THE "ACTION GROUPS." The formation of the action groups took place in three stages.

In the first of these, the insurrectional phase that began in 1934, terrorism came to the fore, and assaults and kidnappings were employed to get arms and supplies. These activities, which entailed the formation of small secret bands, were incompatible with the presence of Grau and his chief lieutenants, who went into exile — the obvious place in which to work out the doctrinal foundations required by all serious political movements. But Grau's oracular style of thought could be transmitted only by word of mouth, and his collaborators proved to be as devoid of ideas — or as full of confusion — as their leader. In consequence, the obvious uselessness of this absentee leadership and the continuation of the cruel and ruthless clandestine struggle in Cuba — the usual means of repression were torture and assassination — engendered a new type of revolutionary. He was an expert in the use of automatic weapons, loyal only to his tiny independent group, full of contempt for those he referred to as the "ideologists" in exile, and thoroughly convinced that violence alone could decide everything.

When it became evident that violence was ineffective against Batista and his generals, these "action groups," as they were already being called, became demoralized by mutual distrust and internecine conflict. In 1938 Grau, elevated by remoteness and by the government's highhandedness to a quasi-mythical status, decided that insurrection would never enable him to accomplish the mission given him by Providence: Inspired by some conciliatory gestures on Batista's part, he returned from exile, thus initiating the second phase in this curious process of historical development. The new phase was marked by the negotiation of the electoral formulas that helped Batista rise to the presidency in 1940 and by the consequences of his election.

It is obvious that Grau's role in legitimizing the new regime and the fortunes amassed by Batista and his generals — he agreed, for instance, that the free and direct ballot established by the recently approved constitution 1940 should not apply to the elections of that year — constituted a setback to the revolutionary movement; and, even though it had been imposed by the iron necessities of politics, it was bound to have pernicious effects on the morale of his followers. Whether or not Grau knew this, there is no evidence that he did anything to avoid it. The result was that the Auténtico politicians elected to Congress from 1940 onward lost no time in reproducing all the faults that they had been criticizing in their new colleagues in the Senate and the House, while the "action groups," who had never completely dissociated themselves from the Auténticos, started to degenerate in a way that was even more marked, as we shall now see.

Grau's decision in 1938 to legitimize the Batista regime put the "action groups" in a quandary. If they accepted the decision they were betraying those who had died for the cause. If they rejected it, however, now more than ever they would multiply their chances of joining the others in the grave. Moreover, very few of them possessed the qualities required for any electoral activity, and fewer still had any inclination to exchange the thrills of revolutionary life and the prestige won by their exploits for the monotony and anonymity of any sort of normal employment. While these "men of action" were pondering which line to take, after coming out of prison, returning from exile, or coming out into the open, they took refuge in the university, the classical center of the revolution from 1930 on, where they were protected against the police by "university autonomy," which prevented the police from entering the campus without the permission of the university authorities.

Here, as the politicians began showing off the benefits derived from the electoral positions they had gained through the agreements between Grau and Batista, the "action groups" came to a *modus vivendi* with the authorities that allowed them both to continue being "insurrectionists" and to exploit the unexpected sources of revenue found in the university.

As a result of this agreement, explicit or implicit, the "action groups" facilitated the apparent restoration of normality, limiting their insurrectional activities strictly to the university campus. The government for its part disregarded the crimes committed within the country's highest center of learning by men, full of revolutionary talk and with pistols in their belts, who monopolized the sale of textbooks, trafficked in grades and free registration, practiced extortion on both professors and students, and raided the Finance Office of the University. They beat up anyone who resisted, and killed each other in quarrels over the division of the booty or in disputes over the elections to the University Student Federation (Federación Estudiantil Universitaria — FEU).

In spite of the behavior of the Auténtico politicians and the crimes of the "action groups" — which he never publicly condemned — Grau was elected President in 1944. Thus his shrewdness in making the electoral agreements of 1938 was vindicated. He had an excellent opportunity to take advantage of popular enthusiasm, now reinforced by his electoral victory, and to introduce the reforms he had been proposing for the previous ten years. Grau, however, did just the opposite. After the first few months of the Auténtico regime, graft reached a higher peak than ever before and the state authorities displayed the same incompetence, frivolity, and irresponsibility that had originally caused the movement of revolt.

It was in this atmosphere of tragic frustration, which the administration of President Prío, elected in 1948, did nothing to dissipate, that the process begun in 1934 reached its final phase.

The masses of the people, who had previously placed their most ardent hopes in the Auténtico leader, lapsed into skepticism when they saw how they had been swindled. After the "success" achieved by Batista's cunning and Grau's deceitfulness — Batista's sergeants and Grau's disciples had enriched themselves equally — the professional politicians of Cuba remained convinced that morals and intellect were none of their business. The intellectual minority, growing constantly feebler in a society that despised and rejected them, took refuge in the pursuit of the purest and most abstract art arriving from abroad. In short, public life was emptied of any ethical or ideological content, and the state, just as in 1920, became a machine alien to the national interests, evoking nothing but indifference or revulsion.

Quite understandably, and as the March 10, 1952 coup was to demonstrate, once the "Grau myth" had disappeared and the formidable power coalition created by Batista from the army, the trade unions, and the traditional political parties had ceased functioning, the pervasive cynicism and corruption encouraged the return of violence.

Let us now examine the behavior of the professionals in violence, the "action groups" in the university, from 1944 on.

When Grau became President he did nothing to prevent the "action groups" from coming out into the open; on the contrary he permitted them to share in the spoils of office with the Auténtico politicians. At this stage, after countless schisms, coalitions, reorganizations, and the formation of new groups, the "trigger-happy kids" (as they were also called in the press) were divided into two chief factions: the Revolutionary Socialist Movement (Movimiento Socialista Revolucionario — MSR), headed by Mario Salabarría, and the Revolutionary Insurrectional Union (Unión Insurreccional Revolucionaria — UIR), under the leadership of Emilio Tró. It was in this second group, which initiated the scheme of leaving alongside its victims a note reading "Justice is slow but sure," that Fidel Castro began his career in 1945, when he came to the university to study law.[17]

When Castro joined the UIR at the age of nineteen, the "action groups" were tiny, rudimentary in organization, and united exclusively by obedience to a chief who had been tested in action. Though they never cut their ties with the university, they were composed for the most part of people foreign to the student body, with a very low standard of education and from the fringes of society, who were either habitually unemployed or had never given any serious thought to working.

They were also anti-Communist. It was they who physically expelled the Communists from the student organizations and loaned their armed men to the Auténtico trade-union leaders so that the latter could implement the decrees passed in 1946 expelling the

---

[17] Ernst Halperin has commented on the frequency with which the word "justice" appears in Castro's speeches. It is not impossible that this preoccupation of Castro's may have been born while he prepared those macabre notes. See Ernst Halperin, "Castroism — Challenge to the Latin American Communists," *Problems of Communism*, Vol. XII, No. 5 (September–October 1963).

People's Socialist Party from the trade-union organization (CTC). The anti-Communist orientation of the "action groups" had originated in the opposition of the Communists to the Grau government in 1933 and had been accentuated by the Communists' opposition to insurrectional tactics and by their agreements with Batista. But one might almost say that there was a psychological basis for this — the fact that the Cuban "man of action" was of an anarchic, semiliterate, and violent character, while the Communists paid tribute to discipline, were arrogantly doctrinaire, and generally displayed exemplary submissiveness.

Moreover, the "action groups" lacked any ideology, program, or doctrinal preoccupation. They devoted all their energy to such activities as getting hold of arms and hiding them and fighting with rival gangs; now that the groups had begun to get a share in the state revenues, they ceased to commit offenses against private property. This was the environment that formed Fidel Castro's political personality. He was the second of five illegitimate sons of a maid servant and a Spanish immigrant, who by hard work had managed to achieve financial security though not riches. There are many who see in Fidel's illegitimacy the key to his whole conduct. However, since his older brother Ramón has demonstrated very different qualities and shortcomings, this interpretation seems unsatisfactory.

Others have interpreted Castro as a typical young intellectual spurred to action by the spectacle of his country's misfortunes. Castro himself, however, has expressly denied this description. "I am not an intellectual," he told Jacques Arnault, "I am a man of revolutionary action."[18] And even before this, in a talk he gave to some Cuban writers and artists, he insisted on his ignorance of the things that preoccupied his audience — problems of form and of the intellectuals' attitude toward the revolution — and maintained that he had come to the discussion as a ruler and as a revolutionary.[19]

As for the ideological influences that might have swayed him, anyone familiar with Castro's speeches knows that he very rarely alludes to them or gives any indication of the reading that might have contributed to his education. We can recall only very few references to any intellectual source in the thousands of pages recording his torrential oratory. It is true that in his "History Will

[18] Interview with Jacques Arnault, *Revolución*, August 17, 1962.
[19] Fidel Castro, *Palabras a los intelectuales* [Talks to Intellectuals] (Havana: Ediciones del Consejo Nacional de Cultura, 1961).

Absolve Me"[20] speech Castro quoted doctrinal precedents from "the remotest antiquity" (China and India) to the Declaration of the Rights of Man in defense of the right to rebel. But this was little more than the enumeration of a long list of names to which he never referred again — he may well have gleaned them from the prison library — and thus can hardly be said to demonstrate genuine erudition.

The only occasion on which Castro made any specific mention of his reading was on December 2, 1961, when he proclaimed himself a Marxist-Leninist. At that point he said he had read Marx's *Capital* up to page 270. He added that it was during his student days that he began "having his first contacts with the Communist Manifesto, the works of Marx, Engels, Lenin, and all that."[21] Castro's speeches do not indicate that these "contacts" were very deep or very frequent. Moreover, since on this occasion Castro had an overriding reason for laying claim to a Marxist-Leninist past, as we shall see, neither this statement nor the example mentioned previously permit us to conclude that Marx's works or any others are in any way the key to Castro's political behavior.

The Cuban leader is not an intellectual but, to use his own words, "a man of revolutionary action," who had only the most superficial smattering of ideology even in 1962, when he described himself in this way, and had much less when he began the meteoric career that has led him to the position he now occupies.

Just at the time Castro joined the UIR, the political ambitions of the groups, which had never completely disappeared, were revived by government funds and by the emergence of the exceptionally favorable situation that has been described. To a certain extent, however, their audacity was kept in check by their dependence on the government treasury; in addition, their experience in 1934–1938 had taught them the great risks inherent in any direct confrontation with the armed forces. It was because of this that they began to extend their influence in public life by penetrating the sphere most easily accessible to them — the police.

In 1947 they obtained from Grau various positions as officers in the police force, among others the appointment of Tró as commander of the Police Academy and Salabarría as chief of the Bureau of Investigation. But in September of that same year Sala-

---

20 As will be noted, it is not entirely accurate to include "History Will Absolve Me" among Castro's speeches.
21 *Hoy*, December 2, 1961.

barría made an error fatal to the "action groups." He thought that his position offered him the opportunity of getting rid of Tró, his rival, and contrived to surprise him when almost alone. But the operation could not be carried out with the requisite speed, and even though Tró was killed after a long gunfight, the public scandal was so great that Salabarría had to be imprisoned.

The disappearance of the two best known and most feared leaders, both veterans of the anti-Machado struggle, came as a crippling blow to the "action groups"; the next year they suffered an equally serious one. The new President, Carlos Prío, appointed Aureliano Sánchez Arango to the Ministry of Education, and the latter at once cut off the copious source of funds these groups had had from his department. Castro tried to mobilize student opinion against the minister; but Sánchez Arango, himself a student leader in 1927, came to the meeting that had been called, and Castro's efforts came to nothing.

With these two setbacks the gangs began declining. Doubtless Castro realized this, since he obtained nomination in the congressional elections scheduled for June 1952 as a candidate of the Ortodoxos. On March 4, 1952 Castro appeared before the courts to denounce those members of the "action groups" still holding government posts.

It would be misleading to deduce from this that Castro had broken off relations with the UIR, because his running for office was not incompatible with remaining a member. Those familiar with the history of the UIR maintain that because this group was most affected by the chain of events that started with the killing of their leader Tró in September 1947, and because it was obvious that their enemies would support the Auténtico candidates in the 1952 elections, Castro managed to persuaded his companions that they should risk everything on the prospect of an Ortodoxo victory.[22]

I think we are now in a position to understand both the ideological emptiness and the character of the "action groups," which specialized in violence and which, in our judgment, constitute the basic elements of the situation that gave rise to such "men of revo-

22 Daniel James, in *Cuba: The First Soviet Satellite in the Americas* (New York: Avon Books, 1961), thanks me for the information on Cuban communism that I placed at his disposal by calling me "a former leader of the Cuban Communist party" (p. 83). To avoid errors such as this, I should make it clear that my knowledge of the "action groups" derives from my participation in the Cuban revolutionary process since 1933 and not from my having belonged to one of these groups.

lutionary action" as Castro. It would be a serious mistake to reduce the Cuban leader to the category of a mere gang chieftain. But it is also misleading to disregard, as has been done until now, the stamp this experience left on him. It was in the "action groups," whose leaders were received by more than one President and by any number of state ministers, who were treated deferentially by police chiefs and magistrates, were given official salaries, and were feared by the majority of the population, that Castro came to know the real weakness of Cuban political institutions, their almost exclusive dependence on force, and the corruption and incompetence of their leaders. It was there that he acquired both the facile conviction that, because the state had survived Batista's devastation as well as the Auténtico disaster, no moral or intellectual qualification whatever was needed to govern it, and also the belief that politics was nothing but a naked struggle for power devoid of any spiritual or ideological principle. It was there, finally, and not in the writings of Lenin, as is assumed by Arnault,[23] that Castro came to realize the decisive role that violence could play in civic life and in this connection the importance of two other elements: firearms and the availability of a group of desperadoes ready to give blind obedience to their leader.

If Castro's political technique is studied attentively, as this work proposes to do, it is easy to verify the traces left on him by this experience. He has changed his main ideas in accordance with circumstances: First he was a "democrat," then he was a "humanist," later he was a "socialist," and at the moment he is a "Marxist-Leninist." He has founded and dismantled organizations. But what he has never abandoned is his personal leadership and the stratagems required to impose it, his weapons, and his handful of followers, devoid of ideology and education and with no known professional training, who first in the Sierra and later in the command posts of the Revolutionary Armed Forces (Fuerzas Armadas Revolucionias — FAR) have carried out the constantly changing orders of their chief.

THE JULY 26 MOVEMENT. On March 10, 1952 Batista staged another coup, installing himself as President in place of Carlos

---

[23] Arnault (in *Cuba et le marxisme, op. cit.*), after saying that Castro while in prison taught his fellow prisoners "history and philosophy" (p. 65), goes on to say that Lenin's *State and Revolution* was bedside reading for him; it was from this that Castro extracted his own "theory of the revolution in Cuba" (p. 53).

Prío. This did not lessen the isolation of the PSP. In 1938, in the face of the growing Nazi menace, the United States had not objected to Batista's alliance with the Communists, but in 1952, when the danger came from the Soviet Union, the re-establishment of collaboration was impossible. As for the opposition, which had begun to reorganize once it had recovered from the surprise effect of the coup and realized that all Batista wanted to do was to remake his own fortune, saw no point in making an agreement with the PSP when the latter was, as we have seen, a force of negligible strength and when, in addition, such an alliance would provoke the ill will of Washington.

Up to the time of Castro's attack on the Moncada barracks on July 26, 1953, the Communists went on publishing their daily newspaper *Hoy* and their ideological review *Fundamentos*. It was in *Hoy* that Blas Roca reviewed the party situation on July 19, 1953. According to him there had been no real change in Cuba as a result of the Batista coup; the decisive and fundamental fact, "the subjection of our country to Yankee imperialism," continued as before. Because the various sectors of the opposition disregarded this circumstance, he said, all their objectives were futile and all their methods of struggle ineffective. For instance, the re-establishment of the 1940 constitution, as demanded by the Auténticos, would not resolve the crisis, while the request for a neutral government to supervise elections, demanded by the Ortodoxos, was nothing but "a slogan of compromise with the *de facto* government." As far as methods were concerned, he asked, what could be expected from terrorism or from a *coup d'état*, these "petit-bourgeois" forms of action, or from "putschism," "these crazy adventures sometimes hatched out on the university campus"? Roca was surely well informed of Castro's activities on the campus, which were to culminate seven days later in the attack on the Moncada barracks.

In contrast to all this confusion, Blas Roca maintained that the program and the methods of the proletariat — that is, of Blas Roca and his party — were both clear and effective: a national democratic front government arrived at by "the action of the masses, which was to lead to elections, a general strike, or a popular uprising."[24]

While the Communists, prevented by the international situation

24 Blas Roca, "Las divergencias en cuanto al Programa, los métodos de lucha y la táctica frente a la crisis cubana" [Differences with Respect to a Program, Methods of Struggle, and Tactics Concerning the Cuban Crisis], *Hoy*, July 19, 1953.

from arriving at an agreement with Batista, reverted to their strategy of 1935, the constitution of an oppositional democratic front, Castro revived the insurrectionist activity of that period, though with one modification learned, as we know, from bitter experience. This was that instead of a direct frontal attack on the armed forces it would be better to outflank them, attacking a provincial barracks by surprise both to obtain supplies and to divide the enemy.

Castro could not count on the UIR for this project. In addition to other reasons, there was the fundamental one that the professional gunmen of this group were most unlikely to accept Castro's leadership because he had never distinguished himself particularly in the actions in which he had participated.[25] Consequently Castro set about recruiting young novices with no combat experience whom he could impress as a "man of action."

These activities culminated in the attack on the Moncada barracks in Santiago de Cuba on July 26, 1953. The operation, planned as a surprise attack to take the position with a minimum of resistance, was a failure for reasons that even today are not clear. And although his losses in action were "insignificant," as Castro later said in court, the army, to the horror of the population, wiped out most of his attacking force after it had surrendered. Castro himself was captured a few days later and sentenced to imprisonment.

The attack on Moncada made Castro's name known to the majority of the Cuban people and especially to his own generation, which in 1952 found all avenues to social advancement closed just as had its predecessor, the generation of the 1930's. Also, with Batista in power once again, there was indisputable evidence of how little things had changed during the intervening twenty years. Given the ideological void, a few words will suffice to outline the intellectual profile of this new generation. It will be enough to quote the statement of one of its most authentic representatives, Armando Hart, the Minister of Education until 1965:

The young people of the 1930's went into revolutionary action against Machado impelled by ideas that they had heard from Varona, or in lec-

---

[25] Castro's participation in the attempts on the lives of Lionel Gómez and Rolando Masferrer and his presence at the time and place of the assassination of "Manolo" Castro, all of whom were members of rival "gangs," have been more than adequately demonstrated. However, no juridical proof of this can be adduced, since a characteristic of this whole situation was the refusal of the witnesses to testify against the members of the "groups," of the police to inform on them, and of the courts to condemn them.

tures given by one professor or another who had visited Havana, or that they had read in Marxist writings. . . . The Cuban generation of 1952, somewhat tired of the discussion of intellectual problems, and fed up with ideological dilettantism, . . . decided to face the situation squarely.

And Hart continued:

We should like to maintain that as regards political creativity our cultural evolution has now reached its peak, and the phase of intellectual speculation is ended.[26]

This in a country at least fifty years behind in its political and social thought! Quite apart from the astounding ignorance of the highest educational authority in the Castro government, which this last sentence demonstrates, the text as a whole shows us why the ex-member of the UIR and the young people of 1952 so easily found common ground.

Since Castro owed his prestige to the Moncada attack of July 26, he decided to perpetuate the date by using it as the name of the new organization he now launched from his prison on the Isle of Pines. In this task his two most efficient helpers were the only two women who took part in the Moncada attack, Haydée Santamaría and Melba Hernández, who had been released from prison after serving a six-month sentence. These women realized that what was needed was a document explaining the aims of the new organization. They asked Castro for one; he replied that "he was engaged in preparing a work that would contain the program of the movement."[27] The work in question turned out to be the *History Will Absolve Me* pamphlet[28] that is still alleged to be the text of the speech made by Castro before the court that sentenced him for the Moncada attack.

When Castro set out for the attack on Moncada he had taken along with him a program signed "The Cuban Revolution." This document, after the usual Cuban rhetorical expressions about the

---

26 See Armando Hart, "En torno a la conciencia nacional" [Concerning the National Conscience], *Revolución*, April 4, 1960. Enrique José Varona was the outstanding exponent of positivism in Cuba; he died in 1933. Hart's description of the "1930 generation," as he calls it, is, to be sure, another indication of his ignorance.

27 Interview with Melba Hernández in *El Mundo*, July 22, 1962, and especially Francisco de Armas, "Como se editó en la clandestinidad la primera edición de 'La historia me absolverá'" [The Secret Preparation of the First Edition of "History Will Absolve Me"], *Hoy*, July 21, 1963. This article, as indicated by its author, was written on the basis of data supplied by Melba Hernández.

28 Fidel Castro, *History Will Absolve Me* (New York: Liberal Press, 1959).

ideals of Martí, the will of the martyrs, and the holy rights of the fatherland, and after declaring its "absolute reverence and respect for the constitution of 1940," stated that the coming revolution adopted as its program the policies of the "Young Cuba" movement, the "Radical ABC" (an unimportant splinter group that broke away from the ABC in 1933 and probably never had a written program), and the Ortodoxos.[29]

It was obvious that the new movement could not begin with such a confused and unoriginal program. Consequently, in *History Will Absolve Me,* Castro not only repeated and amplified the charges against the government that he had made in court but also included the five revolutionary laws that are not mentioned in the July 26 proclamation (despite his having said that they "would have been proclaimed immediately after the capture of the barracks"). These five laws offered something to all social strata of the country except for the "ten or twelve magnates" who in Castro's opinion thought of nothing but "icy profit calculations" in their "air-conditioned offices." The five revolutionary laws provided for the re-establishment of the constitution of 1940; the ownership of land by tenants with less than 165 acres, with compensation to be paid the former owners by the state; the distribution of 30 per cent of the profits among the employees of the "big businesses"; the granting to tenant farmers of the right to 55 per cent of the return on the sale of sugar; and finally, the confiscation of all property of those who had ever abused their power while in government office.

The pamphlet had a very small circulation while Castro was in prison; once he was freed, on May 15, 1955, and realized that he had enough followers to undertake a new revolutionary adventure, neither he nor any of his followers mentioned it again until March 1959, when it was pulled out of oblivion for reasons we shall soon see. Neither in the Mexico program of November 1956, nor when the idea came up of providing the movement with a new program, in July 1957, nor in any document released by Castro himself in his guerrilla period was there any further reference to the apocryphal speech that was to arouse so much admiration later on.[30]

[29] Part of this declaration appears in Jules Dubois, *Fidel Castro: Rebel, Liberator or Dictator?* (New York: Bobbs-Merrill, 1959), p. 33.

[30] The Mexican program, signed in November 1956, appears in Enrique González Pedrero, *La revolución cubana* [The Cuban Revolution] (Mexico City: Escuela Nacional de Ciencias Políticas y Sociales, 1959). On the necessity of

Shortly after he was released from prison Castro left the country; and in March 1956, in Mexico, he and his movement left the Ortodoxo party. Although Castro's prestige had been growing among the youth, from an organizational point of view the July 26 Movement (Movimiento 26 de Julio) had been progressing slowly except perhaps in Oriente province where it had the good fortune to find a very gifted leader in the person of Frank País. In the summer of that year País went to Mexico to discuss the chances of an insurrection with Castro. In these talks País said that he "did not believe in the present organization in Cuba," adding that the domestic leaders were "unprotected, unprepared, and uncoordinated" for any kind of action. But Castro's view prevailed, and País went back to Cuba to organize the November 30 uprising in the capital of Oriente. This was yet another fiasco, and in País' own words it put the July 26 Movement "almost out of the fight."[31]

Castro himself had promised to land in Cuba in time for the uprising, but he and his land party in the boat *Granma* did not get there until December 2. Three days later he was surprised by the army and lost most of his men, and it was not until two weeks later that he managed to collect about a dozen survivors in the Sierra Maestra. His indomitable spirit was not discouraged by this new setback, and when the survivors succeeded in maintaining themselves in the Sierra, the work of reorganizing the movement was resumed. A small executive committee was set up, headed by País, and the formation of workers' sections was begun; no one thought a military victory was possible and there was a vague belief that a general strike would be the best way to finish off the Batista dictatorship.[32]

At the beginning of July 1957 the movement was about to appoint a National Directorate for the first time and to provide itself with a program. We know from Frank País' letter dated July 7, 1957 that in the proposed National Directorate Castro's guerrillas were to have only one delegate, Celia Sánchez, and that he was to have no influence on the definite composition of this organ.

As for the future program, País was hoping simply that Castro would send him "some suggestions."[33] Castro's views on the na-

---

providing a program for the movement see Frank País' letter to Castro dated July 7, 1957, in *Revolución*, July 30, 1962.
[31] *Ibid.*
[32] *Ibid.*
[33] *Ibid.*

tional situation were published in the manifesto of July 13, 1957, which was signed by himself, Raúl Chibás, the brother of the founder of the Ortodoxo party, and Felipe Pazos, ex-president of the National Bank, because Castro realized that a document signed only with his own name would have very little weight. The manifesto called for the creation of a civil revolutionary front, the expulsion of Batista and his replacement by a provisional government to be headed by someone appointed by the so-called civic institutions (that is, mainly professional associations), the holding of elections within one year, and the adoption by the provisional government of a moderate program in which the most radical proposal recommended the "laying of the foundations for agrarian reform," that is, the distribution of uncultivated lands and the transformation into independent landholders of the tenants of small plots of land — always with compensation for the previous owners.[34]

Castro's lack of influence within the movement and with the public was a reflection of his military weakness. At this time the guerrilla forces were still quite unimportant, depending for men, arms, and supplies on what was sent out to them from the cities. In February 1957, when Herbert Matthews saw him, Castro had no more than eighteen men, and his first military operation of any consequence — the attack in late May on the Uvero barracks — was made possible only with the help of a reinforcement of fifty men sent by País from Santiago de Cuba.

On July 30, 1957, before the National Directorate could be elected or the new program issued, Frank País was assassinated. This event, followed by the failure of the strike spontaneously provoked by País' death, plunged the movement into a new crisis. Batista, however, proved quite incapable both of wiping out the guerrilla movement and of finding a solution that would be acceptable to the opposition forces outside the July 26 Movement.

Increasingly savage repression by Batista's regime and the constant increase in corruption created a favorable atmosphere for subversion and revolution. In March 1957 the Revolutionary Student Directorate (Directorio Estudiantil Revolucionario — DER) and other groups launched an unsuccessful attack on the presidential palace with the intention of killing Batista, and on September

[34] The text of this manifesto is reproduced in Fidel Castro, *La revolución cubana* [The Cuban Revolution], selection, Prologue, and notes by Gregorio Selser (Buenos Aires: Editorial Palestra, 1960), p. 119.

5 an abortive military revolt led to the capture of the city of Cienfuegos; the rebels held out against the government forces for
twenty-four hours. Some survivors managed to escape to the nearby
Sierra of Escambray, where they formed the nucleus of a new guerrilla front, called the Second Escambray Front. In early 1958 the
professional associations, which had made no reply to Castro's
manifesto of the previous July, decided to publish a manifesto demanding the resignation of Batista. On March 12 Castro addressed
the whole nation, declaring "total war" against the tyranny and
calling for a general strike.[35]

The strike, scheduled for April 9, was a total fiasco. Its failure
threw all the opposition forces into consternation and sealed the
fate of the underground July 26 Movement in the cities. Faustino
Pérez, the principal organizer of the strike and the only "city
leader" who had achieved any distinction — his name even appeared
as a delegate to the National Directorate of the July 26 Movement
alongside Castro's in the proclamation calling for the "total war" —
was blamed for the fiasco and sent back to the Sierra, from which
he did not return until after Castro's victory on January 1, 1959.
In May the National Directorate (whose origin, functions, and
membership continue to remain a mystery) met in the territory occupied by the Rebel Army; it was agreed that the Directorate would
remain in the "liberated territory" and would choose a delegate,
with the title of General Coordinator, to direct the underground
struggle from Santiago de Cuba. Marcelo Fernández, the present
Minister of Foreign Trade, was selected for this post.[36]

This decision capped the process by which the July 26 Movement
was turned into a mere appendage of the guerrilla forces — which
from then on were called the Rebel Army. In July 1957 Castro had
had only one delegate in the National Directorate of the July 26
Movement, while in March 1958 the call for the general strike
was signed by both Castro, as commander-in-chief of the rebel
forces, and Faustino Pérez, the delegate of the National Directorate.
In May the National Directorate was put under the authority of
the Rebel Army commanded by Castro; there is no evidence that
the Directorate ever took any part in making decisions.[37]

35 *Ibid.*, p. 141.
36 Interview with Marcelo Fernández broadcast by Havana "Rebel Radio,"
April 9, 1964.
37 According to Robert Taber, *M–26: Biography of a Revolution* (New York:
Lyle Stuart, 1961), p. 186, as early as October a mass meeting was held for the

The general prostration of the revolutionary movement after the fiasco of the April strike prompted Batista to mount a massive offensive against the Sierra in the following month. Castro had only 300 men to stand off this attack; yet early in July the government forces were already beginning to lose some of the positions they had won at the beginning of the campaign, and by the end of that month a guerrilla counteroffensive was mounted with complete success. It was at this time that Carlos Rafael Rodríguez, a member of the PSP Politburo and its representative, came to see Castro at his headquarters in the Sierra.

The Communists and Castro's Victory

The reasons for this visit are worth noting.

At the time of the Moncada attack the Communists had declared:

The line of the PSP and of the mass movement has been to combat the Batista tyranny and to unmask the putschists and adventuristic activities of the bourgeois opposition as being against the interests of the people. The PSP bases its fight on the action of the masses, on the struggle of the masses, and opposes adventuristic putschism as contrary to the fight of the masses and contrary to the democratic solution which the people desires.[38]

In February of the following year the Communists repeated their condemnation of terrorism, sabotage, and putschism, declaring that the PSP preferred "the peaceful road and would do everything in its power to achieve it."[39]

The March 1964 conviction of Marcos Rodríguez, a member of the PSP, who confessed that he had denounced to the police four student members of the Revolutionary Student Directorate who had survived the March 13, 1957 attack on the presidential palace, has shed some new light on the extremes to which the Communists

---

purpose of organizing the National Directorate. Taber says "The National Directorate . . . now became a formal entity with at least nominal responsibility for making command decisions." But, he adds, "the word 'nominal' must be stressed. Fidel subscribed to the idea of group decision, in principle. In practice, he continued to issue the orders, both political and military, and to exercise his personal veto on plans of which he disapproved."

[38] *The Daily Worker* (New York), August 10, 1953, quoted by Maurice Zeitlin and Robert Scheer in *Cuba: Tragedy in Our Hemisphere* (New York: Grove Press, 1963), p. 118.

[39] "Carta del Comité Nacional del Partido Socialista Popular al Movimiento 26 de Julio" [Letter of the National Committee of the People's Socialist Party to the July 26 Movement], February 28, 1957, reproduced by Fausto Masó in *Bohemia Libre*, July 7, 1963.

were prepared to go to see that the struggle against Batista did not leave the "peaceful road."[40] Though Rodríguez' motives in informing the police of the whereabouts of the students were mixed and complicated, the decisive elements, as became clear in court, were the Marxist Rodríguez' loyalty to the so-called "mass struggle" and the contempt that had always been felt by the Cuban Communists for the "men of revolutionary action."[41]

Toward the end of the struggle against Batista the PSP kept insisting on the need to create a national democratic front, as can be seen from a letter written by Carlos Rafael Rodríguez to Claude Julien in June 1958, in which he proposed "a coalition that would go beyond the limits of anti-imperialism and necessarily include forces that would not be anti-imperialist."[42] Further, in the message sent by the PSP to the Eleventh Congress of the Communist Party of Chile in November 1958, the PSP, after deploring the "disunity of the opposition forces," went on to call for " 'national unity' in order to overthrow the tyranny and form a 'democratic coalition government.' "[43] The only agreement they managed to reach in this respect concerned the formation of a national front of the trade unions early in November 1958, and this certainly took no part in the overthrow of Batista.

As far as tactics were concerned, the PSP never abandoned the "mass struggle" formula. This does not mean that there were no Communists among the guerrillas, but their number was so small that the second leader of the PSP, Aníbal Escalante, in June 1959 refused to give any statistics on their participation.[44]

Apart from Castro and a few of his closest followers, no one in Cuba ever believed in the possibility of a military victory for the guerrillas; it was always thought that the final blow to the Batista regime would have to come through a general strike or a military uprising. The PSP, although nominally illegal, was treated with

40 The trial of Marcos Rodríguez is discussed in Chapter 8.

41 In December 1955, when the Revolutionary Student Directorate hid weapons at the university for use during a "street demonstration," Rodríguez passed the information on to the Communists, who prevented the demonstration against the police from taking place, because "mass struggle" had nothing to do with actual fighting. On this incident see the statement of Faure Chomón in court during the trial of Marcos Rodríguez in *Bohemia*, March 27, 1964.

42 Claude Julien, *La révolution cubaine* [The Cuban Revolution] (Paris: René Julliard, 1961), p. 84.

43 Ernst Halperin, *Nationalism and Communism in Chile* (Cambridge, Mass.: The M.I.T. Press, 1965), p. 64.

44 *Hoy,* June 28, 1959.

such indulgence by Batista that almost all its leaders — Blas Roca, Aníbal Escalante, Carlos Rafael Rodríguez, Juan Marinello — remained in the country with hardly any interference from the police. In these circumstances, to risk everything for a movement led by someone of Castro's antecedents — a former member of the "action groups," who were their traditional enemies — would have meant nothing less than political suicide for the Communists. It thus seemed advisable to continue following the course of events and to hope for the establishment of the democratic front, inside which the presence of the other opposition groups would afford some safeguard against any decisions that Castro might make.

On July 20, 1958 an opposition front, including Fidel Castro, was set up in Caracas without Communist participation. The front exhorted "all the revolutionary forces of the country, both civic and political," to subscribe to its declaration of July 13, 1957, promising to hold a meeting later "to discuss and approve the bases of unity."[45] Castro immediately began negotiations to have this meeting held in the "liberated territory," that is, the area under his personal control, so as to be able to hamstring the front, as he already had the National Directorate of the July 26 Movement.

Carlos Rafael Rodríguez, as a representative of the PSP, went to the Sierra headquarters in response to Castro's invitation. In Rodríguez' own words, the invitation was "accepted only by our party and the Revolutionary Student Directorate."[46] During this visit Rodríguez found that "in the Sierra Cristal, where Raúl Castro was in command, there was nothing but understanding for the Communists. But when I got to Fidel, to the Sierra Maestra, the understanding had changed to suspicion."[47] Rodríguez fails to mention Ernesto Guevara here, probably because at the time he gave this account, in early 1963, his quarrel with Guevara — which we shall discuss in due time — did not lead to his saying anything in the latter's favor. Nevertheless it is clear that Guevara showed just as much understanding as Raúl Castro, because several of the Communists who had already joined the rebel forces had joined the column commanded by "Che."[48]

[45] Castro, *La revolución cubana, op. cit.*, p. 152.

[46] Statement of Carlos Rafael Rodríguez at the second trial of Marcos Rodríguez (*Bohemia*, April 3, 1964).

[47] Gianni Corbi, interview with Carlos Rafael Rodríguez in "Report on Cuba," *L'Espresso* (Italy), January 26, February 2, 9, 16, and 23, 1964 (JPRS 24,080, April 8, 1964).

[48] For example, Hiram Prats, apparently the only leader of the Socialist

Rodríguez went back to Havana to give his report, then left again for the Sierra, where he stayed until the end of the fighting. Although the failure of the government forces was already known, and although Castro had promised that when the front was formally constituted in the "liberated territory" the PSP would be admitted,[49] the Communists acted with consummate prudence. They gave instructions for a certain number of party activists to join the columns of Raúl Castro and of Guevara but decided to wait for a while before coming to any irrevocable decision.

Events took an entirely unexpected course. The incredible invasion of the central provinces, launched in August with fewer than 250 men, managed to entrench itself in the Las Villas mountains. By the end of December, while some Batista generals were being bribed by the guerrilla leaders to avoid any confrontation, other generals were opening negotiations with Castro, the central cities of Cuba began falling to the Rebel Army, and the imposing military machine of the despotic Batista collapsed.

The flight on December 31, 1958 of the dictator — "The Man," as his followers called him — a man who certainly never went near any front, surprised the Communists, Castro, and the other opposition leaders. By January 1, 1959 the guerrilla movement had won, without the opposition front ever being formally established and without the PSP ever clearly defining its position with respect to Castro, head of the victorious army.

Youth to join the guerrillas, was ordered to serve under Guevara in Escambray on the Las Villas front (see the statement of Hiram Prats at the trial of Marcos Rodríguez in *Bohemia*, April 3, 1964); also Armando Acosta, later secretary-general of the PURS in Oriente province, who was one of the Las Villas Communists, moved to Oriente to return with the invasion column of Che Guevara. There is no doubt about the relations between Raúl and Guevara, and the PSP, at least since the summer of 1958. When Raúl kidnapped several American citizens in June 1958 he sent all the information to the Politburo of the PSP in Havana. The messenger was "Pepe" Ramírez, a Communist with Raúl's forces. (See Raúl Castro, "Operación antiaérea" [Operation Anti-Aircraft], *Verde Olivo*, September 22, 1963.) Guevara, after arriving in the Sierra of Escambray, wrote to Chomón, November 7, 1958, about his conversations with members of the PSP. According to Guevara, those members had a "frankly unitary" position. (See Faure Chomón, "Cuando el Che llegó al Escambray" [When Che Arrived in Escambray], *Verde Olivo*, December 12, 1965.)

49 Castro referred to these promises in his speech of December 1, 1961 (*Hoy*, December 2, 1961). It is impossible, of course, to determine whether at that time he intended to fulfill his promises or was merely trying to provide a valid excuse to offer to the PSP.

CHAPTER TWO

REVOLUTION — POLITICAL OR SOCIAL?

The Sources of Castro's Power

Before fleeing Cuba Batista nominated a government under the presidency of a justice of the Supreme Court to preserve some semblance of constitutionality. General Eulogio Cantillo, who until then had been in command of government forces in Oriente province, now became commander-in-chief of the army. After promising to surrender the capital of the province to Castro on December 31, Cantillo changed his mind for some unknown reason. Castro responded by calling for a general strike and ordering a march on the city that had been promised to him. The officer who had replaced Cantillo in Oriente decided to keep the promise broken by the latter and surrendered the garrison without resistance. As a consequence, on January 2 in Santiago de Cuba, which was occupied by the Rebel Army, a new revolutionary government was formed under the presidency of Manuel Urrutia; this judge had voted in favor of pardoning the members of the July 26 Movement who had taken part in the November 30, 1956 uprising. Castro had proposed him for President when the professional associations failed to reply to his July 1957 manifesto.[1] The new President, given complete freedom to name his own cabinet, appointed as his prime minister José Miró, the coordinator of the opposition front established in July of the preceding year.

Miró was awakened in his Miami home in the early hours of January 1 with the news of the dictator's flight; at first he did not believe it, but before daybreak he left Florida Beach for Oriente to head the new cabinet. The opposition front had never had any

[1] Castro proposed Dr. Manuel Urrutia for President in a letter of December 14, 1957 to the Junta of Cuban Liberation. (See Fidel Castro, *La revolución cubana* [The Cuban Revolution]; selection, Prologue, and notes by Gregorio Selser (Buenos Aires: Editorial Palestra, 1960), pp. 127 ff.) The following day Armando Hart told Urrutia of his appointment. Manuel Urrutia, *Fidel Castro y Compañía, S.A.* [Fidel Castro and Co., Inc.] (Barcelona: Editorial Herder, 1963), p. 26.

formal existence and had had very little influence on the events leading to the collapse of the regime, and with this abrupt and unilateral decision of its coordinator to subordinate himself to the President nominated by Castro, it lost the little respect it still enjoyed and never showed any sign of life again.

In Havana, meanwhile, with the surrender of the army and the disappearance of the police from the streets, the general strike received universal support. The Supreme Court refused to administer the oath of office to the judge whom Batista had appointed as his successor. General Cantillo was arrested; the officer who replaced him, Colonel Ramón Barquín, who had been in prison since April 1956 for his part in a military plot against Batista, decided, in the face of the obvious disintegration of the armed forces, to agree to Castro's demands and to allow him to occupy the two most important army camps, Columbia and La Cabaña.

Batista's coup of March 10, 1952 had been made possible by his influence over the army; and the army had been the sole basis for his power during the six years of his rule. Hence, when the army began to fall apart, state authority practically ceased to exist. President Urrutia was able to transfer his government from Santiago de Cuba to the presidential palace in Havana;[2] but he owed his appointment to Castro, and both he, a judge who was totally unknown until Castro made him his candidate, and Miró, Dean of the Bar Association, were, from any political point of view, two zeroes. Moreover, the very existence of an opposition front had already been forgotten, and only two of the independent revolutionary organizations, the Revolutionary Student Directorate and the Second Escambray Front,[3] had armed men in the field; and these were no match in either prestige or strength for the forces headed by Castro. Thus the real power, and with it the ability to decide the course of the victorious insurrection, fell into the hands of the guerrilla leader.

[2] The Revolutionary Student Directorate occupied the presidential palace and attempted to exercise some influence over the naming of the cabinet, but once the new President arrived in Havana and took control, it abandoned its attempts.

[3] In the first months of 1958 the Revolutionary Student Directorate founded a guerrilla front in the Escambray mountains in Las Villas province. But a little later some men of this front separated themselves and founded a new group, called the Second Escambray Front, in another part of the same mountains. Among its leaders were Eloy Gutiérrez Menoyo and William Morgan (an American). They were not interested in ideological questions, had a very weak organization, and fought very little against Batista.

Castro at this point was the leader of the July 26 Movement, the commander-in-chief of the Rebel Army, and the popular hero who was admired for his victory over despotism. Let us give a brief analysis of these sources of his power.

As far as ideology is concerned, the July 26 Movement had a program — the Mexican one of November 1956. This document stated that "in sound political terminology the word 'imperialism' is now out of place in America." It rejected "economic determinism" and affirmed that the movement was "guided by the ideas of democracy, nationalism, and social justice";[4] but the latter statement was later twisted in an article by Carlos Franqui, the editor of the July 26 Movement's clandestine journal *Revolución,* where it was stated that "in accordance with its goals and as a consequence of the historic, geographic, and sociological reality of Cuba, the revolution is democratic, nationalist, and socialist."[5] Moreover, the Mexican statement had never been promulgated as an official program; and each time Castro was asked to produce a statement of doctrine "he replied . . . that it would emerge from the depth of the events, since tying oneself down to inflexible theories in advance would restrict one within excessively dogmatic limits and would obstruct the necessary dynamism of the revolution."[6] If one also takes into account the July 26 Movement's "Economic Thesis," which was circulated widely but did not have an official character,[7] and the *History Will Absolve Me* pamphlet, which Castro had not yet claimed to be a program, it is apparent that a typically "Fidelista" confusion dominated the movement in the ideological field.

[4] The Mexican program, signed in November 1956, appears in Enrique González Pedrero, *La revolución cubana* [The Cuban Revolution] (Mexico City: Escuela Nacional de Ciencias Políticas y Sociales, 1959), p. 89.

[5] Parts of this modified program appear in Herbert L. Matthews, *The Cuban Story* (New York: George Braziller, 1961), p. 79. Matthews writes: "In mid-February, 1957, when I went up to see Fidel, the underground publication of the 26th of July Movement, *Revolución,* published what I believe was the first program." I have no personal knowledge of the complete document.

[6] Euclídes Vázquez Candelas, "La revolución humanista" [The Humanist Revolution], in *Temas en torno a la revolución* [Themes Concerning the Revolution] (Havana: Editorial Tierra Nueva, n.d.). At the time he wrote the article Vázquez Candelas was the assistant editor of *Revolución.* Moreover, as he says in the article, when he was in the underground he edited a pamphlet entitled *Razones del 26* [Principles of the July 26 Movement] and the declaration of the movement against the November 1958 elections.

[7] *La tesis económica* [The Economic Plan], according to the copy in my possession, was edited by Regino Boti, Minister of Economics until the summer of 1964, and by Felipe Pazos, president of the National Bank until November 1959 and now in exile.

The same confusion prevailed in organizational matters. It is impossible to calculate the strength of the July 26 Movement membership on December 31, 1958; though Arnault says that there were 400 members in Havana,[8] my own experience indicates that this figure is if anything an exaggeration. These members, and also those in the other provinces, took their orders from municipal and provincial coordinators, everyone being subject to the instructions of the National Directorate, the elusive and mysterious body that after May 1958 was subject to the jurisdiction of the Rebel Army. Finally, the National Directorate had created two instruments to extend its own influence: the National Trade Union Front, which as early as January 1959 dissolved the alliance that had been formed with the Communists the preceding November, quickly acquired control of the Cuban Workers' Confederation (CTC), and now became the most effective section of the July 26 Movement; and the "Civic Resistance," made up of professional and business men, which played no role whatsoever after Castro's victory in January. Such was the "organization" of the July 26 Movement.

At the time of Batista's fall the Rebel Army numbered 1,500 men at most.[9] We know that when Batista began his offensive against the guerrilla forces in May 1958, Castro had no more than 300 men. It follows that four fifths of this army must have joined it during the last five months of the civil war, because it was practically impossible for them to have done so while Batista's offensive, which did not end until July, was still in full swing. This means that the great majority of the new recruits were attracted by the rising prestige of Castro and were more inclined to follow his personal authority than that of the July 26 Movement. It should not be assumed, however, that they were willing to obey their chief's orders blindly. The army had, after all, been formed on the basis of the democratic slogan "Liberty or death."

The organizational elements of Castro's power were, as can be seen, extremely feeble. The fundamental source of this power was his personal prestige, the intense attraction he exercised over the people by virtue of being not merely the victor over Batista but the first victorious military leader in Cuban history who had not depended on foreign aid to secure his victory. Yet, intense as popular

---

8 Jacques Arnault, *Cuba et le marxisme* (Paris: Editions Sociales, 1962), p. 103.
9 This is the figure given by Robert Taber, *M–26: Biography of a Revolution* (New York: Lyle Stuart, 1961), p. 297. As a maximum estimate it seems correct to me.

feeling in favor of Castro was, it is obvious that he could consolidate influence over the masses only if he accurately interpreted their aspirations and the real nature of the situation in Cuba.

To sum up the situation briefly: If revolution is to mean a violent, long drawn out, and fundamental transformation of the prevailing social and economic system, brought about through the demands of the "oppressed and exploited masses," who are "aware of the impossibility of going on living as they are living and so demand changes,"[10] then in January 1959 there was no revolutionary situation in Cuba. In 1952 the people had reacted to Batista's coup with indifference. They were never sympathetic to the dictatorship. Nevertheless it was only during 1958 — and in Havana only in December 1958 at that — that opposition began to take on massive proportions. And when that point of exacerbation was reached, there was still an ideological void, and the objective conditions for a revolutionary situation in the Leninist sense — great poverty in large sectors of the population plus their conviction that it was impossible to go on living as they had been living — were still absent. The aspirations of the overwhelming majority of the Cuban people were therefore limited to the removal of the dictatorship and the re-establishment of constitutional legality.

The People and Its Revolution

Accustomed to the later propaganda of Castroism and to the extensive literature that explains everything in terms of economic underdevelopment, the reader may be surprised by our statement that the overthrow of Batista was not due to any demand by the masses for a radical transformation of the socioeconomic structure. Hence a word of explanation is needed.

The two basic arguments generally used to explain the intensity of social unrest in Cuba are, first, Cuba's underdevelopment, which is documented by pointing to the fact that its per capita income is substantially lower than that of the United States — $325 as against $1,908 in 1953; and second, the inequity in the distribution of land. According to the agricultural census of 1946, peasants with 25 hectares of land or less constituted 70 per cent of the peasantry and owned only 11 per cent of the land under cultivation.

With respect to the first argument, those who use it fail to ex-

[10] Lenin's phrase appears in *The Infantile Disease of "Leftism" in Communism* (Moscow: Foreign Languages Press, n.d.), p. 78.

plain why Italy, with a per capita income of $307, Austria with $290, Portugal with $240, Spain with $242, Turkey with $221, Mexico[11] and Yugoslavia with $200, and Japan with $197 — as of 1953 — enjoy a fair measure of stability while Cuba is undergoing the earthquake of Castroism.[12]

As for the Cuban agricultural system, no one can deny its profound injustice; but the whole point is to ascertain what influence it might have exercised on the emergence of a revolutionary situation in January 1959. In this respect, it must be pointed out that the peasants who had 25 hectares or less constituted only 111,000 out of an economically active population of nearly 2,060,000, that is, a little more than 5 per cent. Moreover, though we know very little of the real aspirations of these peasants, the only data we have indicate that land was not the first item in the order of their preferences. For instance, in a survey carried out by Lowry Nelson that covered 742 peasant holdings distributed throughout Cuba, the problems mentioned most often by those who were interviewed were as follows: roads and highways, 250 times; schools, 188; irrigation, 90; housing, 72; machinery, 68; and, at this point only, land, 66 times. In another study, carried out by the University Catholic Association in 1958, "74 per cent thought that the best way to improve living conditions was by increasing employment opportunities."[13] It is difficult to see how a segment that did not amount to 6 per cent of the economically active population and plainly did not have the avid hunger for land that was later discovered by observers (when Guevara started the myth of peasant revolution)

11 Dudley Seers, in his *Cuba: The Economic and Social Revolution* (Durham, N.C.: University of North Carolina Press, 1964), pp. 18–19, voices the opinion that "political stability can hardly be expected in a country which has fallen far behind a neighbor with which it is in close economic and political relations." But this is the case not only with Cuba but also with Mexico, which has a per capita income lower than that of Cuba and has been enjoying enviable stability for the past three decades. According to the *Statistical Abstract of Latin America* (Los Angeles: University of California Press, 1961), Cuban per capita income in 1959 was $338 as against $263 for Mexico. Concerning the closeness of the Mexican and Cuban economic ties with the United States, the *Statistical Abstract* indicates that in 1959 Mexican trade with the United States amounted to 72.94 per cent of its total exports and 72.91 per cent of its imports; Cuban exports and imports amounted to 69.70 per cent and 63.59 per cent, respectively.

12 See Charles P. Kindleberger, *Economic Development* (New York: McGraw-Hill, 1958), table on p. 6.

13 Lowry Nelson's survey appears in his *Rural Cuba* (Minneapolis, Minn.: University of Minnesota Press, 1950), p. 249; the investigation carried out by the University Catholic Association is mentioned by Andrés Bianchi in Seers, *op. cit.*, p. 97.

could have made an important contribution to the revolutionary situation in January 1959, using the term in the sense described earlier.[14]

The fact that a revolutionary situation in the Leninist sense did not actually prevail is indicated quite conclusively by Castro's activity during the first months after his victory. Showing even then his exceptional gift for winning popular support, he began to fortify his ties to the masses not by displaying radical slogans but, quite the contrary, by demonstrating moderation and by threatening that if he were replaced he would be succeeded by others who would be far more radical.[15]

At his first mass rally in Havana, on January 8, 1959, Castro began to create this image of himself as a prudent leader, anxious to re-establish normality and preoccupied by the excesses of those who wanted to continue revolutionary agitation. He vowed that if he or his movement became an obstacle to peace, "then the people itself could assume command over all of us and tell us what we must do." In the name of peace he went on to incite the masses against the Revolutionary Student Directorate. At that time the Directorate was claiming a voice in policymaking because it had fought alongside Castro, and was trying to obtain arms for itself because Castro would not give it access to the military barracks. He kept insisting that it must bow to the will of the people and to presidential authority.

In this speech Castro never once mentioned *History Will Absolve Me,* nor did he promise land reform, nor did he thank the peasants for the outstanding share in the formation of the Rebel Army they were later "discovered" to have had. His promises were quite different — simply peace. And so long as he could "serve as a bridge" between the revolutionaries and the "honest military men" of Batista's army, he promised the latter that they would keep their

14 It is hardly necessary to point out that this by no means signifies any belief on my part that if the Castro regime were to vanish Cuba would return to the land system that prevailed before 1959. I sincerely hope that system has been conclusively wiped out.

15 For instance, in his January 21, 1959 speech Castro said: "There are people behind me who are more radical than myself." (Fidel Castro, *La revolución cubana, op. cit.,* p. 187.) Immediately following this he mentioned his brother, revealing even then the jealousy that has always been characteristic in any question concerning his personal power, that is, he was very careful to mention as leader of the radicals not Ernesto Guevara, who was the real brain among the radicals, but his own brother Raúl, so that everything could be kept within the family.

ranks and positions, while he promised the former free access to the armed forces, retaining "their ranks regardless of the date of their promotion."[16] These were clearly the right words for the revolutionaries (in whose ranks, as Castro himself later complained, a disproportionate number of majors were beginning to appear) as well as for a people that firmly believed in the disappearance of all its afflictions with the flight of the tyrannical Batista.

Castro, continuing this same policy, opposed the attempts made by the President to close the casinos that Batista had allowed to operate for the purpose of attracting tourists, and he rejected the so-called "Urrutia doctrine," the President's proposal not to recognize the right to asylum of Batista's collaborators who had taken refuge in the embassies of the Latin American republics. Castro also ended the boycott on British goods (proclaimed during the civil war as a reprisal against the British government for having sold aircraft to the Batista regime), and asked the sugar workers to begin the harvest (of 1959) without waiting for their demands to be met.[17]

Within this framework of winning the confidence of the people, it was extremely easy for Castro to exploit the critical reaction of the United States to the summary trials of the Batista war criminals. I do not wish, of course, to defend these mock trials, which disregarded the most elementary rules of justice. But it must be pointed out that the Batista dictatorship had provoked profound hatred. Because of this, the "trials" had, if not the approval, at least the acquiescence of the great majority of the Cuban people. In consequence, Castro could exploit the criticism from abroad in order to identify himself with, and at the same time exacerbate, the national indignation. This also provided him with the basis for his first experiment with mass meetings which was held on January 21 to protest against U.S. criticism of the "trials."

While Castro was consolidating his ties to the masses without explaining concretely just what the aims of the victorious movement were, the Urrutia-Miró government remained paralyzed, overwhelmed by the demands of office seekers that threatened to annihilate even the very low level of efficiency at which the Cuban public administration was accustomed to function. By the end of the first month of the revolution this situation was giving rise to a

---

16 *Ibid.*, p. 177.
17 Both speeches are in *ibid.*, pp. 200 and 228.

certain anxiety, aggravated by those who wanted to "deepen and widen" the scope of the revolution. We are referring to the People's Socialist Party (PSP), that is, the Communist Party, and Ernesto Guevara.

The January Theses of the PSP and Guevara's "Armed Democracy"

On January 6, 1959, before Castro made his entry into Havana, the National Committee of the PSP published a statement entitled "The Overthrow of the Tyranny and the Immediate Tasks Ahead." In this document the Cuban Communists promised the new government "all the support and all the cooperation necessary" and called for the "formalization, extension, and consolidation of unity" of all revolutionaries. It proposed a program with the following basic points:

1. "To complete the disintegration of the Batista political machine," making the Rebel Forces the nucleus of the new army.

2. The promulgation of the Land Law issued in the Sierra on October 10, 1958, which granted ownership rights to tenant farmers with 165 acres or less (66 of which to be granted gratis) and always with prior compensation to the previous owners.

3. A quest for new markets for Cuban products in the socialist countries.

4. The restoration of the 1940 constitution to prepare for democratic elections, "after the changes or adjustments deemed necessary by the people."[18]

As we see, this program was not phrased in anti-U.S. terms. In its general modesty it obviously corroborates our view that in the first days after Castro's victory there was no revolutionary situation in Cuba. If the Communists wanted to keep abreast with Castro, they would have to amplify that program once it became clear, first, that he was actually proceeding toward the "disintegration of the Batista political machine"; second, that the Urrutia government remained in a state of inactivity; third, that Castro had begun to utilize mass meetings to protest U.S. criticism of the trials so as to increase his popular support; and finally, that the PSP was challenged from the "left" itself by one of the most brilliant of the guerrilla chiefs, Ernesto Guevara.

18 *Hoy,* January 6, 1959.

Guevara, the author of *Guerrilla Warfare,* is the only veteran of the Sierra Maestra who seems to have found the time to read Marxist texts. Was he a Marxist as early as 1959? J. P. Morray claims that Guevara worked with Communist groups in his own country, Argentina, and in Guatemala;[19] but I have not been able to find a single document showing that Guevara was familiar with the classics of Marxism or could be identified completely with any Communist position before the summer of 1960. His talk to the Nuestro Tiempo association in Havana on January 27, 1959, which will have to serve as a guide to his thinking at that time, was not that of a Marxist. After his trip to Europe and Asia in the summer of the same year, "Che" came back an ardent admirer of Nasser. And in November 1959 he recommended to Latin Americans the adoption of an international posture "similar to that adopted by the Afro-Asian zone, the so-called Bandung pact countries."[20] Finally, there is the evidence of Blas Roca, the secretary-general of the PSP.[21] In his speech to the PSP Central Committee plenum in October 1959 the Communist leader referred to the danger of "exceptionalism." As we shall soon see, Roca gives a tortuous interpretation of "exceptionalism" and also fails to indicate whom he is referring to. But all who lived through this period know that his target was Guevara.

From all this I conclude that Guevara, when he first met Castro in Mexico in 1956 during the preparatory stages of the expedition to Cuba, was a young man of certain intellectual and revolutionary inclinations but with no precise ideological position, and this was still true in January 1959. In contrast to Castro, however, he felt the need for an ideology and he had the strength to create one for himself. Under the impact of the revolutionary process this ideology finally took a Marxist shape.

Now let us turn to the positions of the PSP and of Guevara in January 1959. Under the immediate impact of Castro's victory the PSP had hurriedly come out with its extremely moderate program of January 6. On January 11, the party newspaper *Hoy* published the "Theses on the Present Situation," which were considerably

[19] J. P. Morray, *The Second Revolution in Cuba* (New York: Monthly Review Press, 1962), p. 61.

[20] Guevara praised Nasser and the UAR in his two television interviews reporting on his trip (*Hoy,* September 9 and 16, 1959). On his attitude toward Latin American foreign policy see "Interview with 'Radio Rivadavia,' Buenos Aires," *Revolución,* November 3, 1959.

[21] See Blas Roca's conclusions on the program in *Hoy,* October 9, 1959.

stronger in both wording and content. On January 27 the top leader of the party, Secretary-General Blas Roca, gave a report explaining the Theses to the Central Committee.

Like all Marxists, Roca — it was he who formulated the theoretical documents of his party — took as his starting point a sociological interpretation of events. The Batista dictatorship, in the wording of his January Theses, "was the government of submission to imperialism, of the great landholders, the big import merchants, and the sugar magnates." This government has been swept away and a new one has taken its place based "on popular forces (workers, peasant-bourgeoisie, and national-bourgeoisie) although at present the control and the authority are in the hands of the national bourgeoisie and the petite bourgeoisie."[22] The political significance of this sociological outline was made clear in Roca's report to the party explaining the theses.[23]

Roca stated that what had appeared in Cuba was the phenomenon known as "dualism of power," which is characteristic of every revolution. After the fall of the dictatorship, he said,

. . . power passed into the hands of the rebel armed forces, with the commander-in-chief, Fidel Castro, in supreme authority. . . . Nevertheless these groups then passed formal power over the nation on to President Urrutia and the Cabinet . . . but through a phenomenon of moral authority, through a spontaneous and inevitable political phenomenon, these rebel forces, headed by Fidel Castro, have retained part of the power. . . .

Roca called this power "revolutionary power" because it "is a better and more complete reflection than the provisional government of the social forces that made possible the overthrow of the dictatorship."

If the problem is posed in these terms, the logical solution, from Roca's point of view, would be to support the "revolutionary power," that is, the Rebel Army, in order to solve the duality of power in a sense favorable to the revolution. But the Communist chief could not recommend this, first of all because he knew that the influence of the PSP within the rebel forces was minimal — not a single field commander of the Rebel Army was in Roca's party — and second, because in such a case the one to make all the decisions would be Castro, whose attitude up to that point was, to say the least, doubtful. Hence Roca proposed strengthening the "formal

22 "Theses on the Present Situation," *ibid.*, January 11, 1959.
23 *Ibid.*, February 1, 1959.

power," that is, the Urrutia provisional government. This government should change its composition; the PSP would be disposed to form part of the cabinet. Moreover, the provisional government should expand its functions, and no longer be, "as was originally thought," a government of transition but one of "consolidation of the revolution."

The revolution should bring about the nationalization of the public services, put "into effect the land law issued in the Sierra Maestra in the fall of 1958 until the large landholdings are wiped out," modify the constitutional provision providing for the prior compensation in cash for expropriations, and eliminate from the constitution the provision that a party must have at least 2 per cent of the electorate on its register in order to enjoy legal status. The PSP was still thinking in electoral terms and was afraid of not being able to register a sufficient number of voters to qualify for participation in a coming election.

To achieve all this, "to defend and promote the revolution," the PSP recommended the well-known Communist tactic of "calling the masses into action" for the realization of a program of concrete demands. What was fundamental, however, was not this but unity, the formation "of a broad revolutionary, patriotic, democratic, and popular coalition" that would allow the Communists to appear before the people not with their own name and banner, under which they would be rejected out of hand, but protected by the prestige of the Revolutionary Student Directorate and of the July 26 Movement.[24]

In Guevara's talk of January 27, 1959, on the other hand, nothing can be found of Marxist sociology or of any electoral preoccupation. His language was much more simple and direct. For him the Rebel Army was "the vanguard of the Cuban people, . . . our primary instrument of struggle" and must be the formative nucleus of the whole of the Cuban people, which "must be turned into a guerrilla army" in order to lay a firm foundation for "armed democracy," as Guevara described the current regime.[25] However, Guevara was not in control of the Rebel Army and, like Roca, was surely worried by Castro's moderation. What he needed, therefore, was a "motor" to push ahead the "vanguard." For the PSP the

[24] The phrases in quotation marks are taken from the theses and the report cited in notes 22 and 23, respectively.

[25] Guevara's talk to the Nuestro Tiempo association in Havana (see Fidel Castro, *La revolución cubana, op. cit.,* pp. 427 ff.).

driving force was to be "unity" and "mass action," whereas for Guevara it was to be the peasants. It was they who had prevailed upon the revolution to "do something that at one time had not been thought of" — the land law issued in the Sierra — and it was with the aid of "threats from the peasants" that the guerrillas had marched through Cuba "with land reform as the spearhead of the Rebel Army." Guevara thus launched what was later to become the myth of the peasant origin of the Cuban revolution. It would be the peasants also who would now impose the new program put forward by Guevara, which was practically the same as that proposed by the PSP except that it did not include a demand for elections; it called for the elimination of the big landholdings and the nationalization of the public services, to which Guevara also added "the recovery of our subsoil." It should be noted that in this underdeveloped country (in January 1959) neither Guevara nor the Communists were demanding wage increases or making any other demand on behalf of the workers, who, if one includes the agricultural sugarcane laborers, make up the great majority of the Cuban people.

The basic difference, however, between the PSP and Guevara was in foreign policy.

In his theses of January 11 Roca denied "in general terms . . . the possibility of armed intervention" on the part of the "Yankee imperialists," listing the national and international factors that warranted this statement. Even in his report of January 27, following the mass meeting to protest the criticisms of the trials, in which he pointed out that "the Number One enemy of the Cuban people" was "Yankee imperialism," in describing the various forms that aggression might take he never even contemplated the possibility of an armed attack.

In contrast, it may be said that Guevara not only foresaw this possibility but even needed it, since it was evident that if he wanted to turn the whole Cuban people into a guerrilla army it was indispensable to have an enemy that would justify such a mobilization and that would make aggression seem likely. "If we are attacked," he said, "the attack will be supported by a power that takes up almost an entire continent." Hence the people should be armed. But that was not enough. "The revolution," said "Che," "is not limited to the Cuban nation." It must be extended to "our brothers in America, situated economically in the same agrarian category as ourselves." They will have to learn the "fundamental lesson" of "our revolution," that is, that "agrarian revolutions must be made; we must struggle in the fields, in the mountains, and from there bring the revolution into the cities."

I offer these remarks both to those who would like to turn the Cuban revolution into a mere reaction to the errors and short-sightedness of U.S. foreign policy and to those who would like to explain the whole thing in terms of the perversity of the Communists. In January 1959, when the United States had just recognized the revolutionary government and not even the PSP believed in the possibility of intervention, Guevara was proposing to arm the people to fight against the U.S. Marines and to extend subversion to Latin America. This was because he understood that if he wished to turn the struggle against the dictatorship and for the re-establishment of constitutional legality into a violent and deeply rooted process of social transformation, a domestic program was not sufficient. Something further was needed, a foreign enemy, to justify the scope and rhythm of the domestic upheaval, to impose obedience on the people without paying any attention to their desires, and to crush any dissidents, while constantly invoking the sacred interests of the nation.

It is easy to imagine the alarm Guevara's program aroused throughout the PSP. From the day it was founded the party had had a monopoly of the "left" and of "anti-imperialism," even though from 1934 on both these attitudes never extended beyond mere rhetoric. Now a rival had appeared that demanded of the PSP that it should practice what it preached.

Castro as Prime Minister

On February 16, 1959, Castro took over from Miró the office of Prime Minister. The circumstances that impelled him to this step were the continuing inactivity of the government, the ever-increasing clamor of office seekers, and the pressure brought to bear on him by the radicals, Guevara and the PSP, whose position was strengthened on February 2 by the designation of Raúl Castro as his brother's substitute in command of the armed forces in case of temporary or permanent absence.

Castro's speech on this occasion gave no indication that he had decided to abandon his previous, moderate position. After reiterating his "respect for the system . . . lack of personal ambitions, loyalty to principles, unshakable and profound democratic convictions," Castro denied having proposed a lowering of rents. He said such action would be inopportune (though twenty-four days later he issued a decree to that effect). He also announced a rather feeble program that boiled down to a cutback of the salaries of the members of the Council of Ministers, the ousting of Batista collaborators from public service, and a guarantee of the strictest honesty in his public administration. Finally, by way of demonstrating his total ignorance of economic questions, he gave assurances that "in the course of a few short years" he would raise "the standard of living of the Cubans to a level higher than that of the United States and Russia"![26] Four days later, on instructions from Castro, the Minister of Agriculture had a law passed by the Council of Ministers providing for the total loss of all rights and benefits under the future land reform law of those who had begun a squatters' movement; and on February 24 Castro himself, in Santiago de Cuba, appeared before the peasants to explain and defend the law that had been passed and to demand from them the strictest discipline.[27]

This concluded what may be called the moderate phase in Castro's policy. We must now attempt to explain his subsequent change in attitude.

From the first of January on, the Cuban people had been living through the honeymoon characteristic of popular victories. There was no army, no police, and the people were dedicated to nothing more than the enjoyment of their freedom and the expression of their gratitude to Castro. History has demonstrated that such phases cannot be prolonged indefinitely, and that sooner or later the organs that ensure social discipline must be restored.

The Batista supporters abroad, encouraged by the apparent incapability of the new regime even to organize its own defense, were beginning to raise their heads. Uncertainty was growing among the propertied classes, worsening the economic paralysis that had been started by the intensification of the civil war. The professional politicians — Auténticos, Ortodoxos, and so on — who for six years had been kept away from the national treasury, were now hoping for a return to normal elections that would give them back their offices as senators and representatives. And among the masses of

---

26 *Ibid.,* p. 239.

27 The then Minister of Agriculture, Humberto Sorí Marín, who was later executed by Castro, told President Urrutia that Law 87 was Castro's proposal (see Urrutia, *op. cit.,* p. 54). For the February 24 speech see Fidel Castro, *La revolución, cubana, op. cit.,* p. 273.

the people, with the dizzying rhythm characteristic of such processes, new expectations were emerging that had never even remotely existed in January.

Now that Castro was head of the government, basic decisions could no longer be put off. Either he had to implement the stated aims of the struggle against Batista — the constitution of 1940 and elections within a short time — or he had to take the path of social revolution to justify him in clinging onto revolutionary power, in which case the sympathy and gratitude of the masses were not enough. He had to find incentives and means that would transform mere declarations of support into active and organized participation, and by thus mobilizing the masses provide himself with a solid power base. In short, he needed a new program and the instruments with which to implement it.

As for the first alternative, Castro had probably never contemplated it with any seriousness, and was all the less likely to now that his position as head of the government, supreme commander of the armed forces, and popular idol — something completely new in Cuban history — confirmed the high opinion he had always had of himself. With respect to the second alternative, Castro simply did not know what to do, as is illustrated by his speech when he became Prime Minister. He could, to be sure, adopt one or another of the formulas being put forward by Guevara or the PSP, but it was still very early to identify himself with any of those positions. One must admit that no suggestion worthy of consideration came from any other quarter.

On February 16, the same day that Castro took over the government, the periodical *Revolución*, more or less the official organ of the July 26 Movement, published an editorial signed by Marcelo Fernández, the movement's national organization coordinator. The coincidence of dates, the position of the writer, and the actual contents of the article indicate that this was an attempt to formulate a program for the new cabinet. The editorial was entitled "The Permanent Revolution." The reader must not think, however, that it had anything to do with the well-known theory expounded by Leon Trotsky. Fernández was probably quite ignorant of it because he does not mention it even once as a source. According to Fernández, the revolution was "not an act but a process. It is permanent, or it is no revolution." The revolutionary process was launched when Castro, the "guerrilla-statesman," was named Prime Minister, and it would continue with the promulgation of a whole series of laws that would include land reform, educational reform, customs and tariff reform, the general raising of wages, the lowering of rents, electricity, and telephone charges, and so on. But the provisional government was "transitory." It would have to hold elections, though Fernández did not say when. It was here, he said, that the danger lay. "The old politicians" were already preparing for elections, and it would be necessary to circumvent them by turning the July 26 Movement into "a revolutionary party that could control and ensure the continuation of the work undertaken by the present government." The article ended with these words:

Cuba can have confidence in the July 26 Movement. The revolution will not fail, nor will it become out of date. It will be the permanent revolution the theorists have been asking for.[28]

A few days later Marcelo Fernández opened an office to which all dismissals of public administration personnel had to be reported so that the new "revolutionary party" could allocate the vacancies to its future supporters. Some of the youthful leaders from the underground movement began thinking of their chances in an election.

Given the problem confronting Castro, to mobilize and organize the masses around his own person, it is difficult to see what attraction he could find in a program that was becoming an organized assault on governmental posts and that emphasized the "transitional" nature of his regime.

It was at this point that Castro recalled his *History Will Absolve Me*. In his March 6 television appearance he used it to justify the lowering of telephone rates (a decision passed four days before), as well as intervention in the management of the telephone company, and the lowering of rents by as much as 50 per cent (decreed on March 10). He said the delay in implementing the program had been because "we wanted to do things with moderation and care, and carry out the proposals in an orderly way. . . ." But his recollection of the pamphlet was so vague that, as one can see from the text of the interview, both the journalist interviewing him and Castro himself only occasionally used the right title of the pamphlet and at other times called it *History Will Judge Me*.[29]

[28] The February 16 edition of *Revolución* gave a program of twenty points as the objectives of the new cabinet. In his speech on becoming Prime Minister, Castro disavowed such a program.

[29] Television interview of March 6 in Fidel Castro, *Discursos para la historia* [Speeches for History], Vol. 2 (Havana, n.d.), p. 35.

During the same television appearance in which he rescued his pamphlet from oblivion, Castro also referred to the "cordial and friendly conversations with the Ambassador of the United States" that had taken place the day before and announced his forthcoming visit to Washington at the invitation of the Association of Newspaper Publishers. Nevertheless, on March 22, José Figueres, ex-President of Costa Rica, attempted publicly to get a foreign policy statement out of him. Castro, while avoiding a precise statement, stressed that he was not concerned about aggression that might come from "other continents," that is, the Communist world, but about attacks "by mercenary bands" that could come from "the beaches of Florida or from Santo Domingo."[30]

Moreover, on March 13 the anniversary of the attack on the presidential palace was celebrated "in unity," that is, with the participation of the PSP, the July 26 Movement, and the Revolutionary Student Directorate. This was plainly a victory for the Communists, even though on this occasion Castro avoided the theme of unity.[31] On April 9 he demonstrated his aversion to elections when he said to his audience, "Those who are not interested in elections should raise their hands."[32] Of course everyone did so. Taking all this into account, one is led to conclude that March 1959 marks the beginning of a policy that was quite different from his previous one. To realize how rapidly Castro's intentions had changed it is enough to point out what he had said about elections only one month earlier: "We are going to have elections, and if the people do not want us because they are tired of us or because we are failing, then we shall go. . . ."[33]

This progressive radicalization, which led Castro to positions more and more incompatible with the original aims of the struggle against Batista, was interrupted by his visit to the United States at the invitation of the Association of Newspaper Publishers. It is difficult to determine his reasons for making the trip. In his speech to his hosts he said: "It is incorrect to say that we have come here to look for money. . . . Public opinion is more important to us. . . ."[34] But if the visit was for propaganda purposes why was

30 *Ibid.*, pp. 81–106.
31 "Llamamiento del PSP para conmemorar el 13 de marzo" [Declaration of the PSP to Commemorate March 13], in answer to the declaration made by the Revolutionary Student Directorate, *Hoy*, March 12, 1959.
32 Speech of April 9, in Fidel Castro, *Discursos para la historia*, Vol. 2, *op. cit.*, p. 110.
33 Television interview of March 6, previously cited, in *ibid.*
34 April 17, in Washington (see *ibid.*).

he accompanied by his economic and finance ministers and by the president of the National Bank?

It was during this same trip that Castro began speaking of his "humanist democracy," which according to him offered "liberty with bread and without terror"; though it seems that this "liberty" did not include the right to elect a government, since Castro mentioned the possibility of having to wait as long as four years before holding the first elections. He further amended his remarks of March 22 by stating that in case of a conflict between democracy and communism he would be "on the side of democracy," and adding categorically: "I am not a Communist, nor do I agree with communism."[35]

All this leads one to conclude that at this time, apart from the restoration of any legal system that would be incompatible with his own virtually absolute power, Castro was willing to consider every possible solution, and that among the motives for his visit to Washington might have been the hope of receiving some economic aid.[36] This does not mean, however, that Castro felt impelled to collaborate more closely with the radicals because he did not receive aid or because it was not offered on a scale or on terms that were attractive to him. As we shall see, it was in fact just after this trip that he showed signs of wanting to distance himself both from Guevara and from the PSP.

Castro's visit to the United States must have constituted a serious problem for the PSP, since it had always been a dogma of Latin American communism, at least until Khrushchev's visit to Washington in September 1959, that the mere presence of a Latin American statesman in the U.S. capital was unspeakable treason. In this particular case, however, even though, in the words of the Deputy Director of the CIA at that time, C. P. Cabell, "the Communists

---

[35] In the program "Meet the Press" (see *ibid.*, p. 140).

[36] Even Arnault, a Communist, was puzzled by this visit: "Does [Castro] think it possible to secure the good will of the United States? Or does he want to make a demonstration of the nature of imperialism for those who still doubt? . . . It is difficult to say." (Arnault, *op. cit.*, p. 105.) To give some notion of Castro's state of mind at this time, I think it relevant to mention a statement by former President Rómulo Betancourt of Venezuela in connection with the visit Castro paid him at the end of January 1959: "He wanted a loan of $300 million from Venezuela to free his government from dependence on the U.S. sugar-market quota, loans from U.S. banks, and international credit agencies." (See Rómulo Betancourt, "The Venezuelan Miracle," *The Reporter*, August 13, 1964.) It is beyond belief that Castro would have thought seriously that Venezuela could have loaned him $300 million.

were concerned when, at the time of his trip to the United States, he [Castro] showed evidence of a friendly attitude toward the United States,"[37] and *Hoy* censored Castro's statement that Cuba would remain a party to the Inter-American Defense Pact,[38] the Communists did not come close to condemning the visit for two reasons.

First, the Cubans lived outside the mainstream of world politics and were not involved in the Cold War. After 1946, when the Communists lost control of the trade-union organization and became an isolated group, anti-Communist feelings had no influence at all on Cuban politics. Nevertheless, when the members of the PSP reappeared in 1959, demanding a reward for their participation in a victory that everyone knew they had done extremely little if anything to promote, opposition to communism began to manifest itself with growing virulence, especially in the working-class circles of the July 26 Movement. It was these that had control of the CTC and it was precisely this control that was the primary goal of the Communists.

Of course the PSP could count on the support of Raúl Castro and Guevara, as was later confirmed at the trial of the informer Marcos Rodríguez.[39] But the Communists knew very well that these two men's support would be given only if it had the approval, either implicit or explicit, of Castro. Hence they did their best to avoid irritating him. Take, for instance, their attitude toward the anti-squatters' law. It was in fact the PSP that had encouraged squatting, but once Law 87 of February 20 was published in the official *Gazette*, the PSP, even though it said such a law was unnecessary, nevertheless agreed "that it was necessary to put a stop to the anarchic seizures of land."[40]

In short, the Communists were well aware of their dependence

---

[37] His statement to the U.S. Senate Internal Security Committee on November 5, 1959 (mentioned by Maurice Zeitlin and Robert Scheer, *Cuba: Tragedy in our Hemisphere* [New York: Grove Press, 1963], p. 111).

[38] "Un comentario: Sobre la posición internacional de Cuba" [A Commentary: On Cuba's International Position], *Hoy*, April 9, 1959.

[39] In January 1959 Marcos Rodríguez, who had never been with the guerrillas, obtained a post in the cultural department of the Revolutionary Armed Forces. And even when the widow of Fructuoso Rodríguez, one of the murdered men, found him there and had him arrested, Marcos obtained his freedom by means that are not quite clear. In April Joaquín Ordoqui, one of the principal Communist leaders, sent him to Prague to protect him from further investigation. See the report on the trial in *Bohemia*, March 27 and April 3, 1964.

[40] *Hoy*, February 22, 1959.

on Castro's favor and realized that if they lost this they would run perhaps the greatest risk in their entire history, since they were now confronting not a mere police state but a tremendous popular movement.

Second, the prospects of the PSP were so promising that it would feel inclined to shrug aside Castro's transgression in visiting the center of world capitalism.

As we have indicated, March 13 was celebrated "in unity," and Castro's March 22 speech was so favorably viewed by the PSP that it became the first one reproduced in full in the party newspaper *Hoy*.[41] While Castro was away the opportunities for the "unity" campaign were still better. Castro designated as his substitute in the premiership a protégé of Raúl's, Augusto Martínez Sánchez; and under the latter's leadership the "unity" activities were given a renewed stimulus and reached their peak on May 1, International Labor Day. On this day the militia, which had been organizing since March, paraded for the first time. In Havana Raúl Castro bitterly denounced anticommunism, while in Santiago de Cuba Guevara said: "Our voices must hammer out again and again the word unity."[42]

Yet on May 1 all was not well within the ranks of the partisans of "unity." In his March 22 speech Castro had said farewell to Cuba in the following words: "I am saying goodbye to the working class of Cuba until we meet again on May 1." But instead of keeping his promise, and in spite of all the efforts made by Raúl, who went to Houston to remind him of this among other things, Castro traveled to Argentina to take part in a session of the Inter-American Economic and Social Council, and it was not until May 9 that he returned to Havana. Against this background it is easy to imagine the anxiety with which the PSP awaited Castro's pronouncements. His speech on May 9 was a continuation of the themes he had developed during his visit to the United States. The Cuban revolution, he said, was "entirely democratic . . . the rights of man are the rights of our revolution." He denied that it had anything to do with communism, since "not only do we offer people food but we also offer them freedoms, and that is our clear and definite ideolog-

41 *Ibid.*, March 24, 1959.
42 *Ibid.*, March 5 and April 3, 1959, reports on the organization of the militias. The speeches of Raúl Castro and Guevara appeared in *ibid.* on May 3, and the same edition contained an article by Blas Roca, "Las 4 características del primero de mayo" [The 4 Characteristics of May 1], in which the "unitary" meaning of the celebration is pointed out.

ical position." He promised that the revolutionary tribunals that had aroused so much criticism in the United States would cease, because they had "already fulfilled their essential function." Finally, with a decisiveness he had not shown in this matter since January, he declared:

We have a powerful movement that is called the "July 26 Movement." . . . It won revolutionary power, and holds it . . . firmly in its hands. . . . Can anyone deny that it is the July 26 Movement that is responsible for the present government?[43]

If there was any doubt about the meaning of these words, it was completely dissipated on May 22, when Castro announced a trip that Guevara would make to various countries in Europe, Africa, and Asia. He denounced "the stupidity, the demagogy, the opportunism, and the politicking of all those who today give the appearance of being more revolutionary than anyone else"; and he denounced the public demonstrations, the agitation, and the excessive demands leading to disorders of the sort that had taken place in a town in Oriente province, San Luis. When the journalist who was interviewing him asked whether he "meant, in referring to the group of extremist agitators, the Communists," Castro replied: "There may be quite a lot in that. . . ."[44]

It need hardly be said that these words were just what the July 26 Movement had been waiting for. The following day, May 23, marked the beginning of the congress of the largest trade union in the CTC, the National Federation of Sugar Workers (Federación Nacional de Trabajadores Azucareros — FNTA). Since the election of delegates had not been carried out with joint lists on a "unity" platform, the PSP representation was quite negligible; and not even Ursinio Rojas, the PSP leader among the sugar workers and a member of the Politburo of the party, appeared among the delegates to the congress. Because of this *Hoy* printed an adverse account of the congress. The reaction of the congress was crushing. The "unity" candidate put forward by the Communists was rejected by the executive; the new directorate, headed by members of the July 26 Movement, was elected unanimously; a motion of censure against *Hoy* was passed; and there was even talk about the advisability of giving the newspaper back to the CTC — justifiably

43 *Hoy,* May 10, 1959.
44 *Revolución,* May 22, 1959. *Hoy* on May 23 also published Castro's interview but omitted the paragraphs that were critical of the Communists.

so, since it seems that *Hoy* was founded in 1938 with funds from this organization.[45]

The effect of all these events on the PSP was of course devastating. After Castro's speech on May 22 the Communists had still attempted to escape, as they had done before, by protesting feebly against the accusations of the "maximum leader" (máximo líder) and denying any responsibility for the events that had provoked Castro's remarks.[46] But following the resolutions of the FNTA, which cut the PSP off from the most powerful trade union in Cuba, a report given by Blas Roca to the PSP Central Committee plenum of May 25 showed how great was his dismay. "We stand at a critical moment for the revolution," he said. "All this threatens to degenerate into a general breakdown of revolutionary solidarity." Then he went on, as though everything were already finished, "This revolution has had better opportunities and possibilities than any other revolution in America. . . ." Thinking he had lost Castro's approval, the veteran leader of the PSP was so disturbed that he no longer knew what to suggest to his comrades: "We must not create or aggravate any conflicts . . . but it is also impossible for us to retreat."[47]

In the next chapter we shall see how the differences between Castro and the PSP were resolved. At this point we must inquire into Castro's motives for sending Guevara out of Cuba immediately after his own return from the United States, for publicly criticizing the Communists, and for allowing them, moreover, to be eliminated from the FNTA.

With respect to Guevara he has never given any explanation. But it should be noted that Castro took advantage of Che's absence to disperse the forces that had been under his command: after his return in September Guevara, who had led one of the two columns that had marched across Cuba, had been commander of the La Cabaña fortress until he left Cuba, and was the theoretician of guerrilla warfare, never again had any military forces under his control.

As for his skirmish with the PSP, in his December 1, 1961 speech Castro explained that he had been the victim of some misinformation concerning the disorders in San Luis (as he was later to estab-

---

45 Report on the FNTA congress in *Hoy*, May 24 and 26, 1959.
46 *Ibid.*, May 23, 1959.
47 See Blas Roca's report, not quoted directly, in *ibid.*, May 26, 1959.

lish that the Communists had had nothing to do with them).[48]
Nevertheless, when he came back from his trip and went to see
President Urrutia at the palace, Castro asked him: "Do you know
that the Communists intended to stage a coup against me"?[49] There
is not the slightest evidence of any such intention.

In our opinion there was never any danger of a coup during
Castro's absence, and the measures he took on his return are to be
explained as follows. As we have seen, after Castro's departure the
"unity" movement, under the aegis of Raúl Castro and Guevara,
acquired great momentum. Castro had not begun any serious organization of the Revolutionary Armed Forces just because any form
of organization would mean delegation and hence diminution of
his power; but on his return he came to the conclusion that the
intimate collaboration of his brother, Guevara, and the PSP, extending to the creation of a semimilitary apparatus outside his own
immediate control, implied a danger he could not allow to grow.
With his usual decisiveness he took appropriate steps to block any
possible rivals and to re-establish his absolute power.

In the midst of this friction the land reform law was passed on
May 17; it had been drawn up without the slightest participation
of the public. In general terms the law established an upper limit
of ownership at 30 caballerías (some 400 hectares), with 100 caballerías in exceptional cases; the rest was to be expropriated with
compensation to the landowner in twenty-year bonds at an interest
rate of 4 per cent. The land acquired in this way was to be distributed among the peasants in plots of no more than 2 caballerías
or handed over to cooperatives for their use. Tenants, subtenants,
lessees, and sublessees were to be granted free ownership of the
land they occupied provided that it did not exceed 2 caballerías.
The law further provided for the setting up of the National Institute of Agrarian Reform (Instituto Nacional de Reforma Agraria —
INRA), a body with immensely broad powers, presided over by
Castro himself. It was laid down that "wherever possible" INRA
would encourage cooperatives "under its own direction, preserving
the right to designate the administrators."

The implementation of the law would harm only an insignificant
number of landowners[50] but would immediately benefit about

[48] *Ibid.*, December 2, 1961.
[49] Urrutia, *op. cit.*, p. 54.
[50] According to the 1946 agricultural census only 12,749 estates comprised more

100,000 tenants, subtenants, and the like, and, if the land was actually distributed, perhaps some 200,000 new farmers.[51] Implementation, accordingly, meant the initiation of a social revolution.

The law, though criticized by some, still had the clear support of the great majority of the Cuban people; and with this support Castro had in five months transformed the struggle for the overthrow of the dictatorship and for the restoration of constitutional legality into a gigantic mass movement aimed at radically changing the socioeconomic structure of the country. The big landowners — whom it is difficult to designate as a class because, according to the 1946 census, only 994 people held more than a thousand hectares — were to lose their economic influence. (They had not had political influence at least since 1933.) The urban groups, especially the workers, who with their organization and electoral strength had imposed on the country social legislation incompatible with the level of its economic development and had prevented any rise in agricultural prices, would now be faced with really serious counterpressure from these 300,000 new smallholders.

As for the constitution and the organizational forms through which the masses were to participate in political activity, all this continued to be wrapped in the deepest of mysteries. Castro's "humanist democracy" never mentioned elections, and though in his May 9 speech he seemed to be backing the July 26 Movement he never did anything to organize it. On the other hand, now that Castro had distanced himself from Guevara and the Communists, and the masses were totally fascinated by his powerful personality, there was no longer any possibility of preventing him from doing what he wanted.

---

than 100 hectares. Of these, 10,433 had between 100 and 499.9 hectares. It cannot be ascertained how many of these exceeded the limit of 400 hectares set by the law, but it is obvious in any case that such estates were very few in number.

51 According to Andrés Bianchi, at the beginning of 1961 the Castro regime had already expropriated 4,500,000 hectares (in Seers, *op. cit.*, p. 103).

CHAPTER THREE

THE FIRST PHASE OF CASTROISM

On July 3, 1959 Castro made the following statement during one of his frequent television appearances:

Our position in regard to this problem of the Communists is very clear. . . . It is that in my opinion it is hardly honorable for us to start campaigns and attacks against them just in order to prevent people from accusing us of being Communists ourselves.[1]

In the same edition of *Hoy* that printed these words the PSP hastened to grasp the hand thus held out to it by agreeing to "ratify and reinforce the party's position of support for the government and for Prime Minister Fidel Castro."[2] A few days later, on the anniversary of the attack on the Moncada barracks, while the peasants were raising their machetes in an oath of loyalty to their leader, the Communist organ reproduced some excerpts from *History Will Absolve Me* and ended its declaration with "Long live the alliance of the workers and peasants."[3] From then on, until March 1962, when he attacked the second-in-command of the PSP, Aníbal Escalante, Castro did not make a single public criticism of the Communists. Moreover, there are many indications that the differences of opinion that had occurred in May were settled even before the July reconciliation. Hence it is worth casting a glance at this interval, between May and July, that was so decisive for the course of the Cuban revolution.

The PSP Conclusions

At the same plenum of the Central Committee of the PSP that had listened to Blas Roca's depressing report referred to in the previous chapter, the so-called "May Conclusions" were discussed

1 *Hoy,* July 4, 1959.
2 *Ibid.,* July 4, 1959.
3 *Ibid.,* July 26, 1959.

and approved, that is, the Communist diagnosis of the character of the revolution, the situation in mid-1959, and the prospects and future conduct of the party. But something must be clarified before we discuss the content of this document.

In a Communist party no one can aspire to leadership or maintain it without justifying his aims in ideological terms. Hence all Leninist political documents are not only a Marxist analysis of the situation but a reflection of the internal state of the party, of the leader's or dominant faction's need to pacify rivals by taking up a conciliatory position or to destroy them by appropriating their program or maneuvering them into an untenable situation from an ideological point of view. Thus in order to understand the May Conclusions it is essential to give some background concerning the internal life of the PSP; without this it would be impossible to grasp their true meaning.

As pointed out in Chapter 1, Cuban Communism, established after Lenin's death, was conclusively Stalinized in 1934. From then on the Communist Party in Cuba was one of the most Stalinist parties of the international movement.[4] Hence it is easy to imagine the impact produced by Khrushchev's speech at the Twentieth Congress of the Soviet Communist Party and by the subsequent process of de-Stalinization. Blas Roca's position as leader and the unity of the party itself were seriously threatened. There was danger that the exposure of his "errors" might lead to his being purged; and so, in 1956, when Castro was preparing the *Granma* expedition, or was even already in the Sierra, Blas Roca "took a ship," just like an ordinary citizen, in spite of the allegedly clandestine character of the party at the time. He left Cuba, to return the following year. This time, however, he did not make a trip to Moscow, as he usually did, but to Peking. This change of itinerary is revealing.[5]

The meeting with Mao was doubly successful for Roca. In the first place, he found out that the Chinese leader did not go so far as Khrushchev in denouncing Stalin, and in consequence he himself could count on the sympathy or support of the second power in the socialist bloc to counteract attempts to intensify the de-Stalinization

---

[4] It is significant that in Robert J. Alexander's work, *Communism in Latin America* (New Brunswick, N. J.: Rutgers University Press, 1957), the chapter devoted to Cuba is called "Stalinism in the Pearl of the Antilles."

[5] Roca mentioned this trip in a television interview published in *Hoy*, May 6, 1959. In response to a journalist's question as to how he had left Cuba, he said "I left as anyone else would. I took a ship, went away, and then came back. . . ."

movement in Cuba. In 1959 *Hoy* echoed the new position of Cuban communism: conformity with the international line laid down at the meeting of Communist parties in 1957; loyalty to the memory of Stalin, who, as Roca said, "deserves criticism for having violated the rules of socialist legality" but "whose historical merits are great and incontestable";[6] admiration for Mao, "a true genius who has contributed to the development and the enriching of the theory of Marxism-Leninism";[7] and the recognition of the Chinese Communist Party as practically equal in the hierarchy to the Soviet Communist Party.[8]

In the second place, Blas Roca's trip to China gave him another advantage, but one that he could not have foreseen in 1956. It allowed him to become familiar with a revolutionary experience that in mid-1959 was to help him work out a doctrinal position that would lessen the possible attraction a "deviationist" group might exercise among the PSP cadres. This we shall now discuss.

The PSP had maintained its "monolithism" at least until January 1959: we know that Carlos Rafael Rodríguez, who was to head the "deviation" referred to, supported the January theses.[9] Nevertheless, even at that time "objective" conditions already existed for the future internal conflict.

Even though, as we know, Blas Roca had been appointed secretary-general of the PSP by the Comintern, he had not retained this post for more than a quarter of a century merely because he had the support of the international apparatus — which seems to have let him down at least once[10] — but because he had the qualities needed for the legal activity to which the party had dedicated itself since 1938 and because he represented the real spirit of Cuban communism during its electoral and politicking phase. Carlos Rafael Rodríguez also belonged to this era. A young student who

6 *Ibid.*

7 Blas Roca, "Calidad humana de Mao Tse-tung" [Mao Tse-tung's Human Qualities], *ibid.*, September 4, 1959.

8 Analysis of the 1959 issues of *Hoy* shows an almost mathematical equilibrium between the space devoted to the two great states of the socialist bloc; the references to China are consistently more enthusiastic.

9 An interview with Carlos Rafael Rodríguez (*Hoy*, January 11, 1959): "My opinion is the same that has just been expressed by the document of the party that we have given to the press," that is, the "theses" published on the same day.

10 In 1945 or 1946 a dissident faction, in which the future Senator Rolando Masferrer took part, arose within the PSP. He was apparently favored by the Soviet embassy in Cuba. In spite of this Roca continued as leader, and the dissidents were expelled.

had taken part in the struggle against Machado, a member of the Communist Party probably since 1934, a member of the party Central Committee since 1939, and later of the Politburo, as well as Secretary of Propaganda and Education, Rodríguez was an authentic intellectual and the only Cuban Communist leader who was really familiar with the Marxist texts. He made his way up in the party hierarchy through his loyalty to Roca and because he refrained from any show of intelligence that might have aroused the suspicions of the secretary-general of the PSP.

By 1959, however, things had changed. Rodríguez wore a beard — the sign of the guerilla fighter; Roca lacked one. The former had been in the Sierra, while the latter had only been a dubious fighter in the urban underground. Rodríguez had personal contacts with Castro and with the other guerrilla commanders. Roca probably had none, or they were very superficial. Finally, Rodríguez was surely one of the "comrades" who, according to a later statement by Roca, "wanted us to undertake a critical and self-critical evaluation of our whole past activity" — referring obviously to the party's position during the struggle against Batista — but Roca did not feel the slightest regret for this past activity.[11]

From the "unity" celebration of March 13 onward, Rodríguez' fascination with Castro's personality became completely clear. Things went so far that by the end of that same month he felt obliged to defend himself. "We pay no tribute to a heroic conception of history," he said, adding that his high praise for Castro's speeches, especially the one made during José Figueres' visit, was because the leader's words expressed "a state of conscience representing the best forces of the country. . . ."[12]

---

[11] "Conclusiones de Blas Roca ante la VIII Asamblea Nacional" [Conclusions of Blas Roca before the National Assembly], Hoy, August 28, 1960. Roca declared that no member of the PSP would necessarily be "prejudicially affected" because of not having taken part in the civil war.

This leads me to the conclusion that Carlos Rafael Rodríguez was one of the "comrades" who wanted to criticize the conduct of the PSP during the struggle against Batista, since at various times he had tried to demonstrate that the party had openly supported the armed struggle. For instance, in his article "Un esclarecimiento necesario" [A Necessary Explanation], Hoy, April 15, 1959, he mentioned the instructions given "publicly" in February 1958 to PSP members to join the guerrillas. He never again, however, mentioned this document, nor is there the slightest proof that it ever existed. It is possible that Rodríguez invented this directive in order to defend himself in his polemic against the July 26 Movement; such was the object of his article.

[12] See, for instance, Rodríguez' articles in Hoy: "La gran jornada del día 13" [The Great Occasion of the 13th Day], March 15, 1959; "Cubanos y no

Rodríguez maintained this attitude during Castro's visit to the United States, despite the PSP's reticence concerning the visit. Even after Castro's speech on his return, Rodríguez, in the midst of Roca's and the PSP's silence, maintained that Castro's "clarification" had been "definitive," since he was the first Latin American statesman to "reaffirm his programmatic principles," after visiting the United States, although in fact he had behaved, at least on the "Meet the Press" program, like any other "lackey of imperialism," to use a favorite Communist expression.[13]

But the most convincing proof that there were differences within the PSP was the reorganization carried out by Roca at the beginning of April. The new Secretariat, that is, the key part of the *apparat*, was made up of Roca and two of his faithful supporters, Aníbal Escalante and Manuel Luzardo. Rodríguez was confirmed as editor of *Hoy*, but he was replaced as chairman of the commission on education and propaganda by another follower of Blas Roca, Joaquín Ordoqui.[14] Finally, Rodríguez, the only member of the Politburo who had been in the Sierra, was given the insignificant position of member of the commission on plans and ideas for national development, presided over by Jacinto Torras, and was entrusted with the study of a "Social Security Plan."[15]

I must repeat that this reorganization, in which Roca appointed his faithful supporters to the key positions of the *apparat*, while entrusting Rodríguez with two totally irrelevant tasks — the editorship of *Hoy* was under the supervision of the new chairman of the commission on propaganda and education — is a definite indication of conflict within the PSP.[16] What, then, was this conflict about?

Cubanos" [Cubans and non-Cubans], March 18, 1959; and "¡A las filas!" [To the Ranks!], March 27, 1959. The passages quoted occur in the last article.

13 See the article of Carlos Rafael Rodríguez, "La clarificación de Fidel Castro" [Fidel Castro's Clarification], *ibid.*, May 10, 1959.

14 Practically all the details of Carlos Rafael Rodríguez' party career are taken from his article "El Times engaña al pueblo americano" [The *Times* Is Deceiving the American People], *ibid.*, November 22, 1960. In this article he says he "held the office of secretary of education and propaganda for ten years," a post actually held by Joaquín Ordoqui. However, in the April 1959 resolutions Ordoqui is mentioned as president of a commission. I presume that the commission was created in order to justify Carlos Rafael Rodríguez' replacement by Ordoqui, since as editor of *Hoy* he would of course be under the jurisdiction of the president of the commission.

15 The resolutions making known the reorganization appeared in *Hoy*, April 8, 1959.

16 The existence of two factions within the PSP, one headed by Carlos Rafael Rodríguez and the other by Roca, was publicly known. For instance, the journa-

The only documentation we have is in Rodríguez' articles in praise of Castro and in Roca's version of the situation. According to Roca, the danger that had threatened the PSP up to the time of the May Conclusions was "exceptionalism," that is, a position attributing to the Cuban revolution a unique character, outside the rules of Marxism, and inclining, moreover, toward a Tito-type "revisionism," that is, a rightist deviation.[17] However, the elements later mentioned by Roca, who wanted to censure the caution of the PSP during the struggle against Batista, could not be considered representative of a rightist deviation. And in the May Conclusions, as we shall now see, the major emphasis was on the dangers of "any leftist extremist tendencies" and of "any exaggerated measures." Hence it must be concluded that the disagreement arose from the left and not, as Roca made out, from the right.

This hypothesis is confirmed by the contents of the May Conclusions. These contain two positions: a moderate one, applicable to the present, and a radical one, whose application is to be postponed to an indeterminate future. In our view this second portion was a dialectical subtlety contrived by Roca to make it more difficult for his opponents to defend the radical position.[18]

Let us now summarize the content of the May Conclusions.

Blas Roca first pointed out that the character of a revolution is defined by its objectives, which in turn are determined by the situation in which the revolution takes place. The aims of the Cuban revolution, he wrote, are full independence, the transfer of land to the peasants, industrialization of the country, and the "realization and strengthening of democracy." Hence this cannot be a workers' socialist or Communist revolution but only a "patriotic and democratic national liberation and agrarian" revolution. Castro calls it "humanist"; it can be given many names as long as there is agreement on the objectives.

Given the stated goals, the classes that are interested in the revolutionary movement are the peasants, the workers, the urban

---

list who interviewed Roca in May asked him about them. Roca of course denied their existence. (See *ibid.*, May 6, 1959.)

[17] Blas Roca, "Conclusiones sobre el programa" [Conclusions on the Program], *ibid.*, October 9, 1959.

[18] In *ibid.*, Roca pointed out that it had taken two months, because of the discussions involved, to secure approval of the May Conclusions. However, the article by Roca, "¿Que clase de revolucíon es esta?" [What Kind of Revolution Is This?], in *Hoy*, April 11, 1959, that is, almost two months before the Conclusions, contains almost in its entirety the position I have called "moderate."

petite bourgeoisie, and the national bourgeoisie. Under Castro's government it is the petite bourgeoisie that exercises "hegemony." "In spite of the vacillations and the contradictions inherent in the petite bourgeoisie the revolutionary role of these people must not be underestimated." Hence the "proletariat" — that is, the PSP — "must make all necessary efforts to maintain an alliance with them against the big landowners and against imperialism."

The revolution, the document went on to say, is threatened by two dangers: the blunders of the revolutionaries themselves and the campaign of the imperialists against them. With respect to the imperialist threat, the first thing that must be kept in mind is that "imperialism in general has weakened." The existence of the "socialist camp" and the growth of anti-imperialist sentiment throughout the world, including Latin America, "prevent the Yankee imperialists from having recourse to the old method of landing Marines and to military or diplomatic intervention." Therefore, the best strategy is to be against the Cold War and for peaceful coexistence. The Cold War is being used by "the imperialists" in order to justify their meddling and their demands on the Latin American peoples. "Hence the role of Cuba in the sphere of international relations is not to aggravate or support the Cold War but to work toward its termination and for the establishment of peaceful coexistence."

Finally, it is vital not to forget the specific difficulties of the Cuban revolution:

We are a small country, situated only a very short distance away from the United States. The deformation of our economy through imperialist influence has made us very dependent on imports, even for the most basic foodstuffs of the people. In view of this, any leftist extremist tendency, any exaggerated measures . . . to be applied or implemented by the revolution, and any attempt to disregard the realities and the concrete difficulties confronting the Cuban revolution must be rejected.

Because of these difficulties the revolution demands of its leaders not only "a profound revolutionary consciousness, a great firmness of conviction, and an invincible determination" but at the same time "great flexibility and skill in tactics. . . ."[19]

Up to this point the contents of the document were relatively

---

[19] "Conclusiones del pleno del Comité Nacional del PSP, realizado en los días 25 al 28 de mayo de 1959" [Conclusions of the Plenum of the National Committee of the PSP That Took Place Between May 25 and 28, 1959], *ibid.*, June 7, 1959.

moderate. Now let us examine the "leftist" appendix, the ideological formula designed to foil the extremists, who maintained that the Cuban revolution was unique and that such general laws of Marxism as the "leading role of the proletariat" were not applicable to it.

According to the appendix, one peculiarity of the Cuban revolution, "which had already occurred in the Chinese revolution," was that the working class was not the chief factor in the overthrow of the dictatorship; the overthrow took place through the action of a guerrilla army that had advanced from the countryside into the cities. From this it follows that in Latin America, "even in small countries like Cuba," it is possible to reproduce the Chinese method. But this by no means implies a refutation of the principles of Marxism. It had already "been laid down by Mao Tse-tung that the duty of revolutionaries is to apply the universal truth of Marxism to concrete practice within a given situation." What Marxism teaches is that the working class is "the most important and the most profoundly revolutionary class in contemporary society." Moreover, whatever the conditions under which a revolution begins, only the working class is in a position to sustain it in order

to make it advance without interruption, to place itself at the head of all the revolutionary elements of society in alliance with the peasants, to destroy capitalist exploitation, and to construct socialism.[20]

I call the reader's attention to the use in the document of the concept of "uninterrupted revolution." As far as I have been able to ascertain, this was the first time the expression appeared in Cuban Communist usage. It is a concept used by the Chinese. In the countries that Leninists call underdeveloped, colonial, or semicolonial, it is analogous to the Parvus-Trotsky theory of "permanent revolution," according to which no revolution can stop at the democratic phase but, independently of the degree of socioeconomic development, must proceed without interruption until it arrives at socialism. The Chinese, however, do not use the expression in this specific sense but rather as a generalization of their revolutionary experience, applicable to all countries in a similar stage of development.

It is probable that Blas Roca became familiar with this theory during his trip to Peking in 1956, and its use in the May Conclusions tends to confirm the intimacy between the Chinese Com-

[20] *Ibid.*

munist Party and the PSP during these years. In 1959 the PSP used the leftist phrase "uninterrupted revolution" to foil the extremist critics both within and outside of its ranks. While insisting on moderation in the present, it accepted the theoretical possibility of radical developments in an unspecified future. But this leftist phraseology turned against it when Castro, without having read either Mao or Liu Shao-ch'i, actually decided to put into effect his own "uninterrupted revolution" in Cuba.

The Dominican Invasion

At the same time that Castro was censuring the Communists, sending Guevara abroad, and promulgating land reform, he was also engaged in an underground operation: the organization of an expedition to Santo Domingo, which landed on the coast of the Dominican Republic on June 14, 1959. There is ample evidence that Castro personally prepared and arranged this operation. It is enough to mention here that in his enthusiasm he one day forgot all prudence and made an open appeal for public support, which he had to disavow the following day.[21]

We thus see that from his trips to North and South America Castro brought home his own "conclusions": to initiate the social revolution, to confirm his personal power in such a manner as to dissipate any doubts that might have cropped up in the minds of Guevara and the PSP, and to extend the revolutionary movement abroad by force of arms.

Castro's program was thus no more than a bad copy of Guevara's in January. Leaders who believe that it is sufficient to improvise when confronting great historic crises find themselves taking over other people's ideas. But in putting them into effect, since they have no respect for the ideas as such, they render them ineffective by falsification. Guevara had demanded land reform, the organization of the Rebel Army as a vanguard, the preparation of the masses for the struggle against "imperialism," and the search for allies in Latin America by preaching the Cuban examples of land distribution and guerrilla warfare. Castro adopted land reform, but he warped everything else. He rejected Guevara's concept of the Rebel Army as a "vanguard," because this would have meant giving to the Rebel Army a role that sooner or later would have obliged him

21 *Ibid.*, June 16 and 17, 1959.

to acknowledge the authority of its commanding officers to the detriment of his own personal power. And in his program for extending the revolution to the continent, he omitted the appeal to the peasants advocated by Guevara because he knew very well that he himself had won without it simply by arming a band of loyal followers and launching them against a hated dictatorship.

It is no accident that social revolution, the reaffirmation of his personal power, and revolutionary expansion appear united in Castro's program. There was a logical connection among these proposals.

Castro could implement a radical transformation of the Cuban social structure, while maintaining his personal power intact, only if he kept up his close and constant relations with the masses. The lowering of rents, the granting of land to the tenants, and similar acts of course reinforced these ties; but, like every internal reform, they also ran into opposition. The opposition was, to be sure, insignificant, but even so it was potentially dangerous, for two reasons: It could evoke against Castro's autocratic tendencies the original democratic program of the revolution, and it would be able to find powerful support abroad.

Castro saw that to succeed in his aims he had to become the symbol of a great national cause that would enable him, by accusing his domestic opponents of being agents of the CIA, to crush them before they were able to organize. If he merely accused them of defending their property, public opinion would indignantly reject the use of the one punishment effective in revolutionary periods — execution.

In mid-1959 it was still too early for a charge of treason through collaboration with U.S. intelligence to appear plausible. Castro had just returned from the United States, and the American reaction to his land reform was described by *The New York Times* as follows: "The American note to Havana is courteous and within the legitimate bounds of friendly relationship. It will surely be treated as such."[22]

Castro's plans, however, could not wait, as much because of their very nature as because of the international situation. Given the proximity and the influence of the United States on Cuban affairs, the implementation of a social revolution in Cuba was an extraordinarily delicate task, as Blas Roca had already noted. The difficul-

[22] *The New York Times,* June 13, 1959.

ties were multiplied still further if, as in Castro's case, such a revolution was associated with a political regime that gave no sign of wishing to proceed toward constitutional normality. Thus it must have been evident to Castro that what he planned for Cuba would meet with resistance from the United States.

Washington had to protect the numerous American interests that would be affected by such a revolution. Furthermore, the United States, a gigantic power, was not prepared to accept the possibility that tiny Cuba was capable of creating serious difficulties for it. "Arrogance," as Reinhold Niebuhr has said, "is the inevitable consequence of the relation of power to weakness."[23] The serious aspect of the matter is not that this defect was present in U.S.-Cuban relations, as it undoubtedly was, but that neither American public opinion nor the U.S. government was capable of appreciating Cuban problems, of devoting to them the attention and time that they deserved, or even of contemplating with equanimity events that might result in a loss of prestige for the United States.

Castro therefore had to take U.S. resistance into account. Moreover, the situation did not permit him to let his adversary take the initiative, first, because of the enormous disparity of power between them, and second, although this may seem paradoxical, because of the fundamental weakness with which his revolution has always been afflicted.

In only five months Castro had transformed a movement designed to restore constitutional normality into a social revolution that was bound to collide with the United States. He obviously lacked cadres prepared for such a confrontation; and the masses that adored him would be paralyzed with terror if they suspected that the happiness they were enjoying — the mass meetings, the demonstrations, the demands, the strikes, and the freedom from meeting obligations — might end in a conflict with their mighty neighbor to the north.

In these circumstances Castro could not remain idle. Since it was up to him to take the initiative, the attack on Santo Domingo seemed an excellent solution. The United States would be obliged to rush to the defense of Trujillo; Castro would reaffirm his posture as liberator in the eyes of the Latin American peoples. Victory seemed certain, for the Dominican tyranny was hated at least as

23 Reinhold Niebuhr, *The Irony of American History* (New York: Charles Scribner's Sons, 1952), p. 112.

much as that of Batista. Castro would direct the operations from the eastern tip of Cuba, and his military triumph would decisively convince both the July 26 Movement and the Rebel Army that they must allow him to carry out his designs, because destiny itself had singled him out to accomplish a great historical task.

However, confident as he was, Castro had to take certain measures to guard against failure in his first foreign adventure. This was all the more necessary because on June 8 Hubert Matos, the military chief of Camagüey province and one of the most distinguished commanders of the Rebel Army, had, with the support of President Urrutia, publicly voiced his concern over the activities of the PSP. Both Castro and the Communists realized that Matos constituted a potentially serious rival,[24] and Castro had to guard against the possibility, in case the Dominican invasion failed, that the forces rallying around the banner of anticommunism would be able to impose their conditions. The situation called for a reconciliation with the PSP.

Everything indicates that this took place long before July 3, the date on which the *rapprochement* was made public. In the resolutions of the plenum that listened to Blas Roca's report on the crisis in relations with Castro, although "any attack on any revolutionary organization" was considered "serious and inappropriate," a firm stand was taken against "the provocations and the armaments of Trujillo and other tyrants."[25] On June 6 the PSP issued a declaration "on the growth of the struggle for freedom in our continent and against the savage reactionary and imperialist repression of our peoples"; and the following day *Hoy* published a manifesto of the party "against the plotting and the activities of the counter-revolutionaries and the imperialists."[26]

It was no accident that these resolutions, declarations, and manifestos appeared just at the time that Castro was putting the final touches on the plan for the Dominican invasion, and, moreover, that they came from a party that only a few days before, in its Conclusions, had reduced the "imperialist" danger to "threats to the sugar quota" and to "economic sabotage." This impression of the timing of the reconciliation is reinforced by two events that

---

[24] The Communists, of course, noticed this at once, as is shown by the article by Carlos Rafael Rodríguez, "En torno a un discurso de Hubert Matos" [On a speech by Hubert Matos], *Hoy*, June 12, 1959.

[25] "Comunicado sobre la situación" [A Report on the Situation], *ibid.*, May 28, 1959.

[26] *Ibid.*, June 6 and 7, 1959.

took place almost simultaneously. On June 12 Castro reorganized the cabinet. Among those who left the government were the Minister of Agriculture, who had opposed land reform, and the Minister of Foreign Affairs, called by *Hoy* a "Plattist"[27] and a "retrograde element." Those who replaced these officials — a total of four — are still in Cuba, though some have left the Council of Ministers. It was evidently a reorganization on the basis of "unity," but, it must be observed, not in the sense given to this word by the Communists — who interpret it as coparticipation in political decisions — but in Castro's sense — that is, as the elimination of the elements that inhibited his own freedom of action — because at that time he was bent on preserving his collaboration with the PSP.

Finally, on June 17, after an interview with Castro in the presidential palace, the Executive Committee of the Revolutionary Student Directorate declared its full support for the "unity" movement.[28]

There seems to be no doubt, then, that during the first two weeks of June, once the PSP had demonstrated its obedience by offering to collaborate in the Dominican adventure (even though this violated the line of the May Conclusions), and once Castro had made a few "unity" gestures that did not take away any of his power, cordial relations were restored between Castro and the Communists.

It was a timely reconciliation from Castro's point of view, because it turned out that he had made a lamentable error in assuming Trujillo to be just another Batista. The invaders had scarcely landed before they were taken prisoner or annihilated. The Domin-

---

27 The Communists used the term "Plattists" for those who seemed to be subservient to "imperialism." Roberto Agramonte, the Minister of Foreign Affairs, was repeatedly called a "Plattist," for instance, in Aníbal Escalante's "El Plattismo, dolencia pertinaz" [Plattism, a Lingering Disease], *ibid.*, May 5, 1959. This accusation was leveled at Agramonte because he had refused visas to a Chinese acrobatic troupe that was in Santiago de Chile.

28 On the interview see *Hoy*, June 14, 1959, and the statements in the June 17 issue. I make so bold as to say that everything said by Maurice Zeitlin and Robert Scheer in their book *Cuba: Tragedy in Our Hemisphere* (New York: Grove Press, 1963) concerning the Revolutionary Student Directorate is incorrect, especially their description of it as "an independent political group with strong ideas of its own" (p. 74).

The Directorate never had any ideas of its own; it was a "unity" organization from March on, and in the statements made on June 17 it came out expressly in favor of "the constitution of a united front," a thing that even Castro had never demanded. Its leader, Faure Chomón, as we shall see, has been one of the most faithful instruments used by Castro in his political maneuvers.

ican commander of the expedition was killed, and his Cuban aid, Delio Gómez Ochoa, was captured — and became a collaborator of the Dominican despot.[29] Castro had suffered a defeat; and the consequences of his failure would have been serious if it had not been for the secrecy of the operation and the fact that his opponents were still incapable of assessing how dangerous he was.

On June 26, twelve days after the invasion, Cuba broke off relations with the Dominican Republic, and the latter immediately turned to the Organization of American States, setting in motion its cumbersome machinery and thus involving the United States.

On July 1 President Eisenhower stated, in answer to questions on the Caribbean situation: "I think that if America is going to be true to itself and its pledges, it must depend primarily upon the OAS to take cognizance of these difficulties."[30] A few days later Secretary of State Herter confirmed the anxiety felt by the United States: "I think that the whole problem of the intervention of one country in the internal affairs of another country [is one] we always regard with real seriousness."[31]

All this obviously put Castro on the defensive. On July 3, at the same public appearance at which he held out a friendly hand to the Communists, he said: "Our strategy . . . is to repel aggression, not to attack, but to defend ourselves on our own territory. . . ." He then went on to demonstrate his sorrowful surprise at his air force Major Pedro Díaz Lanz's defection to the United States, at Eisenhower's statements, and at Santo Domingo's denunciation of Cuba to the OAS. "All this is too much coincidence," he said, suggesting that there had been a sinister plot against him and pretending to forget that he himself had provoked this reaction. Lastly, taking advantage of the opportunity to wave the flag of nationalism, he added: "Cuba will accept no kind of intervention, nor any investigation . . . that might in any way harm its sovereignty or its dignity."[32]

While in foreign affairs Castro took to the defensive, the opposite

---

[29] For instance, in his report to the Politburo of the PSP (*Hoy*, November 8, 1959), Roca said that Gómez Ochoa had made certain recommendations to Trujillo in connection with the chances of forming a conspiracy in Cuba. It is strange that Zeitlin and Scheer, in their listing of the accusations against the Cuban government of "alleged support of attempts to overthrow other governments in Latin America" (*op. cit.*, pp. 101 and 102), omit any reference to the invasion of the Dominican Republic.

[30] *The New York Times*, July 2, 1959.

[31] *Ibid.*, July 10, 1959.

[32] *Hoy*, July 4, 1959.

was the case at home. By the last week of June, on Castro's return from Oriente province, where he had gone to direct the military operations in Santo Domingo, he personally initiated the expropriations of land, affecting at least 2,300,000 acres, the property of "counterrevolutionary" landlords, thus disregarding the conditions he himself had laid down in Article 53 of the agrarian law.[33] On June 29 he restored the death penalty for crimes that were counterrevolutionary and harmful to the national economy.

Meanwhile, at the end of June the air force major who had defected to the United States and President Urrutia both denounced Communist activity in a television appearance. A few days later the President repeated these charges, even though Castro had said he thought it "not very honorable" to attack the members of the PSP. On July 16 Castro resigned as Prime Minister, thereby provoking a crisis; he deposed the President the following day.[34]

Urrutia was replaced as President by Osvaldo Dorticós, an ex-member of the Unión Revolucionaria Comunista (the 1939–1945 name of the Cuban Communist Party). He, like so many others, had left politics and then returned to it — although not as a member of the PSP — because of the excesses of the Batista dictatorship. The first postrevolutionary Prime Minister, Miró, had appointed him to the Council of Ministers with the task of formulating the revolutionary laws. While Dorticós' appointment as President did not pass unnoticed, it did not produce any lasting commotion. The masses continued to be fascinated by Castro; and Urrutia had proved incapable of winning the sympathy of even the members of his own cabinet.

The crisis did, however, allow one to get a glimpse of the true features of Castro, cruel and implacable, during his savage speech of accusation against the unfortunate ex-President. And the crisis probably also convinced Castro of something that he had already suspected. In spite of his resignation as Prime Minister (a post to

[33] Article 53 of the agrarian reform law allowed INRA sixty days to present to the Council of Ministers a draft for the implementation of the law. Obviously no one expected that the law would be applied before this draft was published.

[34] The Communists kept on attacking Urrutia after his appearance with Matos on June 8 in Camagüey. See Aníbal Escalante, "Divagaciones sobre la justicia y la defensa propia" [Digressions on Justice and Self-Defense], *Hoy*, June 30, 1959, for a discussion of the President's first television appearance; Carlos Rafael Rodríguez, "Los comunistas y el interés nacional" [The Communists and the National Interest], *ibid.*, July 15, 1959; and Blas Roca, "El anti-comunismo es un pretexto" [Anti-Communism Is a Pretext], *ibid.*, July 17, 1959. All these articles are against Urrutia.

which he returned on July 26) and his television effort to arouse
the masses to a maximum degree of exultation, the latter remained
wholly passive and did not respond to his call for street demonstrations in his support and for expressions of hatred toward the ex-
President. From this he must have drawn the conclusion that a
more powerful motive, the defense of the imperiled fatherland, was
needed to arouse the masses to the pitch of passion required for the
purposes of his revolution.

The Decision to Seek Soviet Aid

In the last week of August a conference of the foreign ministers
of the OAS was held in Santiago de Chile to discuss the Dominican
protest against Cuba. Nothing came of this meeting except an agreement to make a full study of the current situation in the Caribbean.

Some weeks before, Castro had "discovered" a most peculiar
conspiracy, which he attributed to Trujillo. It was in the light of
this alleged conspiracy that the Cuban leaders interpreted the
conference. According to Raúl Castro, the OAS conference had
been,

as is known, a move against Cuba. The plans of Trujillo and his cronies
were to coordinate a counterrevolutionary uprising at home and an
invasion of mercenary forces from abroad with the meeting of the Foreign
Ministers. In this way, if the counterrevolutionary plan succeeded, the
conference would give its approval to the new antipatriotic government.[35]

Blas Roca was even more specific: "The opening of the meeting
was to coincide with the uprisings in Cuba, bombardments of cities,
the assassination of Raúl and Fidel. That is how it was planned."[36]

However, we who watched Castro's television appearance when
he described all the details of the conspiracy, came to the conclusion
that the only serious element in it was the involvement of Castro's
agents, who inveigled imprudent people to join the alleged conspiracy, only to hand them over to the police as soon as Castro
found it opportune.[37] As for the objectives attributed by Raúl

---

[35] *Hoy,* September 16, 1959.

[36] *Ibid.,* September 1, 1959.

[37] I am not saying that there was no conspiracy. After aiding Batista by
giving him arms and money until December 31, 1958, Trujillo began to plot
against Castro in January 1959. José Suárez Núñez, *El gran culpable* [The
Great Guilt] (Caracas, Venezuela, 1963). According to Robert D. Crassweller,
two guerrilla leaders of the Second Escambray Front, Eloy Gutiérrez Menoyo
and William Morgan, collaborated with Trujillo in this plot. Morgan received

Castro and Blas Roca to the foreign ministers' meeting, it has been impossible for me to find a single source that backs up their interpretation.

It hardly matters whether the Cuban leaders really believed in such a fairy tale as the alleged OAS conspiracy. More important is that after the Dominican fiasco, Castro needed the conspiracy in order to create the atmosphere of a besieged fortress, thus enabling him to suppress the domestic opposition while at the same time accelerating the rhythm of the revolution.

Castro's defeat at the hands of Trujillo had been shattering. The OAS was alerted and in motion. In March — months before the Dominican invasion — Castro had broken with former President Figueres and thereby with the one possible ally he had in Latin America: the so-called "democratic left," represented by Figueres himself, Rómulo Betancourt of Venezuela, and Muñoz Marín of Puerto Rico. Knowing perfectly well what he himself would do against an adversary who was weaker and isolated, Castro very naturally felt gravely threatened and wanted to open the eyes of his own people, who were still acclaiming him jubilantly, to that threat.

In such a situation Castro needed a means of protection strong enough to deter his opponents. Above all, he needed weapons that he could distribute to his enthusiastic followers, thus preventing a recurrence of the Guatemalan events of 1954 — namely, the crushing of Arbenz' government by the army, with the help of the U.S. government. This does not mean that Castro had not already taken steps to increase his armed strength over what it had been in January, when the entire equipment of Batista's army had fallen into his hands. Early in the spring he opened negotiations to acquire war materials in Europe.[38] And in June 1959 the man who in his January 8 speech had asked the mothers of Cuba the rhetorical

---

$500,000 from Trujillo for this operation. Later it became clear, according to the same source, that "the whole project had been an elaborate "double game" played by the Cubans." (R. D. Crassweller, *Trujillo: The Life and Times of a Caribbean Dictator* [New York: Macmillan, 1966], pp. 349–351.) Morgan was executed in 1961 by Castro, and Menoyo today is in a Castro prison for attempting to enter Cuba to initiate a guerrilla war. It may be that both Morgan and Menoyo began to conspire seriously against Castro in 1959, got Trujillo's help, and upon being discovered by Cuban police pretended that everything had been a "double game from the beginning."

38 Nicolás Rivero, *Castro's Cuba* (Washington, D. C.: Luce, 1962), p. 56. At the time Rivero was working in the Foreign Ministry. The author, who at that same time was working in the Treasury, is in a position to confirm Rivero's report.

question, "arms for what?" was planning to spend no less than 9 million dollars for the purchase of destroyers and other equipment[39] in the United States itself. After the fiasco in the Dominican Republic, Castro's need for arms was greater than ever, but by now the U.S. government was not only opposed to letting its own country satisfy these needs but applied pressure in Western Europe to cut off that source from him as well. So the Cuban leader began to look toward the only source of arms not reached by American influence — the Soviet Union.

The PSP Position

It is true that in the summer of 1959 the international situation did not appear to favor the establishment of Soviet-Cuban cooperation against the United States. In August Khrushchev's impending visit to the United States was announced. This visit appeared to mark the beginning of a *rapprochement* between the two world powers.

The PSP saw in the announcement an excellent opportunity to return to the peaceful policy of the May Conclusions, which it had been obliged to abandon temporarily during the Dominican crisis. The party newspaper *Hoy* cited two fundamental reasons for its support of the Khrushchev visit, which it described as "the outstanding international event since the end of World War II."[40] First, Washington was making use of the anti-Communist argument to justify its opposition to the "patriotic, nationalist, and democratic" revolution. Second, Cuba needed to devote all its attention to the tasks of economic development, seeking new markets for its products, including of course markets in the "socialist world." In both cases a Soviet-American *rapprochement* would prevent Washington from continuing to make use of the anti-Communist bogey. It would create an atmosphere of peace in which the Cubans could devote themselves to fruitful labors and would eliminate any objections the United States might make to the establishment of trade relations between Cuba and all other countries.

39 *The New York Times*, June 26, 1959.
40 "Nuestra Opinión: La visita de Kruschev" [Khrushchev's Visit], *Hoy*, September 17, 1959. On the same theme see "El encuentro de Kruschev y Eisenhower" [Khrushchev's Meeting with Eisenhower], *ibid.*, August 5, 1959; Blas Roca, "Visitas a Moscú y Washington" [Visits to Moscow and Washington], *ibid.*, August 9, 1959; and the greetings of the PSP Politburo on the visit and on the rocket to the moon in *ibid.*, September 18, 1959.

Time and again *Hoy* harped on these two themes. The number of articles devoted to the subject is in itself a clear indication of the difficulties the PSP encountered in dispelling the Cuban leadership's uneasiness about the visit.

In October, when another plenary session of the Central Committee of the PSP was held, Blas Roca thought it timely to insist once again on the specific difficulties of the Cuban revolution. Once again he alluded to the "dependence" of Cuba on imports. And he added a reference to another problem: "Certain sectors of the population have become accustomed to a way of life that does not correspond to the development of the country." Under such conditions any acceleration of the revolutionary rhythm of development involved the risk of a failure; and, of course, "the proximity of the imperialist forces and of flunkeys like Trujillo and Somoza" constituted a danger, but "we must take a good look at what this danger consists of and how it can be overcome." In 1959 the forces of "imperialism" were incomparably weaker than they had been decades before. "Today it is very difficult for imperialism to embark on an open and brutal intervention. It is still more difficult for Yankee imperialism to organize an action similar to that which it brought about against Guatemala." To show that "imperialism" had become enfeebled, he said, "Despite its aggression and its blackmail, in Santiago the United States was unable to arrive at any agreement directed against Cuba similar to the one it had approved in Caracas." In his report Roca did not allude to the sinister designs he himself had attributed to the Santiago meeting in his television appearance early in September. From this strange omission we may draw the conclusion that he had never taken his accusations seriously.

Roca ended his report by emphasizing the danger of "leftism," which wanted to pass on to more advanced stages of the revolution, disregarding the fact that the Cuban revolution "depended more than other revolutions on the international situation." In Cuba, accordingly, the "uninterrupted revolution" did not depend solely on "the achievement of national liberation and the transformation of the colonial economic structure." It needed in addition some specific external "objective conditions" such as

the advance of a similar revolutionary process in other Latin American countries in which anti-imperialist governments will establish themselves so that there will be not merely popular but also official, governmental mutual support and concurrent strengthening of the forces for peace and anti-colonialism in the world, even in the United States. . . .[41]

One cannot interpret this speech of Roca's as anything but a polemic against all those inside and outside the PSP who were following a policy of revolutionary extremism. This impression is confirmed by the statement of the plenum of the Central Committee on the conversations between Krushchev and Eisenhower. "In our country," said the PSP,

some doubts and reservations have been expressed concerning these conversations, on the supposition — for which no evidence has been produced — that these talks could lead to some agreements between the "Big Two — the United States and the Soviet Union — at the expense of the small countries like Cuba, or against the interests of these latter. There are no grounds whatever for such a supposition.

And further:

Any raising of doubts like the ones alluded to can serve no one but the partisans of the Cold War and of international reaction.[42]

Three days after the PSP report had appeared in the press, the first attack on Cuba took place, carried out by airplanes based along the U.S. coastline and manned by anti-Castro Cubans.[43] Furthermore the attack coincided with determined U.S. moves to prevent the Cubans from buying jet planes in Great Britain. These moves caused the Cuban ambassador in Washington to state on October 17 that

if any foreign government should attempt to hinder or obstruct such legitimate desires [i.e., to obtain military materials] there can be no doubt that it is going against the basic interests of Cuba . . . and would probably oblige the government of Cuba to try to make up the lack by supplies from such sources as might remain open to it.[44]

I think this makes it sufficiently clear why, and for what, Soviet aid was sought. We do not know if Castro had already initiated the

[41] Report of Blas Roca to the October plenum on the party program in *ibid.*, October 7, 1959.

[42] "Saludo del pleno de la dirección del PSP a las conversaciones de paz entre Kruschev y Eisenhower" [Welcome of the plenum of the PSP Leadership on the Occasion of the Peace Talks Between Khrushchev and Eisenhower], *ibid.*, October 8, 1959.

[43] This date, October 11, 1959, as that of the first air attack on Cuba is taken from Leslie Dewart, *Christianity and Revolution* (New York: Herder and Herder, 1963), p. 47. In view of Dewart's partiality toward Castro, I am sure he would not have failed to mention a previous attack.

[44] *Hoy*, October 18, 1959.

first contacts. The sources at our disposal appear to indicate that there was still a period of delay caused by obstacles that arose in Cuba itself.

The Eclipse of the July 26 Movement

Neither the reconciliation between Castro and the Communists nor the deposition of Urrutia was sufficient to make the July 26 Movement follow Castro's "unity" line. For example, within two weeks of the replacement of the President, the July 26 Movement's newspaper *Revolución* deliberately reminded its readers of the PSP's shady past collaboration with Batista. It did this by reprinting the dedication to one of the works of the poet Juan Marinello, president of the PSP. This was couched in particularly cordial terms and addressed to Santiago Rey, Minister of the Interior in Batista's cabinet. Marinello was obliged to confess his "error," but the incident led to an extensive polemic that went on until September.[45]

The tension between the July 26 Movement and the PSP was particularly noticeable on three fronts: the Rebel Army, the University Student Federation (Federación Estudiantil Universitaria — FEU), and the CTC.

There was much talk of Communist infiltration in the Rebel Army. Although the presence of Marcos Rodríguez, the Communist informer we have mentioned before, in the department of culture of the armed forces indicates that there was some such infiltration, the accounts of its extent were highly exaggerated. Even today, we know of only two former members of the PSP who held important posts in the Revolutionary Armed Forces: Flavio Bravo and Joaquín Ordoqui, respectively Chief of Operations and Deputy Minister (and after this was written Ordoqui was purged).

In our opinion the tension within the ranks of the Rebel Army was caused by the fact that the army constituted the initial and fundamental germ of Castroism. The guerrilla army was Castro's personal handiwork. Its commanders were men whom he had selected from among his first followers — those who took part in

---

[45] The dedication was published in *Revolución*, July 29, 1959, and Marinello's acknowledgment of his "error" in *Hoy*, August 1, 1959. Carlos Rafael Rodríguez ended the polemic in the middle of September, calling the assistant editor of *Revolución* "a little Caesar who has just come on stage" and "the defender of Carlos Prío in his worst period" ("Punto y aparte" [Period and Paragraph], *Hoy*, September 15, 1959).

the Moncada attack, the survivors of the *Granma* expedition, and a few others who joined him during the civil war. Almost all of them — Camilo Cienfuegos, Juan Almeida, Calixto Garcia, Efigenio Ameijeiras, Ramiro Valdés, William Gálvez, Universo Sánchez, Guillermo García — were young men with no money and with very little or no education, who rose in the military hierarchy both because of the services they had rendered and because of their loyalty to Castro. There were a few exceptions, products of inevitable error, such as Hubert Matos, a schoolteacher who had joined the movement without passing through the Moncada or the *Granma* experience.

Through the victory of January these men, who had had enough faith in Castro to accompany him in his desperate revolutionary adventures, became the high command of the armed forces of the republic. And the unanimous admiration of the Cuban people for Castro convinced them once and for all of the exceptional qualities of the man they had acknowledged as their chief. Not one of them, as far as I have been able to ascertain, was or had been a member of the PSP. They were "Castroites" or "Fidelistas" in the sense that they attributed quasi-magical powers to Castro and were ready to follow him as long as victory confirmed that faith, whether their leader was a partisan of "unity," a Communist, a Papist, or a vegetarian.

This attitude was bound to lead to a clash with Hubert Matos, an officer who had some educational background and who seems to have been impervious to Castro's charismatic qualities. It was also quite logical for Matos to have confused the Castroite officers with the Communists, first, because, at that time it was believed that the danger was communism, not Castroism, and, second, because Matos was obviously unable to accuse anyone publicly of being a "Fidelista."

In October Raúl Castro was appointed Minister of the Armed Forces. For Hubert Matos this was a confirmation of his worst fears. He decided to hand in his resignation to the commander-in-chief.

We know very little about the real aims of this resignation. Everything seems to indicate that it was part of a plan by which Matos was to secure the backing of certain leaders of the July 26 Movement in order to force Castro into a clear definition of the revolution's aims. If this was the plan, those who took part in it showed that they had a totally erroneous understanding of Castro's personality. On receiving the resignation Castro went to

Camagüey and arrested Matos before the latter's friends could come out publicly in his support. Moreover, taking advantage of the raid of another "pirate" airplane, this time over the capital, Castro linked the two events together; he called a mass meeting and in his speech announced the arming of the people and the imme-diate restoration of the revolutionary tribunals.[46]

With the arrest of Matos and his subsequent sentencing to twenty years' imprisonment, Castro corrected the only mistake he had ever made in choosing his commanders and allowing them to have forces of their own.

The conflict in the FEU and the CTC came to a head on the occasion of elections to the governing bodies of the two organizations. The July 26 Movement was certain to win both elections and was by no means prepared to share its victory with the Communists by the nomination of "unity" candidates.

In the University Student Federation elections in October the candidates for the presidency were, for the July 26 group Pedro Boytel, a member of the underground, and for the "unity" move-ment Rolando Cubelas, an officer from the ranks of the Revolu-tionary Student Directorate. The former's victory was certain until Castro himself publicly declared that the July 26 Movement would "not support any particular tendency in the struggle for the presi-dency of the FEU" and recommended that the students "give each other a revolutionary embrace, proclaim a president unanimously, and all unite in a genuine plan for reform."[47] After this the tri-umph of the "unity" candidate was assured.

That same day it was announced that Augusto Martínez Sánchez had been appointed Minister of Labor in order to impose the "unity" line on the elections for delegates to the congress of the trade-union organization (CTC). In spite of this the "unity" ten-dency in the trade unions remained insignificant. Castro therefore had to use his personal influence as he had in the case of the University Student Federation. First, he brought about a vote of confidence for the secretary-general, David Salvador. Then he pre-vailed upon Salvador to propose candidates who had been hand-picked by Castro for the CTC directorate. With the exception of Salvador himself, who proved unreliable and is now in a Castro

---

[46] After Castro's return in May the organization of the militias had been discontinued. At the same time the tribunals sitting in judgment on Batista's accomplices had come to an end.

[47] *Hoy*, October 18, 1959.

jail, the new directorate fulfilled Castro's requirements. That is to say, they were partisans of "unity" in the same sense as the ministers he had designated in June and the new president of the FEU — partisans of "unity" in Castro's sense only, united behind Castro and obedient to his commands. In practice this meant that the Communists played no role either in the political leadership of the country or in the leadership of the students or of the trade unions. The best proof that this type of "unity" was unsatisfactory for the Communists is that their delegates to the trade-union congress abstained from voting for the directorate that was elected; the PSP at once demonstrated its disagreement with the new directorate on the pretext that it did not correspond "to the positions required by Fidel Castro" — as if Castro were likely to permit any of his requests to be rejected![48]

Castroism Takes Shape

Meanwhile the internal rhythm of the revolution did not slacken at all. The method in which land reform was applied may be assessed from the following résumé, made by an observer sympathetic to the Cuban experiment:

INRA officials negotiated directly with the landowner on the land which the latter could retain and seized the rest; cattle were similarly divided, and in many cases buildings, trucks, and farm equipment were also seized. Inventories were rarely taken, receipts not given. Few bonds were actually issued.[49]

On November 24 the Minister of Labor was authorized to seize any factory that was not working satisfactorily. Two days later Ernesto Guevara was appointed president of the National Bank, and in December a law was issued making total confiscation of property the penalty for crimes against the revolution.

Against the background of these events, Castroism by the end of 1959 constituted a form of personal power, based essentially on the charismatic qualities of the leader and made possible by the complete collapse of the old state authority on January 1, 1959. Castroism had assigned itself a revolutionary task, one of infinite and boundless dimensions: the only thing that Castro was able to say

[48] *Ibid.*, November 24 and 25, 1959.
[49] Andrés Bianchi in Dudley Seers, ed., *Cuba: The Economic and Social Revolution* (Durham, N. C.: University of North Carolina Press, 1964), p. 402, note 9.

about it was that "our revolution is profound, it is a radical revolution," and "a revolution different from all other revolutions ever made in the world."[50] Apart from its radicalism, two of the most outstanding characteristics of the regime were the unprecedented scale on which state means were used for patronage and its profound allergy to any form of organization. In the armed forces, for instance, not only did most of those who had served under Batista receive pay but also all the members of the Rebel Army and of the other armed groups that had taken part in the civil war. In the civil administration the so-called "supplementary staff" lists soon began to appear; these were endless lists of personnel who for one reason or another had lost their jobs in government service but went on receiving their pay checks with no obligation other than that of passing by the appointed place on the appointed day to receive them.

As for the regime's dislike of organization, it is enough to note that the July 26 Movement, which had thought it was the victor on January 1, practically ceased to exist when two of its best-known leaders, Manuel Ray and Faustino Pérez, resigned from the posts of Minister of Public Works and Minister for the Recovery of Property, respectively, at the end of November. They were replaced by Osmani Cienfuegos, whose only claim to fame was that he was the brother of Major Camilo Cienfuegos who had disappeared in somewhat mysterious circumstances at the end of October, and Rolando Díaz Aztaraín, of whom nothing at all was known. The reorganization of the armed forces failed to make any progress. Moreover, in the first days of January 1960 a chief of the Revolutionary Militias, Captain Rogelio Acevedo,[51] was appointed, and that body, although not much more organized than the army, began to take on a shape that allowed it to contest the army's monopoly in the use of force. Finally, the Castroite victories in the FEU and in the CTC by no means meant that these organizations were going to play a more important role in events. On the contrary, they became mere appendages to the personality of the "maximum leader."

[50] Castro's statement at the trial of Hubert Matos (*Hoy*, December 17, 1959). This statement is an excellent summing up of Castroism at the end of 1959. It boiled down to the following: If the Sierra campaign ended in victory it was because he was the commander and all the others obeyed him. Castro does not expressly state the logical conclusion from this, but it is obvious: Let everyone follow him blindly once again, and everything will be put right.

[51] Acevedo's appointment was announced in *Revolución*, January 9, 1960.

From this it may be seen that by the end of 1959 almost the only organized force remaining in the country was the PSP, even though within it also "Fidelismo" was making headway, as we shall see further on. And quite apart from this danger, which could not of course escape the expert eye of Blas Roca, the general situation confronting the PSP was so unclear that the secretary-general could not extract any great satisfaction from the fact that his party had managed to escape the general disorganization thus far.

Beginning in July, Blas Roca endeavored to convince his followers that the example of the Soviet Union, where a single party monopolized government, could not apply to Cuba, but that what was relevant to Cuba was the experience of China. In China, according to him, the bourgeoisie was collaborating in the construction of socialism, and an alliance of parties representing diverse social classes was in charge of government, not merely during the bourgeois democratic phase of the revolution but also thereafter.[52] In October it became quite clear that Castro had no interest in preserving the July 26 Movement. Roca stopped talking about "the diverse parties in China" and mentioned the possibility that "the more advanced elements of the radical sector of the petite bourgeoisie, which are now leading the revolution, might move toward the proletariat, adopt its socialist point of view, and continue to lead in the transition to socialism."[53] This was, as can be seen, a delicate hint to Castro.

Castro, however, has always been rather impervious to delicacy. "Unity" in the Communist sense, that is, any type of collaboration with Castro that allowed the PSP to take part in decisionmaking, made no progress at all. Furthermore, Roca could not fail to realize that the very radicalism of the revolution was threatening to convert his conception of the "uninterrupted revolution" into an ideological justification of this dizzying process, in spite of all his repeated warnings against "leftism" and against any belief that the socialist phase of the revolution was imminent.[54] Moreover,

---

[52] See, for instance, "Nuestro camino" [Our Path], *Hoy*, July 9, 1959, and "Los varios partidos de China" [The Diverse Parties of China], *ibid.*, October 6, 1959.

[53] Report on the program in *ibid.*, October 7, 1959.

[54] *Ibid.* In this report Roca explained the concept of the "uninterrupted revolution": "This does not mean, of course, that anyone should think that Cuba can go on at once to the socialist phase of the revolution, or even that this phase is imminent." He went on to enumerate the "objective conditions" on the international scene (already mentioned) that were indispensable for the transition to the socialist phase.

Castro was now establishing his initial contacts with the Soviet Union, and the concept of the "uninterrupted revolution," inspired as it was by Chinese thinking and by Roca's admiration for Mao, was bound to create serious obstacles in the way to winning Khrushchev's confidence. Consequently, from the time of the PSP plenum in October, the expression "uninterrupted revolution" vanished from the language of the secretary-general of the PSP, and his references to the "Chinese example," or to Mao, became fewer and briefer until they were replaced by references to the Soviet experience and by praise for the Soviet Premier.

Meanwhile Castro resumed his audacious foreign policy maneuver to ensure Soviet protection as soon as the internal obstacles had been overcome. Soviet Vice-Premier Mikoyan was scheduled to travel to Mexico to open a trade exhibition, and on November 3 *Revolución* suggested that advantage be taken of this to invite him to Havana. On that same day, and in the same issue of *Revolución* — showing, to my mind, the relation between the two questions — the British were threatened with the loss of the Latin American market, and even of their investments there, if they persisted in refusing to supply jet planes to Cuba so as not to antagonize the United States. Two weeks later apprehension was so great that *Revolución* suggested that Mikoyan, who was due to arrive in Mexico the following day, should proceed at once to Havana.[55]

In December, Alexander Alexeyev, the present Soviet ambassador in Cuba, turned up in Havana and, with the ease with which Soviet officials take on the most variegated disguises, registered as a "correspondent of the Tass agency."[56]

55 *Revolución,* November 3 and 17, 1959.
56 *Ibid.,* December 15, 1959.

CHAPTER FOUR

THE ESTABLISHMENT OF RELATIONS WITH THE SOVIET UNION AND CHINA

We can sum up in a few words what we know of the relations between Cuba and the countries of the socialist camp up to February 1960.

A delegation of the Central Council of Soviet Trade Unions left Moscow to take part in the celebration of May 1, 1959 in Havana but because of visa difficulties arrived after the celebrations had taken place.[1] In November 1959, when the Tenth Congress of the CTC was held, Agramonte was no longer Minister of Foreign Affairs, the visas were given in time, and the Soviet trade-union delegation was able to take part in the sessions of the congress.

In June of the same year, at a banquet given in Castro's honor by Cuban journalists, Kung Mai, "the representative in Cuba of the Chinese News Agency," sat next to Carlos Rafael Rodríguez.[2] The following month a Chinese press delegation spent three weeks in Cuba,[3] and from then on the arrivals of journalists from Peking became so numerous that by November, according to C. P. Cabell of the CIA, the Chinese correspondents had set up their general headquarters in Havana.[4]

For their part Cuban visitors to the Iron Curtain countries, almost all members of the PSP, initially showed their preference for Peking, as was to be expected in view of the excellent relations maintained by the PSP with their Chinese comrades, as we have seen. In July 1959 Violeta Casal, the popular announcer of "Rebel Radio" in the Sierra, paid a visit to China, and at the end of that month Juan Marinello returned from a trip there. In October the PSP sent a delegation to China, headed by Aníbal Escalante, on the occasion of the anniversary of the Chinese People's Republic. It

[1] *Hoy*, May 12, 1959.
[2] *Ibid.*, June 9, 1959.
[3] Statement of the Chinese journalists on leaving Cuba (*ibid.*, July 29, 1959).
[4] Associated Press cable, *Revolución*, February 1, 1960.

included artists and intellectuals. A little later the Chinese capital was visited by a delegation from the Revolutionary Student Directorate, headed by Faure Chomón. This was surely a reward to Chomón for the "unity" position he had adopted in June.[5]

As for trade relations, the Soviet Union bought half a million tons of sugar in 1959, approximately the same as in 1955, but much more than it had bought in 1956, 1957, and 1958, when the figures were 235,000, 395,000, and 207,000 tons, respectively. At the end of 1959 the Chinese bought 50,000 tons.

We have cited these data simply as part of our function as historian. They are of no import. All such visits and transactions could have continued without affecting the evolution of Cuban affairs. What were really decisive were the decisions taken by Castro when the Dominican debacle prevented him from continuing his offensive abroad and when, believing more than ever that destiny had singled him out for a special mission, he decided to pursue his radical revolution without yielding any of his personal power.

Relations with Moscow

The Soviet Union failed to respond to Castro's overtures with the speed or in the form he wanted. One reason was surely that after the conversation between Khrushchev and Eisenhower in September 1959 Soviet-American relations were dominated for a time by the optimistic "spirit of Camp David" — so named for the presidential retreat where the two leaders conferred. At such a time Khrushchev would hardly endanger the chances of achieving some or all of his objectives through negotiation by showing an excessive interest in the Caribbean. Hence Cuban contacts with the Soviets developed slowly.

That there were difficulties involved is suggested by Castro's initiative, at the beginning of December, in calling a conference of underdeveloped countries.[6] This was apparently a maneuver to heighten his own importance in Khrushchev's eyes by suggesting the role that Cuba might play in cooperating with Soviet foreign policy among the countries of the "third world." It seems unlikely

5 For Violeta Casal see *Hoy*, July 29, 1959; Marinello's return, *ibid.*, July 30, 1959; the PSP delegation in China, NCNA, September 27, 1959 (SCMP 2103, October 2, 1959); and the delegation of the Revolutionary Student Directorate, NCNA, October 3, 1959 (SCMP 2111, October 7, 1959).

6 Statement of Foreign Minister Raúl Roa at the United Nations (*Hoy*, December 4, 1959).

to me that Castro would have launched this plan — which ended in a resounding failure — if he had been certain of a favorable Soviet response to his blandishments.

If closer relations were to be established between Cuba and the Soviet Union, it was no longer possible to go on criticizing the policy of peaceful coexistence and of *rapprochement* between the latter and the United States. Hence Guevara acknowledged that there had undoubtedly been "a certain relaxation" in the international situation, even though this had not yet affected Cuba.[7] In exchange for this admission, *Hoy,* still advocating a policy of peace in the interests of the revolution, conceded that "the actions of the U.S. imperialists against Cuba . . . were not in accord, let us say, with the spirit of Camp David."[8]

On December 15 it was announced that the Soviet trade exhibition would arrive in Cuba in January 1960. At the beginning of that month there arrived the "directors sent to prepare the exhibition," probably among them other Soviet agents who with Alexeyev had been instructed to report on the state of affairs in Cuba.[9] Finally, on February 4, Mikoyan arrived to open the exhibition. Nine days later he signed a trade agreement with the Cuban government. The Soviet Union undertook to buy 425,000 tons of sugar in 1960 and a million tons per year in the following four years. Further, the agreement provided for a Soviet credit to Cuba of $100 million, at an annual interest of 2.5 per cent, for the purchase of plants, machinery, materials, and technical assistance. The communiqué issued on this occasion expressed "the interest of the two governments in active cooperation within the U.N. in favor of coexistence, cooperation, and friendship among all the peoples of the world." The communiqué announced that both nations would soon discuss the resumption of diplomatic relations, which had been broken off by Batista a few days after his successful coup of March 1952.[10]

Even before Mikoyan had left Cuba, a delegation arrived from East Germany. On February 20, 1960[11] this delegation signed a

---

[7] *Ibid.,* January 15, 1960.

[8] "Nuestra Opinión: El espiritu de Camp David y las amenazas y los ataques contra Cuba" [The Spirit of Camp David and the Threats and Attacks Against Cuba], *ibid.,* January 27, 1960. On the position of the PSP in these months see also "Nuestra Opinión: Las medidas de desarme soviético, demostración efectiva de paz" [The Soviet Disarmament Measures, an Effective Demonstration of Peace], *ibid.,* January 16, 1960.

[9] *Ibid.,* December 15, 1959 and January 10, 1960, respectively.

[10] Text of the communiqué in *ibid.,* February 14, 1960.

[11] The arrival of the East German delegation was announced in *ibid.,* February 9, 1960.

financial and commercial agreement with Cuba. This was followed at the end of March by a similar agreement with Poland, thus showing that the establishment of ties with Cuba was now a general policy of the socialist camp, or at least of its European members.

There is no need to emphasize the effects of these agreements on the relations between the United States and Cuba, which had already been worsened by the "revolutionary," that is, totally arbitrary, application of the agrarian reform law,[12] by the growing frequency of air attacks on Cuba by planes coming from U.S. territory, and by the first rumors of what *Revolución* called the "new Platt Amendment,"[13] that is, the congressional moves to cut the Cuban sugar quota in the U.S. market. On January 28 the Cuban press had announced that U.S. Ambassador Bonsal was leaving Cuba for good.[14] Bonsal did return to Havana the following month, but relations between the two countries at that stage had already deteriorated so much that Daniel M. Braddock, Minister-Counselor of the U.S. Embassy in Havana, requested the mediation of the Argentine ambassador, Julio A. Amoedo, to present the Cuban government with certain proposals for the resolution of differences between the two countries.

According to Amoedo, these proposals included a halt to the campaign of insults against the United States and an agreement by Castro to receive Bonsal after his return so as to study ways and means of returning to normal relations. They also indicated the desire of the U.S. government "to assist the Castro regime in the financing of the agrarian reform, as well as other economic and social matters."[15] The U.S. State Department, however, has denied having made any offer of economic aid.[16]

In spite of the Argentine ambassador's statement it seems to me

12 I do not consider it necessary to emphasize that one characteristic of the Cuban revolution was the consistent failure of the government to implement its own laws. Today all the revolutionary leaders acknowledge this. It will be sufficient to mention something said by Castro: "We realize that one of the weaknesses of the revolution has been that things have been done outside the law . . . by self-styled lawmakers. The revolution must and can legislate so that nothing shall be done outside the law." (Speech to the sugar workers of Camagüey, *ibid.*, May 16, 1962.) There is no need to say that since then everything has been going along in exactly the same way as before.

13 E. V. Candelas, "Cuba contra la nueva Enmienda Platt" [Cuba Against the New Platt Amendment], *Revolución*, March 4, 1960.

14 *Hoy*, January 28, 1960.

15 Julio A. Amoedo, "Negotiating with Fidel Castro," *The New Leader*, April 27, 1964.

16 See "A Postscript by Theodore Draper" in the same issue of *The New Leader*.

highly unlikely that an unofficial offer of economic aid would have
been made at a time when American property was being expropriated and Washington was demanding prior cash payment for
the expropriations through official channels. It is futile to specu-
late on what might have happened if at the time of Castro's visit
to Washington in April 1959 the United States had made the
spontaneous offer of, say, one billion dollars, something that at
least some of the people with Castro had in mind. But by February
or March 1960 it is hardly likely that any offer of economic aid
could have persuaded Castro to desist from his plans.

The methods chosen by his adversaries, the threats to the sugar
quota, and the denunciations of Castro as a Soviet agent did nothing
to weaken Castro's power. On the contrary, they even consolidated
his popularity with the Cuban people and gave an air of plausi-
bility to his charges that his opponents were all agents of the CIA.
Meanwhile the clumsiness of the U.S. State Department in the
face of the Cuban-Soviet *rapprochement*, the U.S. government's
failure to shake the Castro regime, and the growing admiration of
the Latin American peoples for this David fearlessly braving the
blows of Goliath must all have contributed to Castro's growing
conviction that he might have overestimated the enemy and that it
might be worthwhile to see whether history had destined him to
play the role of liberator of the entire continent. It seems to me
puerile to assume that under such conditions any offer of economic
aid could have persuaded Castro to renounce his "historic mission."
If one wanted to negotiate with him, the only possibility was to
accept his conditions, namely, to recognize "Cuban sovereignty,"
Castro's right to govern Cuba for life, without a Congress, without
courts, without elections, and not prevent him from fulfilling his
destiny, which was to repeat the revolution of 1810 and lead the
Latin American peoples into battle against the new colonial power.
If one wished to oppose him, on the other hand, there was also
only one way: to disregard his provocations, carefully watch his
plans for expansion, and denounce him before the world for what
he really was, a tyrant who was about to impose on his people the
gigantic catastrophe that they have now in fact suffered.

Whatever might have been its content, the mediation attempt of
the Argentine ambassador collapsed at the end of February, when
Castro's government demanded that previous to any negotiations
the United States must pledge itself not to adopt any measures

harmful to the Cuban economy; and the United States rejected this condition as unacceptable.

The U.S. note was dated February 29, 1960. Four days later the French ship *Le Coubre,* which was unloading war material in Havana harbor, was blown up, and many people were killed or wounded. In the speech he made at the funeral of the victims on March 5, Castro said that the explosion had not been accidental but had been brought about by "those who do not wish our country to be in a position to defend its sovereignty," indicating that "among those who had a great interest in our not receiving those arms" were "the functionaries of the North American Government." In conclusion he launched a new slogan: "Fatherland or death!"[17]

Jean-Paul Sartre, who listened to this accusation, said that all at once the meaning of the Cuban revolution was revealed to him: "At that moment I understood that the enemy, with all his maneuvers, was doing no more than accelerating an internal process that would develop in accordance with its own laws. The revolution was adapting itself to actions coming from abroad, and improvising its own replies."[18] There has been no proof that foreign sabotage caused the explosion — everything seems to indicate that it was the result of unpardonable carelessness[19] — and it is clear that before Castro spoke no one had voiced the slightest suspicion and that after his speech the masses did not take to the streets to demonstrate in front of the U.S. embassy, or attack American property, or make attacks on any of the numerous Americans living in Cuba at the time.

17 The text of Castro's speech in *Hoy,* March 6, 1960. Before the *Granma* expedition Castro had been accustomed to repeating that in 1956 "we will be free or we will be martyrs." His war manifesto against the dictatorship, dated March 12, 1958, ended with these words: "The whole nation is ready to become free or to perish." Beginning in March 1960 no further allusion was ever made to freedom, and the two-pronged slogan then became "Fatherland or death!" However, it appears that either Castro himself or someone else thought this disjunctive slogan was too tragic sounding; hence it was decided to add an optimistic note: "¡Venceremos!" (We shall overcome!). This is the form in which the slogan is now used.

18 *Sartre visita a Cuba* [Sartre Visits Cuba] (Havana: Ediciones R., 1960), p. 8.

19 On this point the author has personal knowledge that on the same night that the explosion took place, when the Council of Ministers was in session, neither the Prime Minister nor the Minister of the Armed Forces Raúl Castro nor anyone else present knew the nature of the cargo on *Le Coubre.* This was ascertained only when the director-general of customs found the cargo documents. It is thus obvious that not even the most elementary precautions had been taken.

This seems to me to show that there was no spontaneous "reply" by the revolution but that it was Castro himself who had to accelerate events at a dizzy pace because he wanted to make a social revolution without possessing the indispensable ideological and organizational cadres. Because of this and because of the weakness of his territorial base, he had to keep constantly on the offensive; now that the Soviet Union was beginning to smile on him, while the United States seemed incapable of action, and Latin America was looking toward him, he needed to convince all of them of his audacity and resolution.

Coming after the trade agreements with the Soviet Union and East Germany, and the Cuban note to the United States of February 22 laying down unacceptable conditions for negotiation, Castro's speech on March 5 appears to have convinced Washington that the Cuban question was serious. It was now, on March 17, that the CIA was authorized to equip a force of Cuban exiles, although no particular sense of urgency appears to have been attached to the project.[20]

Castro's accusation, even if it failed to arouse the people, also had important consequences in Cuba. *Revolución,* the organ of the July 26 Movement, which had carried on a lively polemic against *Hoy* and the Communists throughout 1959, published two editorials on March 22 and 26, entitled "Anti-Communism, Spearhead of Imperialism," and "Pretexts and Intentions of the Enemies of the Revolution." In these it withdrew from the position it had maintained until then, vigorously rejected anticommu-

[20] Haynes Johnson, *The Bay of Pigs* (New York: W. W. Norton, 1964), reports the parsimonious manner in which the CIA proceeded. At the end of March 1960 Manuel Artime, a defector from the Rebel Army, who had joined the guerrillas on December 27 or 28, 1958, and who from March 1960 on continued to enjoy the confidence given him by the CIA because of his docility, was appointed to organize a committee together with some other Cuban exiles. Early in June the first group of officers left for the training camps. On August 22 a camp was set up in Guatemala, and on September 19 the first arms arrived — 13 Springfield rifles from World War I and a few pistols. By the beginning of November the total force came to 430 men. On November 4 it was decided to abandon the original plan of starting a guerrilla war in Cuba, replacing it with the organization of Brigade 2506, which was the force that undertook the chaotic invasion of the Bay of Pigs (*ibid.,* pp. 25, 29–30, 34, 39, 48, 54, and 55). Castro was probably always well informed of the slowness of this whole proceeding. For instance, on September 28 *Hoy* reproduced a protest by the Guatemalan Labor Party to the effect that Roberto Alejos had bought the "Helvetia" estate and would use it for the training of "Batista henchmen." It was, in fact, on this estate that the exiles' camp was set up. See also Arthur M. Schlesinger, Jr., *A Thousand Days: John F. Kennedy in the White House* (Boston: Houghton Mifflin, 1965), pp. 226 ff.

nism, called for "the unbreakable union of all Cubans around their leader Fidel Castro," and justified that union with arguments that were typically Castroite: "In confronting foreign aggression only one attitude is possible — the unshakable unity of the people under the slogan 'Fatherland or death!' "[21]

It is obvious that these editorials were received by the PSP with great satisfaction, but one may be fairly sure that Blas Roca did not participate in that satisfaction, for reasons we shall see later.

On February 28, four days before the explosion on *Le Coubre,* another plenum of the Central Committee of the PSP took place. Blas Roca gave the same report he usually did. According to him the situation was characterized by the following features: (1) "the advance and the deepening of the revolution," evidenced by the increase in confiscations and in the number of state-held properties, which had been undertaken "as a fundamental method of avoiding economic sabotage"; (2) the growing aggressiveness of the enemy, due chiefly to the activity of the "imperialists," who were now the "axis of the counterrevolution"; and (3) "the definition of the revolutionary and counterrevolutionary camps." He then went on to define the growing aggressiveness of "imperialism." He said: "It would be wrong to think that the imperialists are going to launch any military intervention in our country. . . . Such a line of thinking is capable of giving rise to serious errors, and it is incorrect. . . ." The chief danger, he said, lay in economic aggression, but even with respect to that it should not be forgotten that the "United States needs Cuban sugar; it cannot do without it. . . ."[22] Roca spoke on February 28; on March 4 the explosion on *Le Coubre* occurred and on March 5 Castro made his speech.

The resolution of the Central Committee plenum "on the situation, national development, and the defense of the fatherland and the revolution" was not published until March 16, a very unusual delay in PSP Central Committee matters that can be explained only by the content of the resolution. "Before our own people, before the people of the United States, before the peoples of Latin America, and before all the peoples of the world, we say once again: Cuba needs fighter planes and radar equipment, as well as other arms, for the defense and protection of its territory and of its sovereignty against the growing and evident threats of its enemies, and she

21 "El anticomunismo, punta de lanza del imperialismo" [Anti-Communism, Spearhead of Imperialism], *Revolución,* March 22, 1960.
22 Roca's report in *Hoy,* March 1, 1960.

insists on buying them wherever they are being sold. . . ." The document went on: "The socialist countries have given us priceless solidarity. . . . We, all patriotic and revolutionary Cubans, understand the extraordinary importance of the solidarity given us by the socialist countries, and we are duly thankful. But at the present moment we need still greater solidarity, and we are sure that it will be."[23]

The text of this resolution requires no comment: The majority of the National Committee of the PSP, despite the opinion of its secretary-general, who thought it a "serious error" to ascribe excessive importance to military threats, had succumbed to the martial interpretation of history supported by Castro, and like him was hoping that the Soviet Union would provide "fighter planes, radar equipment, and other arms."

Two other resolutions of the plenum reveal the crisis that had occurred within the leadership of the PSP. On March 1, in a resolution on "the problems of national development and the activities of the working class, the peasantry, and the masses of the people in general," it was agreed that "in the articles published under the title 'Our Opinion' [in *Hoy*] collective opinions were expressed and orientations given that the whole party must heed."[24] In other words, in the organ of the PSP somewhat unorthodox opinions were being put forth under the editorship of Carlos Rafael Rodríguez, and it was thought necessary to orient the party with respect to those articles that harmonized with the authentic "line."

Finally, in its resolution of March 15 the plenum denounced "the attempts of the imperialists to revive in our country the Trotskyite groups in order to use them as provocateurs, spies, and confusionists against the Cuban revolution." Every student of the international Communist movement knows the meaning of such references to Trotskyism in a party document. Unless there is proof to the contrary, they are a sure index of the existence of serious internal differences. Given this background, I have not the least doubt that this was the reason for these references in the resolution.

It was doubtless the abrupt turn taken by events, with the Castro accusation of March 5 and the unusual rebellion within the ranks of the PSP, as evidenced by the resolution of March 15, that showed

23 Text of the resolution in *ibid.*, March 16, 1960.
24 Text of the resolution in *ibid.*, March 4, 1960.

Blas Roca the wisdom of collecting the opinions of the main leaders of the international Communist movement; and with this in view he left Cuba at the end of the same month for the countries of the socialist camp.

At the end of April he was in Peking, where he was received by Mao, who for the first time offered the support of his 650 million compatriots to the Cuban revolution. Roca was lavishly honored and entertained by the leaders of the Chinese Communist Party.[25] His visit to Peking was closely followed by that of Major William Gálvez, at that time inspector-general of the Rebel Army, a position eloquently testifying to his Castroite allegiance.[26]

Roca then went on to Moscow where he met Khrushchev for the first time.[27] At this stage Roca must already have been informed of the growing Sino-Soviet friction and known that Mao was going through a "leftist" deviation similar to that he himself was facing in Cuba. It is significant that after his interview with Khrushchev, even though Roca continued to refer to Mao as an "admirable and wise leader,"[28] he began to stress Khrushchev's good humor, capability, practical sense, and, above all, his "definite stature as a great Leninist."[29]

After the shooting down of a U-2 airplane over Soviet territory had been announced on May 5, 1960, Khrushchev apparently decided to use this incident as an excuse for wrecking the summit conference projected for the middle of May in Paris. One reason must have been that he was no longer as optimistic as he had been in 1959 about the outcome of his negotiations with Washington and thus felt the necessity for bringing further pressure to bear on the United States, by way of Cuba, for instance. We cannot determine the degree to which Roca's reports helped toward the selection of Cuba as one of the main points of the new Soviet offensive, but it is significant that Soviet-Cuban diplomatic relations were restored at the time of the Khrushchev-Roca interview on May 7, 1960.

[25] Support expressed for Mao in *Hoy* and *Revolución*, May 5, 1960. On Roca's stay in Peking, see NCNA, April 24 and 29 (SCMP 2247, April 29, 1960, and SCMP 2251, May 5, 1960), as well as *Hoy*, April 30 and May 4 and 5, 1960.

[26] Gálvez' visit and his interview with Mao in NCNA, May 5 and 10, 1960 (SCMP 2255, May 11, 1960, and SCMP 2258, May 16, 1960).

[27] In his television interview Roca said that this was the first time he had met Khrushchev (see *Hoy*, June 1, 1960).

[28] Letter of Roca in *Hoy*, May 19, 1960.

[29] Letter of Roca in *ibid.*, May 24, 1960.

Soviet Arms in Cuba

Roca returned on May 23. On April 19 Soviet oil had begun to arrive in Cuba; on May 16 diplomatic relations were established with Czechoslovakia; and two days later, from Paris, Khrushchev sent his greetings to the Cuban people, "which through its heroic struggle had secured its liberty and independence."[30] All this shows the speed with which relations between Castro and the Communist bloc were progressing.

On May 25 the Politburo of the PSP issued a communiqué "On the Summit Meeting." Since the document was issued shortly after Roca's return, one may assume that it contained the latest impressions — or instructions — received by Roca in his conversations with the main leaders of the international Communist movement.

The communiqué attributed the collapse of the Paris conference to "the maneuvers of imperialism," but it reaffirmed the PSP's confidence in the policy of peaceful coexistence. As for Cuba, its conclusions were as follows: "The struggle against imperialism" had to be reinforced; a state of alert against any Yankee aggression had to be maintained, "more than ever"; and "the movement to promote and reinforce the solidarity of the peoples of Latin America and of the whole world in support of the Cuban revolution" had to be intensified.[31]

The contents of this document were far removed from the warlike spirit that animated the March 15 resolution of the PSP (which called on the countries of the socialist camp to show their solidarity by sending airplanes, radar equipment, and other arms); hence we must conclude that by invoking the authority of the Soviet leaders Roca had managed to re-establish his control of the PSP and bring it back to his usual "centrist" line.

We have no proof whatsoever that Castro has ever read any PSP document, much less that he has ever been guided by one. At the end of May what worried him was the refusal of the oil companies to refine Soviet oil. Hence, just as William Gálvez had followed Roca to Peking, now another trusted follower of Castro, Antonio Núñez Jiménez, the second figure in the National Institute of Agrarian Reform, left for Moscow in order — as was publicly stated — to invite the Soviet Premier to Havana.[32] It was probably Núñez

---

30 *Ibid.*, May 19, 1960.
31 Communiqué of the PSP on the summit meeting in *ibid.*, May 25, 1960.
32 *Ibid.*, June 8, 1960.

Jiménez who made arrangements with Khrushchev over fuel supplies, which were to make Cuba independent of British and American oil deliveries and thus enabled Castro to confiscate the Texaco refinery on June 29 and the Shell and Standard Oil refineries two days later. We may also assume that it was he who arranged the details of Raúl Castro's journey, which was to take place during the last week in June in order — as the Cuban press stated — "to attend the Spartacus games" in Czechoslovakia.[33]

If there is some doubt as to the real goals of Núñez Jiménez' trip, there is none whatever concerning that of Raúl. On July 8 Fidel Castro announced the imminent arrival of arms for the militias, and on July 26 he stated: "This will be the last time the worker and peasant militias will parade without rifles, because the militias' rifles are already in Cuba."[34] From a later statement by Guevara we know that the first arms came from Czechoslovakia.[35]

On July 6, in retaliation for the confiscation of the oil refineries, President Eisenhower reduced the Cuban sugar quota for 1960 by 700,000 tons. This in its turn caused Khrushchev, three days later, to make his historic statement: "In a figurative sense, if it became necessary, the Soviet military can support the Cuban people with rocket weapons. . . ."[36] That same day the Soviet Premier sent a cable to Castro committing himself to take over the 700,000 tons of sugar by which the American quota had been reduced. On July 10 a huge mass meeting took place to demonstrate the Cuban people's gratitude for Khrushchev's offer of aid. Castro happened to be ill at the time and could not be present at the meeting, but at the end of the proceedings the television cameras were brought to the clinic — to allay fears about his absence — and, as always happens whenever Castro has a chance, he spoke at length. Two things emerged from this talk: The Soviet offer had been "absolutely spontaneous" — words Castro repeated at least half a dozen times; and the Soviets had offered real, not "figurative," rockets.[37]

Castro was obviously eager to reassure public opinion, which had been stunned by the promise of missile aid, of his absolute inno-

---

33 *Ibid.,* June 29, 1960.

34 For Castro's television appearance see *Revolución,* July 9, 1960; his July 26 speech in *ibid.,* July 27, 1960.

35 Guevara's speech of September 18 from *Events in United States–Cuban Relations,* a Chronology, 1957–1963, prepared by the U.S. Department of State for the Committee on Foreign Relations, U.S. Senate.

36 *Revolución,* July 11, 1960.

37 For Castro's television appearance see *Hoy,* July 12, 1960.

cence in the matter, although his insistence on this point seems to me in itself highly suspicious. As to his statement that the Soviets had offered real and not "figurative" rockets, this was certainly a deliberate attempt at confusion. We shall see his aim later.

The Soviet Premier, for his part, hastened to clarify the real meaning of his promises. Taking advantage of Raúl Castro's visit to Moscow, supposedly to thank the Soviet government on behalf of the Cuban people for the outstanding Soviet offer of help,[38] a communiqué was issued in which the Soviet government declared that it was in a position "to undertake the transfer of oil and of any other products to the extent necessary to satisfy fully all Cuban demands." But there was no reference, symbolic or otherwise, to nuclear weapons; the communiqué stated only that the Soviet Union would use "all measures to prevent any armed intervention against Cuba."[39] In the message sent by Khrushchev to Castro on July 26 to commemorate the anniversary of the Moncada attack, he made use of a similar expression: "If any armed intervention is undertaken against Cuba, the necessary aid will be forthcoming."[40]

Castro, of course, paid no attention to all this. "Against all comers,"[41] he alone had routed Batista's army. Against all comers, he alone had proposed having Soviet weapons put in his hands, and now he had them in his arsenal. The moment would come to oblige Khrushchev to deliver real missiles.

Meanwhile, on July 26, 1960, at the scene of his military triumphs, he proclaimed his new ambitions to the world with renewed audacity: "Here, facing the unconquered mountain range, facing the Sierra Maestra, let us promise one another that we shall continue to make our fatherland an example that will make the Andes mountain range into the Sierra Maestra of all America."[42]

The First Nationalizations[43]

At the end of June Castro had said: "If they take our quota away from us pound by pound, we shall take away their sugar mills one

---

[38] This was the explanation given by Raúl in his television interview, published in *ibid.*, August 7, 1960.

[39] Text of the communiqué in *ibid.*, July 22, 1960.

[40] The greeting from Khrushchev in *ibid.*, July 26, 1960.

[41] This is the title of an article written by Castro on December 25, 1955 and published in *Bohemia* (Havana).

[42] *Revolución*, July 27, 1960.

[43] The Castro government does not distinguish, but we must, between:

by one. . . ."[44] On July 6, as has been noted, President Eisenhower "took away" 700,000 tons, and on the same day the Cuban Council of Ministers authorized the President and the Prime Minister to nationalize U.S. properties. It was not, however, until August 6 that Castro actually began to implement his threat. Why the delay? It was due to a number of factors.

First of all, a new attempt at conciliation was made by President Frondizi of Argentina, about which we have very little information.[45]

Second, however ignorant Castro may have been of economic affairs and however much he may have simply trusted to luck, he must have understood that Eisenhower's decision was a declaration of economic war. If he picked up the gauntlet by implementing the nationalization of American properties he would be joining battle with an economic power that in 1958 had provided Cuba with $543 million of its total imports of $777 million, and to which Cuba had exported $491 million of its total exports of $733 million.

Finally, he was also bound to be affected by the resistance within his own ranks, not among the commanders of the Rebel Army, who as far as we know have never yet opposed his decisions, but in the remnants of the July 26 Movement and in the PSP, or at least that faction of it that was led by Blas Roca. In speaking of resistance I do not mean organized opposition but a reluctance to follow the leader along a path strewn with obstacles toward an end probably unknown even to himself.

As Castro progressed in his *rapprochement* with the Soviets, the discontent of the remaining July 26 figures became more and more evident. In the course of the first six months of 1960, Marcelo Fernández was replaced as "coordinator" of the movement by Emilio Aragonés,[46] a figure of the third or fourth order in the strug-

---

Intervention: the government appoints an official who "intervenes" in the enterprise, national or foreign, that is, controls all its operations, but the ownership of the enterprise is not affected. This procedure was used before Castro in Cuba and by Castro until 1960.)

Confiscation: expropriation without any indemnity.

Nationalization: The government seizes foreign property, with or without indemnification.

44 Speech at Artemisa (*Hoy*, June 30, 1960).

45 According to an Associated Press dispatch (*The New York Times*, July 6, 1960), President Frondizi told British Prime Minister Macmillan of this attempt. It was mentioned by *Hoy* in an editorial on July 30, 1960.

46 The signature of Aragonés appeared on the address welcoming Mikoyan to Havana (*Revolución*, February 6, 1960).

gle against Batista. In June Fernández also gave up his government position, that of Undersecretary of Foreign Affairs. His successor, Carlos Olivares, was a loyal Castroite.[47] On July 1 Enrique Oltunski, who had been the coordinator of the July 26 Movement in Las Villas province, resigned as Minister of Communications. Raúl Curbelo, who succeeded him, was not one of the known leaders of the July 26 Movement.

The July 26 Movement had had six representatives in the January 1959 government: Faustino Pérez, Manuel Ray, Enrique Oltunski, Armando Hart, Humberto Sorí Marín, and Luis Orlando Rodríguez. Of these only one, Hart, was still in the government on July 1, 1960.[48]

Finally, the chief labor leader of the July 26 Movement, David Salvador, abandoned his post as secretary-general of the CTC in March 1960 and initiated a clandestine struggle against the regime, which came to an end with his arrest before the end of the year.

It cannot be doubted that these resignations and replacements reflected the discontent of the July 26 Movement with a policy that continued to insist on the autonomy of the revolution and at the same time steadily tightened Cuba's ties with the Communist world. Castro could not disregard this discontent: If it gained enough strength to become a real movement led by the majority of the figures just mentioned, all known as genuine July 26 leaders, the "unity" of the revolutionaries would no longer be so believable. Castro's popularity would be affected, and he would have to rely more and more on the PSP for the implementation of his policy. After the reduction of the sugar quota, moreover, the nationalization of U.S. properties implied that Cuba would soon become economically dependent on the Soviets; hence Castro was obliged to move with extreme caution.

As for Castro's other supporter, the PSP, this too, paradoxically, does not seem to have been very enthusiastic about expropriating

[47] Olivares had originally been a protégé of President Urrutia and then became an informer for Raúl Castro in order to keep the President's activities under surveillance.

[48] Armando Hart, who had been in prison on the Isle of Pines during the last year of the struggle against Batista, tried to mediate between Colonel Ramón Barquín, the temporary commander of the army, and Castro on January 1, 1959. When Castro refused to negotiate, Hart gave in and returned to Havana to become Minister of Education. I myself spent January 1, 1959 in Camp Columbia, together with Colonel Barquín, and was a witness to Hart's repeated calls, Castro's refusals to come to the telephone, and Hart's "wise decision," which won him the ministerial post.

the "imperialist companies." At any rate, we do not know of a single PSP statement in favor of expropriation throughout the critical month of July 6 to August 6; our sources, rather, reflect considerable perplexity.

Roca's report to the enlarged Politburo of the PSP, after the publication of the nationalization law of July 6, emphasized that it was not "applicable to enterprises belonging to Cubans or nationals of any other country." Roca limited himself to pointing out that "the economic war" would not be an "internal civil struggle" and recommending that preparations should be made for it, since it "will be a long one."[49]

During the Congress of Latin American Youth at the end of July the Trotskyites — flesh-and-blood ones this time, almost all of them Argentines and Uruguayans — circulated a manifesto declaring that the Cuban people were "taking over the property of the imperialists" and calling on "People's China to move up and make itself the most powerful state in the world." The Cuban delegation, which included some members of the PSP Youth (Young Socialists), replied with a denial, maintaining that expropriation had taken place only "in cases where Cuban laws were violated" and that the revolutionary government had "proceeded to confiscate [properties] in order to keep them in production." As for the mention of "People's China," the document said only that no one would be deceived by such invocations, since everyone knew that "under the cloak of radicalism . . . there will appear the dagger of betrayal."[50]

This statement, signed by the Cuban delegation consisting of July 26 people, the Revolutionary Student Directorate, the Socialist Youth, and the CTC, appeared in the press on the morning of August 5. That night Castro, at the same congress, announced the nationalization of thirty-six sugar plants, two oil refineries, and the electric and telephone companies, all of them U.S. property. It is impossible to ascertain what made Castro override once again all obstacles and all opposition, but the fact that after only a few short hours he was strongly contradicting the statements of his own representatives at the congress, thus confirming the Trotskyite views, is plain proof that he took the decision against all the expectations of his supporters.

The signature of the Socialist Youth on the statement formulated by the Cuban delegation to the Latin American Youth Congress did not prevent the PSP from greeting and supporting "with great emotion . . . the historic decision"; and, since Castro was ill — he had partially lost his voice during the reading of the nationalization law — they ended on a delicate note of tenderness: "We ask dear Fidel to take care of himself."[51]

The first nationalizations illustrate what I may term the predominant administrative character of the Castro revolution. They were not preceded or followed by any meetings, demonstrations, or other public expressions of the popular will. The Prime Minister simply dictated an order. And once his followers and the masses saw that there would be no serious and immediate American reprisals, and once they had recovered from the shock, they found one more reason to trust Castro blindly. Castro, of course, hastened to distribute official positions as administrators of the nationalized enterprises, jobs that, together with the public offices, including the "supplementary staff lists" — freely proliferating by now — constituted the rewards with which the leader strengthened the faith of his followers.[52]

The PSP Eighth Party Congress

In spite of the emotional reaction of the PSP, it is evident that the nationalization law could not give Blas Roca any great joy, much less on the eve of a party congress, the Eighth National Assembly of the PSP that convened on August 16. In fact this law demonstrated the growing "leftist" tendency of Castro; it increased his influence within the PSP and weakened Roca's "centrist" position still further in the face of the complex problems plaguing him. These problems were the following:

First, after the Le Coubre explosion and Castro's speech, Chinese interest in Cuba grew substantially — and almost coincidentally with the aggravation of the Sino-Soviet conflict, which took place

51 "Saludos del B.E. del PSP al Comandante Fidel Castro" [PSP Politburo Hails Commander Fidel Castro], Hoy, August 9, 1960.

52 I much regret having to disillusion those who, like Herbert Matthews, hold that one advantage of Castroism has been political probity. On the contrary, one feature of Castroism is the use of patronage to a degree unknown in Cuban history. Since Castro became Prime Minister dismissal from public administration has become unknown. Posts, salaries, and functions in public administration have been reserved for "revolutionaries." Anyone replaced went on being paid, without working, by means of an "auxiliary allowance." The same procedure was also extended to confiscated or nationalized private enterprise.

during the meeting of the World Federation of Trade Unions in Peking at the beginning of June and the so-called Bucharest Conference the same month. The PSP adopted a position of strict neutrality. *Hoy*, for instance, not only reproduced the communiqué of the Bucharest meeting and the speech of Khrushchev but also the reply made by the Chinese delegate P'eng Chen[53] and the speeches by the Soviet and Chinese delegates at the Congress of Latin American Youth in which they put forth their respective points of view. Roca could not fail to realize, however, that the Chinese were suffering from a "leftist" deviation similar to that of Castro, which constituted a serious danger to the unity of the PSP. The dissident Cuban Communists never in the course of their "heresy" came to the point of identifying themselves with the Chinese position, but Roca could not anticipate this. Hence, in August 1960, the possibility of a convergence between Castro, the dissidents within the PSP, and the Chinese constituted a serious concern of Roca's.

Second, as already noted, after the October 1959 plenum Blas Roca never again alluded to the idea of the "uninterrupted revolution." But the second figure in the party, Aníbal Escalante, did make use of it in his report to the plenum in March 1960, in his lecture on "Marxism-Leninism and the Cuban Revolution" in April, and in his report on the program to the party congress in August.[54] Zagoria refers to this last report as "some indication of an incipient Left-Right split in the Cuban Communist Party."[55] This confirms what I said in the preceding paragraph and suggests the possibility that there was some agreement between Escalante and Carlos Rafael Rodríguez, who was the leader of those Roca called "the young ones" and we call Castroites or "Fidelistas."

Roca's third problem was just this: Carlos Rafael Rodríguez and "the young ones."[56] After the March resolution indicating which

[53] *Hoy*, June 23, 24, and 30, 1960. It must be noted, however, that on July 3 the communiqué and Khrushchev's speech were republished, but not that of P'eng Chen. This was replaced by an article by Soong Ching-ling (Mme. Sun Yat-sen), "Los pueblos derrotarán por completo al imperialismo" [The Peoples Will Completely Overthrow Imperialism].

[54] The report to the March plenum in *ibid.*, March 2, 1960; the lecture in *ibid.*, April 10, 1960; the report to the congress in *ibid.*, August 21, 1960.

[55] Donald S. Zagoria, *The Sino-Soviet Conflict, 1956–1961* (Princeton, N.J.: Princeton University Press, 1962), p. 268.

[56] For instance, in his conclusions at the Eighth Congress Roca said: "They have called dear Carlos Rafael Rodríguez a 'young one' so as to contrast him to me as representive of the 'old ones.'" Immediately following this he invoked the thirty-five years of existence of the party to emphasize the importance of party unity.

of the articles published by *Hoy* were "orthodox," the editor of the PSP organ practically ceased contributing to it, interrupting his silence only from time to time with an article reiterating his admiration for Castro.[57] I have been unable to find a single mention by Rodríguez of the idea of the "uninterrupted revolution" in any of his writings, nor, except for his stated admiration for Castro, is there any indication of what his differences really were with the secretary-general's "line." In November, as we shall see, the editor of *Hoy* was to make a public profession of his "Fidelista" faith. I attribute Carlos Rafael Rodríguez' conversion to "Fidelism" to his personal psychology. For twenty-five years he had subordinated himself totally to Blas Roca: From the first months of 1959 onward he felt impelled to show the same submission to the stronger personality that had now appeared on the scene.[58]

Furthermore, it should also be taken into account that faced with all these deviations, differences, and rebellions, Roca was unable to offer any concrete evidence to his comrades that the party's influence in the nerve centers of the revolution was growing. The type of "unity" proposed by the Communists, whether in a pact or by fusion, had made no progress whatsoever by August 1960. And even though there is proof that the PSP members were beginning to infiltrate the administration — for instance, we know that Escalante played a decisive role in appointing the personnel to the Cuban embassy in Czechoslovakia[59] — it is certain that at this time there were no active party members in the Council of Ministers, the command posts of the Rebel Army, the top-level administrative positions, or the directing positions of the mass organizations.

The concern that weighed on Blas Roca's mind, as the Eighth Congress of the PSP drew near, became evident in an article published by him two days before the opening of the congress, entitled, significantly enough, "Enemies behind the Mask of Extremism." The anarchists in Cuba have been an insignificant force since 1930. Yet Roca's article was devoted to a polemic against a "Libertarian Syndicalist Group," and on this pretext he recalled that the PSP had "been able to resist all attacks" because its members had con-

[57] For instance, "Otra gran batalla" [Another Great Battle], *Hoy*, July 29, 1960, written in commemoration of July 26 in the Sierra.

[58] I must add that Carlos Rafael Rodríguez' Fidelism lasted until the crisis of October 1962 and had completely disappeared by the time of the trial of Marcos Rodríguez in March 1964.

[59] This is known by the statement of the same Marcos Rodríguez at his trial (see *Bohemia*, March 27, 1964).

sistently rejected "the factionalism, the divisionism, the deviationism of the Trotskyites, of the opportunists, of the dogmatists, and of
the revisionists." He gave this warning about the real danger facing
party unity: "Since the attack on the revolution from rightest positions did not produce the results hoped for by the imperialists, what
they need now are auxiliaries from leftist positions, using extremist
phraseology."[60]

At the Eighth Congress, party unity was not shaken, but neither
did Roca succeed in imposing his own views. Apparently the compromise formula included approval of the report given the assembly by the secretary-general as well as of his conduct and that of
the party throughout the entire struggle against Batista and also
incorporated the opinions of the several factions in the final resolution of the congress. This is the conclusion to be drawn from a
comparison of Roca's speeches during the congress with the content
of the final resolution.

The most important points were these: Roca continued to char-
acterize the revolution as "national, emancipatory, agrarian, patriotic, and democratic"; and this sentiment was reflected in the final
resolution — but with this addition: "The Cuban revolution is
radical, it uses radical methods, is developing in a rapid rhythm,
and is advancing without interruption." The secretary-general had
stated that the social forces supporting the revolutionary movement
were "the peasants, the workers, the urban petite bourgeoisie, and
the national bourgeoisie"; and even though he had acknowledged
that the "class content of the revolutionary government" had been
changing, he had maintained that "in essence" that government
continued to represent the interests of all these classes. On this
point the final resolution omitted any reference to the "national
bourgeoisie"; it enumerated as the "moving and guiding forces"
of the revolution "the workers, the poor and medium peasants, and
the radical wing of the urban petite bourgeoisie"; it then added a
remark that can only be described as astounding since the Communist Party was not part of the government: "At the head of the
government at the moment is the bloc of the poor and medium
peasants, the radical urban petite bourgeoisie, and the proletariat."
Finally, and most important of all from a practical point of view,
Roca had insisted in his report that "personalities move, mobilize,
and decide the masses, but only a revolutionary organization can

---

[60] "Los enemigos tras la máscara extremista" [Enemies behind the Mask of
Extremism], *Hoy*, August 14, 1960.

give stability and continuity to their action"; and in his concluding remarks he warned against "precipitation," against "the temptation to form unity committees," because he was beginning to realize that it was just this that Castro wanted — "unity at the base" and Castro alone at the top, directing everything. The final resolution of the congress, on the other hand, stated: "The revolutionary unity that was first forged . . . in the ranks of the Rebel Army is now being realized around the revolutionary government. . . . The leadership and the guidance of Fidel Castro are guarantees of maximal unity. . . ."[61]

I doubt very much whether another decision like this can be found throughout the history of the international Communist movement before 1960. Without a pact, without fusion, without the slightest guarantee, the Cuban Communist Party, forged in a struggle that had lasted more than thirty years, agreed to place itself under the orders of a leader whose Marxist-Leninist antecedents were so scanty that he ran into great difficulties when he finally decided to reveal them in his speech on December 1, 1961. In the course of this study we shall examine the effects of this singular decision.

Relations with China

As has already been mentioned, it was after Castro's speech following the explosion on *Le Coubre* that the Chinese began to see that something worthy of their closest attention was taking place in Cuba. It is no exaggeration to say that the Chinese discovered the revolutionary possibilities of Latin America via Cuba. The creation of the Association of Latin American–Chinese Friendship in Peking on March 16, 1960 supports this statement.[62]

A few days later, at a demonstration of solidarity with Cuba, Kuo Mo-jo, president of the China Peace Committee, after reading some extracts from Castro's speeches and pointing out that the Cuban revolution had shown "that any people with the courage to struggle for its liberation will surely be capable of achieving it," concluded: "The storm of the democratic and national revolution

---

[61] There is an English version of Roca's report to the Eighth Congress in Blas Roca, *The Cuban Revolution: Report of the Eighth National Congress of the People's Socialist Party of Cuba* (New York: New Century Publishers, 1961). See the conclusions and the final resolution in *Hoy*, August 28, 1960.

[62] SCMP 2222, March 23, 1960.

has reached Latin America. . . ."[63] On May 14 the Sino-Cuban Friendship Society was founded in Havana.[64]

In 1959 hardly anyone but PSP members made their way to Peking, while in 1960, except for Roca and Ursinio Rojas,[65] it was the Castroites who visited Communist China. A delegation from the Cuban trade-union organization (CTC) took part in the celebration of May 1; we have already mentioned the visit of William Gálvez; a little later student leaders and functionaries of the government visited the Chinese capital; and in June José María de la Aguilera and Vicente Cordero, representing the CTC, took part in the session of the World Federation of Trade Unions in Peking, which was the scene of one of the first public clashes between the Chinese and the Soviets.[66]

On July 16, 1960, in the joint statement issued in Peking by the CTC and the Federation of Chinese Trade Unions, the Cubans for the first time openly supported the Chinese view. For the Cubans this statement was signed by Odón Alvarez de la Campa, secretary of foreign relations of the Cuban trade unions.

Since the Cubans from now on were to find themselves involved in the conflict between the Chinese and the Soviets, it is necessary to give a brief summary of the fundamental themes of the Sino-Soviet polemic in 1960.

Both sides had subscribed to the policy of peaceful coexistence and supported the Moscow Declaration of November 1957. But the Soviets now insisted on the necessity for "creatively developing" Leninism and pointed up the new factor in the world situation — the appearance of nuclear weapons — that compelled the modification of the Leninist dogma on the inevitability of war under imperialism. They limited the accusation of "warmonger" to certain imperialist circles, concentrated their efforts on the adoption of international agreements for disarmament and the control of nuclear weapons, and trusted to economic competition for the final defeat of capitalism. The Chinese, on the other hand, reaffirmed

63 For Kuo Mo-jo's speech see *Jen-min Jih-pao,* March 20, 1960 (SCMP 2228, March 31, 1960).

64 *Hoy,* May 12, 1960, announced its establishment two days later.

65 Ursinio Rojas accompanied the CTC delegation to the WFTU meeting in Peking (*Hoy,* June 22, 1960). He was probably not a member of the delegation, since, when it left Cuba, only Aguilera and Cordero were mentioned (*ibid.,* May 27, 1960).

66 On the delegation to the May 1 celebration see NCNA, April 17, 1960 (SCMP 2243, April 25, 1960); the student delegation, SCMP 2259, May 17, 1960; and the official delegation, NCNA, May 15, 1960 (SCMP 2262, May 20, 1960).

their fidelity to original Leninism, pointed to the danger of "revisionism," and saw in the United States — not in certain "imperialist circles," as did the Soviets — "the most ferocious enemy of all peoples." They believed that the world situation was decidedly favorable to the socialist camp (the "wind from the East will overcome the wind from the West") and maintained that in spite of its apparent power "Yankee imperialism" was no more than a "paper tiger." They placed the whole emphasis of their propaganda and action on "the peoples of Africa, Asia, and Latin America," and even though they were not advocates of war, as the Soviets falsely accused them of being, they did not contemplate the prospect of a nuclear conflict with too much apprehension; they maintained that if such a conflict were to break out it would serve only to bury capitalism and give rise to a new socialist mankind out of its ashes.[67]

As I have said, the Cubans for the first time subscribed to some of these Chinese views in the joint statement of the two trade-union bodies in July 1960. "United States imperialism," as the document put it, "is expanding its armaments and its preparation for war . . . ," thereby demonstrating "that this imperialism is not only the most ferocious enemy of the Cuban people and of the peoples of Latin America but also the most ferocious enemy of the peoples of China and of all the countries in Asia and Africa, and that it is also the common enemy of all peace-loving peoples." The Cuban revolution, the document went on, "demonstrates in a convincing manner that United States imperialism is not so awe inspiring, and that by means of a struggle . . . one can strike the enemy over and over again and achieve victory." After expressing its support for all those in the world who were struggling against "United States imperialism," and after manifesting the conviction that "with the determined support of the socialist camp headed by the Soviet Union . . . the just struggle of the peoples of Asia, Africa, and Latin America" would be "crowned with final victory," the statement concluded with promises to "consolidate and continue to develop the unity and the reciprocal support between the working classes of Cuba and China.[68]

[67] On the Sino-Soviet conflict see Zagoria, *op. cit.*; G. H. Hudson, Richard Lowenthal, and Roderick MacFarquhar, *The Sino-Soviet Dispute* (New York: Praeger, 1962); Alexander Dallin, ed., *Diversity in International Communism* (New York: Columbia University Press, 1963); William E. Griffith, *Albania and the Sino-Soviet Rift* (Cambridge, Mass.: The M.I.T. Press, 1963); *The Sino-Soviet Rift* (Cambridge, Mass.: The M.I.T. Press, 1964), and *Sino-Soviet Relations, 1964–1965* (Cambridge, Mass.: The M.I.T. Press, 1966).

[68] Text in *Hoy*, August 3, 1960.

The ties between the Chinese and Castro were drawn a little tighter that same month of July by the signing of a commercial and tariff convention, an agreement on technical and scientific assistance, and an agreement for cultural cooperation. Among other things China promised to buy half a million tons of sugar a year for the following five years.[69]

In September diplomatic relations were established between Cuba and China. Castro announced this in the "Declaration of Havana," his reply to the "Declaration of Costa Rica," which had been drawn up on August 28 by the foreign ministers of the Americas, and which, without mentioning Cuba, had vigorously condemned the intervention of an "extra-continental power."

At the time the Havana Declaration was hailed by the Castroites as a "historic document." Since then it has been replaced by the Second Declaration and is scarcely ever heard of. It was essentially an *ad hoc* document, like all the others that Castro drew up or ordered drawn up whenever he needed an ideological cover for his actions.

Since the revolution continued to be "radical" and Castro had not yet decided to call it "socialist," all that was condemned in the Declaration was "the exploitation of man by man." In order to back up his claim to the leadership of the Latin American revolutionary movement, Castro charged U.S. imperialism with the exclusive responsibility for the backwardness, lack of education, and poverty of the Latin American masses. Disregarding the Soviets' retreat from their missile offer of July, the Declaration repeated once more that the Cuban people "accepted and thanked the Soviet Union for its missile aid." And finally, in order to heighten the pressure on Khrushchev and to show Mao that it was he who could advance the Chinese "line" in Latin America, the Declaration said that it was agreed "to establish diplomatic relations between the two countries" — Cuba and China — while suspending "relations that up to now Cuba has had with the puppet regime being kept in power in Formosa by the ships of the Yankee Seventh Fleet."[70]

The reaction of the Cuban Communists to this agreement shows the path followed by the PSP in its relations with China since 1959. The tenth anniversary of the establishment of the Chinese People's Republic on October 1, 1959 had been hailed by an enthusiastic declaration of the National Committee of the PSP. The establish-

69 NCNA, July 27, 1960 (SCMP 2307, July 29, 1960).
70 Havana Declaration in *Hoy*, September 3, 1960.

ment of diplomatic relations, however, failed to merit more than one editorial in *Hoy* — three days later in the column "Our Opinion."[71] The eleventh anniversary of Mao's victory was given another editorial, also in "Our Opinion," which for the first time alluded to the Sino-Soviet differences, even though it declared that they were "imperialist speculations" and asserted that "the Soviet Union, China, and all the socialist countries would never break up for any reason."[72]

[71] "Nuestra Opinión: China y Cuba," *ibid.*, September 6, 1960.
[72] "Nuestra Opinión: Saludo a China Popular" [Greetings to People's China], *ibid.*, October 1, 1960.

CHAPTER FIVE

CASTROISM DECLARES ITSELF "SOCIALIST"

The Issue of Nationalization

One of the very few things on which all the delegates present at the Eighth Congress of the PSP had been in complete agreement had been the attitude adopted by the party toward the nationalization of foreign enterprises and the intervention in Cuban private enterprises. The first nationalizations of "imperialist" properties on August 6 had been welcomed by the party congress as a "historic step." However, as far as the future was concerned, extreme caution had been advised. For example, Roca had stated that "Private enterprise that is not imperialistic or monopolistic or of a parasitic nature is still necessary." And as for the interventions in Cuban enterprises, although he had found that "in general" they were justified, "some of them could possibly have been avoided."[1] Aníbal Escalante had recommended that "the revolutionary forces should and do endeavor to keep the national bourgeoisie within the revolutionary camp."[2] It is obvious that such an attempt could not succeed if the nationalizations and interventions continued to take place. The final resolution of the congress had said, "We should avoid interventions that are not fully justified,"[3] without adding a single word about the propriety of continuing the nationalizations.

The final resolution of the congress was published on August 28. On September 13 the first national television network, CMQ, was "intervened." Two days later all the cigar and cigarette factories suffered the same fate. On the seventeenth of the same month the U.S.-owned banks were nationalized.

Meanwhile, on September 13, a study group of workers in a

---

1 Blas Roca, *The Cuban Revolution: Report to the Eighth National Congress of the People's Socialist Party of Cuba* (New York: New Century Publishers, 1961), pp. 105 ff.
2 Escalante's report on the program, *Hoy*, August 19, 1960.
3 *Ibid.*, August 28, 1960.

tin can production plant had, incredible as it seems, sent Blas Roca a telegram asking whether the Chinese regime was socialist. Four days later his reply was published: "Socialism is being built in China. Politically, the regime in existence in China is a socialist regime. In economics, however, there is not yet a socialist regime; that regime is in the process of being constructed on the economic plane." After pointing out that in the vast territory of China all forms of economic systems coexisted, from the patriarchal to "private and socialist enterprises," Roca ended by saying "Today the revolution is unifying the entire country; it is extending progress to every region and will construct socialism throughout the territory."[4]

Possibly Roca was trying in this letter to lower China's status in the socialist camp. But there can be no doubt that he wanted to make two points: First, even China, with its enormous area and with its population of 650 million, both factors mentioned by him, was unable to leap directly into socialism but had to go through and was going through the phase of the "construction" of such a system. Second, a regime could be "socialist" politically even if there existed on the economic plane "enterprises that were socialist, enterprises made up jointly of state and private property, and private enterprises." All these were listed by Roca in his letter of September 13, 1960.

The letter, however, produced no effect: Cuba was already irresistibly entering a new stage, one in which Castroism would declare itself socialist.

Two events in the last days of September foreshadowed new and important decisions. First, on September 19 Euclides Vázquez Candelas, the most prolific ideologist of the July 26 Movement and the most caustic debater against *Hoy* in 1959, ceased to be the assistant editor-in-chief of *Revolución*.[5] The second important event took place when Castro announced on September 28, 1960: "We are going to establish a system of collective vigilance."[6] The Com-

---

[4] Roca's letter, dated September 13, 1960, was published in *ibid.,* September 17, 1960.

[5] Carlos Franqui, editor-in-chief of *Revolución* and one of Castro's most loyal henchmen, at least until he was removed from his post in 1963, thought he had found a way to make amends for his newspaper's anticommunism during the preceding months—he changed the spelling of the name Khrushchev. On September 24, 1960, *Revolución* declared that "Khrushchev's name has appeared with the spelling used in the United States, a negligence we must no longer permit. From now on it will be "Jruschov."

[6] *Hoy,* September 29, 1960. The announcement occurred on Castro's return

mittees for the Defense of the Revolution (Comités de Defensa de la Revolución — CDR) were thus officially created. These committees were established block by block throughout the republic. Their function was to spy on the rest of the population and to report to the authorities any symptoms of discontent with the regime. By 1964 the regime claimed that they numbered 2 million members.

The Communists knew that something of decisive importance was brewing; they suspected, at the very least, what it was going to be. *Hoy* reproduced an editorial from *Jen-min Jih-pao* of Peking entitled "Perspectives of the Bourgeois Parties in China." The article explained that the bourgeoisie had a "dual nature," a term by which the Chinese meant that the bourgeoisie was torn between positive (nationalist) and negative (exploitive) impulses. This was why Chairman Mao had developed the policy of "seeking unity through struggle," and the Chinese were even "buying the means of production" so that the bourgeoisie would not withdraw from the revolutionary process.[7]

The resolutions of the PSP congress, Blas Roca's illuminating letter, and the editorial from *Jen-min Jih-pao* were all of no avail. On October 13 Castro nationalized the Cuban banks and 382 of the most important privately owned Cuban enterprises. The next day he proclaimed the urban reform law, which provided that every tenant, whether pleased or not with his dwelling, must buy it by paying the established price to the government, and not to its previous owner — with payments arranged on a monthly basis.[8] On October 24 all the rest of the U.S. properties were nationalized. This time there were no cheers from the PSP, no eulogies by the poet Nicolás Guillén.[9] In the same edition of *Hoy* in which these laws were published, Blas Roca, rather than comment on this momentous event, busied himself over a heated polemic with the Cuban exile journal *Bohemia Libre* of New York.

---

from the September session of the U.N. General Assembly. This was the eventful session in which Castro first met, and publicly embraced, Nikita Khrushchev.

7 "Perspectivas de los partidos burgueses en China" [Perspectives of the Bourgeoisie Party in China], *ibid*.

8 The law established that the proprietors would be given a monthly sum by the government up to a maximum of $600.00. This promise has been kept, with the irregularities characteristic of all governmental action in Castro's Cuba.

9 In *Hoy*, August 9, 1960, Nicolás Guillén (the dean of Cuban Communist poets) had published some verses on the nationalization of U.S. enterprises. The last lines were:

> Martí promised it to you
> And Fidel accomplished it for you
> It is done.

The Communists did not come out openly against the new laws. After the proclamation, *Hoy* pointed out the anxiety with which the Cuban people awaited "the word of their great revolutionary leader to explain to them how these measures jibed with the objectives of national freedom, economic progress, and social well-being that constituted the revolutionary aims." It added, with an irony that was surely intentional, "at least these same revolutionary laws have successfully silenced those hatemongers who cried out that governmental confiscations would reach all levels"; and when Castro went on the air to explain his laws, the only thing *Hoy* found encouraging in his statement was the promise that such measures would not be repeated. "To be able to destroy the enemy so closely bound up with Yankee power, the revolution had to be drastic. To reconstruct a new fatherland with the support of all its patriots, the revolution should be temperate — and it will be."[10] Roca, for his part, insisted that "in its new phase the revolution does not need to use drastic methods in the fields of economic and social transformation." As Castro had already liquidated the national bourgeoisie, Roca could console himself only by saying that "the revolution must have the support of the middle class and of the individual peasant."[11]

It is easy to understand the uncomfortable position of the PSP when faced with Castro's decisions in October. In mid-1959 Blas Roca had adopted from the Chinese the concept of the "uninterrupted revolution" in order to pose as a leader of rampant radicalism and to appease the new extremists in the PSP. After October 1959 he abandoned this concept because he realized that it could become the ideological justification of the "deviationism" that threatened the PSP. Aníbal Escalante then appropriated the formula. Possibly he did this because, owing to his limited intellectual capacity, he did not realize the inherent danger to the PSP or because he hoped to challenge Roca for the leadership of Cuban communism. He stuck to this concept until the August 1960 congress. But after that congress even Escalante fell into a profound silence that was broken only in May 1961, when the Communists reached a new *modus vivendi* with Castro that they regarded as promising. Thus, when Castro in October 1960 took one more step

---

10 "Nuestra Opinión: Tres leyes históricas" [Three Historical Laws], *ibid.*, October 15, 1960, and "Un Comentario: El Pueblo unido es inexpugnable" [A United Nation Is Unconquerable], *ibid.*, October 18, 1960.

11 Blas Roca, "Unes fuerzo básico en la nueva etapa" [A Basic Effort in the

in his own "uninterrupted revolution" (which obeyed no ideological formula and was to be stopped only by economic catastrophe and the decay of revolutionary possibilities in Latin America), the PSP, although visibly worried, had to accept it.

Carlos Rafael Rodríguez gave an interview to Max Frankel of *The New York Times* in the following month that revealed his doubts about Castro's October laws. He mentioned recent "errors" committed by the leader that had frightened the middle class and the technicians.[12] These confidences were published. As *Hoy's* director knew how susceptible the "maximum leader" was to the slightest criticism, he rushed to erase any suspicion that might have arisen in Castro's mind and made a public profession of his "Fidelista" faith. In an article entitled "The Vipers Also Bite," he did not deny the statement attributed to him by Frankel but stressed that Castro was a man of "caution and prudence, proof of which has been given time and time again," and accused *The New York Times* of attempting to create a wedge between the Fidelistas and the Communists. He ended by saying: "Instead of being so presumptuous as to boast of having Castro on our side, as the *Times* said, we Cuban Communists, like the rest of the Cuban people, are on Castro's side."[13] It seems significant to me that in the same issue of *Hoy* that contained Rodríguez' abject capitulation, Blas Roca, the man to whom he owed his position in the Cuban party, discussed such an utterly untopical subject as the life of Friedrich Engels. Thus it is evident the PSP reacted with considerable coldness to the October nationalization laws. We do not need to add that no other organizations had demanded them. Although Guevara may have privately suggested these radical policies to Castro — at that time Che had already started on the road that was to make him a radical Marxist very close to the Chinese — it would be childish to assume that the Cuban leader made such important decisions only because the theoretician of guerrilla warfare had suggested them.[14] Why

New Period], *ibid.*, October 22, 1960.

12 *The New York Times*, November 27, 1960.

13 C. R. Rodríguez, "Tambien muerden las víboras" [The Vipers Also Bite], *Hoy*, November 29, 1960. See also "Un Comentario: El 'Times' engaña al pueblo americano" [The 'Times' Deceives the American People], *ibid.*, November 22, 1960, written by Rodríguez, as he himself announced in the second article.

14 In my opinion Guevara began to familiarize himself with Marxist thought in the middle of 1960; see his speech to the Congress of Latin American Youth (*Revolución*, July 29, 1960). His article, "Cuba: Caso excepcional o vanguardia en la lucha contra el colonialismo" [Cuba: An Exceptional Case or Vanguard in the Fight Against Colonialism], published in *Verde Olivo*, April 9, 1961 (see

then, if no one, with this possible exception, thought that the moment had come to pass to a more radical stage of the revolution, did Fidel make this move?

There must have been other considerations. In the first place, after the nationalization of 37 per cent of the sugar industry in August and numerous interventions, which reached a climax with those in the cigar and cigarette factories in September, a mass exodus of businessmen and technicians intensified the confusion. Economic reorganization was imperative. For leaders so lacking in economic sophistication as Castro and his collaborators, the easiest solution was to copy the Soviet model.

In the second place, in spite of all the warning voices, Castro maintained his popularity. His influence abroad continued to grow, and, furthermore, the admiration that Sartre, C. Wright Mills, Matthews, and others bestowed on him unbalanced his judgment.

Finally, the myth of the "inevitability" of the "socialist" triumph may have influenced him. At any rate, an editorial in *Revolución* in December used this argument to justify the new radicalism of the Cuban revolution; and that myth, together with the statement "If Fidel is a Communist then I'm one too," was one of the favorite justifications of those who stayed by Castro's side.[15]

But none of these reasons separately or the three of them together are sufficient explanation. Castro is a political animal, and neither economic disorganization nor revolutionary intoxication nor the myth of the final victory of communism, and even less the admiration of Sartre, C. Wright Mills, and Matthews, would have dictated the drastic measures taken in October unless concrete and urgent political motives had prompted him.

The First Differences with Moscow

From the moment in 1957 when the Soviet Union took the lead in missile production until the Cuban missile crisis of October 1962, Khrushchev exploited this advantage (which has now disappeared)

Monthly Review, July–August 1961, for an English translation), abjuring "exceptionalism" is one more proof that Blas Roca had had him in mind when he censured "exceptionalism" in October 1959. It is also obvious that Guevara moved swiftly in his evolution toward Marxism, maneuvering so that he would not be reproached for his attitude during the first months of the revolution.

[15] The editorial appeared in *Revolución*, December 2, 1960. It was entitled "Saldo de un viaje al mundo socialista" [Summing Up a Trip to the Socialist World]. It would seem to me that Faure Chomón used this myth to justify abandoning his violently anti-Communist stand in January–February 1959.

by threatening to use rockets whenever a crisis appeared in U.S.-Soviet relations. Even though in the case of Cuba Khrushchev spoke of rockets only "figuratively," Castro chose to believe him literally. We mentioned in the last chapter that in his speech on July 10, 1960 the Cuban leader omitted the "symbolic" nature of the rockets Khrushchev had promised in the event of a U.S. attack on Cuba. Twice during the same month the Soviet Premier made clear the real meaning of his promise, by substituting the phrase "all needed help" in case of aggression in place of the threat of rockets. Disregarding this, Castro, in the first manifesto to Latin America, known as the Declaration of Havana, gratefully acknowledged "the support of Soviet rockets."

Late in September 1960 the Soviet Premier and the Cuban Prime Minister met at the United Nations in New York. We can only surmise what took place between them, but in view of Castro's situation in September, and knowing what happened later, we can deduce with a high degree of probability both Castro's requests and Khrushchev's replies, the Cuban leader's dissatisfaction with these replies, the resulting conflicts of opinion, and Castro's decisions.

Two fundamental matters must have been in Castro's mind. First, neither the Soviet rocket threat of July 9 nor the Cuban nationalization law of August 6 had elicited any response from the United States. Moreover (and even more important to Castro), in the August meeting of the OAS in Costa Rica, Washington proved unable to bring about a condemnation of Cuba by the other Latin American nations. Thus "imperialism" showed signs of weakness. Under these conditions, it was important to continue the attack, that is, to have Khrushchev dispel any doubt as to the validity of his promise by repeating it. This would allow Castro to enjoy some tranquillity in Cuba, while directing all his efforts as "specialist in the region" to Latin American subversion. Second, the U.S. market was closed to Cuban sugar in 1960, and since at the end of September the U.S. embassy began to advise its citizens to leave the country, there seemed no prospect of the market being reopened the following year. Castro thus needed a Soviet commitment to buy the Cuban sugar surplus. Such a commitment would also serve as new encouragement for the Latin American countries to rebel; they would see that Khrushchev was in a position to help those who revolted against imperialism.

Castro needed Soviet assistance for both reasons and had persuasive arguments with which to justify such aid. If, however, Khrushchev remained impervious to these arguments, the Cuban leader had only one means left to exert pressure on him: to declare himself a "socialist." Moreover, by publicly identifying himself with the countries of the bloc, he would also be able to solicit Chinese support, thus exploiting the "contradictions" of the socialist camp from within.

We cannot demonstrate that such requests were actually put to Khrushchev by Castro. But we know that Khrushchev clearly backed down on his missile promise; that economic help was not obtained easily, if it did finally materialize it was only because of Castro's exceptional skill; and that consequently the first Soviet-Cuban differences, which had arisen over the nature of the rocket promise of July 9, were aggravated and were still not completely resolved in the Soviet-Cuban communiqué of December 1960. Lastly, we know that as soon as he realized Khrushchev's reluctance, Castro embarked on the road to socialism.

Let us now look at the evidence.

1. The first "socialist" law and the nationalization of the banks and the 382 Cuban-owned private enterprises were decreed in mid-October, only two weeks after Castro's return from the United Nations. These measures could not have been suggested or even approved by Khrushchev, since "Castroite socialism" was not accepted by the Soviet Union until April 1962. We already know the negative manner in which the PSP reacted. Its coldness was particularly significant because at that time, in late October, the PSP was about to make a complete break with the Chinese and return to the Soviet fold, a shift of allegiance that was completed during the Moscow meeting of Communist parties in November–December 1960. It is obvious that if the "socialist laws" had had the approval of the Soviet Union, Blas Roca would never have missed this excellent opportunity to speed up his reconciliation with Moscow by supporting them. We must therefore conclude that Castro took the socialist road immediately after his meeting with Khrushchev at the United Nations without the Soviet leader's approval.

2. At the end of October the editor of *Revolución*, Carlos Franqui, saw the Soviet Premier in the Kremlin. He pointed out to Khrushchev that the "imperialists" were saying that "the possible use of missiles in case of armed aggression against Cuba has a purely symbolic meaning" and asked, "What do you think about

this?" The reply was so vague that Franqui persisted: "If this happens, if the threat materializes, are the missiles sufficiently prepared?" Once again Khrushchev avoided an answer by saying that "the principal thing is not annihilation of people but life, blossoming of life."[16]

In spite of this statement, Castro, after warning his followers not to "go to sleep" because of the rockets, some days later repeated that "without our efforts, without our invincible resistance, it would not have been possible to count on the support of the Soviet missiles."[17] On November 7 the hollow shell that remained of the July 26 Movement, presided over by Emilio Aragonés, Castro's puppet, sent a congratulatory message to the Soviet government on the anniversary of the October Revolution, thanking the fraternal nation that had "repeatedly offered the use of its scientific progress [missiles]" if the United States launched an armed attack.[18] It is understandable that such insistence exasperated the Soviets; according to a Havana report by Max Frankel, which was "based on the most reliable diplomatic sources," they had told the Cubans "to quit rattling Soviet rockets."[19]

3. At the trade-union celebration of that same day, José María de la Aguilera, the propaganda secretary of CTC, declared: "It is time to state without fear, with unshaking knees, with untrembling voice, and with our heads held high, that we are marching inexorably toward socialism in our Fatherland." It is significant that in reporting his speech *Hoy* omitted this sentence.[20]

It would be a mistake to dismiss Aguilera's words as unimportant. He had been the first trade-union leader of the July 26 Movement publicly to urge unity with the Communists in the CTC (in September 1959);[21] he had headed the Cuban delegation that attended the Congress of the World Federation of Trade Unions in Peking; and he was also one of the preferred instruments of Castro's maneuvering.

16 *Ibid.*, October 28, 1960.

17 *Ibid.*, November 9, 1960.

18 "Saludos del 26 de Julio por el 7 de Noviembre" [Greetings of the 26 of July to the 7 of November], *ibid.*, November 7, 1960.

19 *The New York Times*, November 19, 1960.

20 *Revolución*, November 7, 1960. *Hoy*, November 8, 1960, reported on the meeting and Aguilera's speech but did not transcribe it. The text was taken from *Revolución*.

21 As secretary-general of the Federation of Bank Workers (Federación Sindical de Trabajadores Bancarios). See *Hoy*, September 12, 1959.

4. On October 19 the United States had prohibited all exports to Cuba with the exception of nonsubsidized foodstuffs, medicine, and medical supplies. Two days later Guevara left for the "socialist" countries. The purpose of this trip was obvious. After losing the U.S. market Cuba had been able to sell only one and a half million tons of sugar, a million to the Soviet Union and half a million to China; and since 1957 the sugar crop had never been less than five and a half million tons.

Guevara remained in Moscow until mid-November without accomplishing anything. From there he went to Peking. Here the situation was completely different. The Chinese press explained why. "The Cuban people has exposed the aggressive nature of United States imperialism and, at the same time, have seen clearly that, despite its appearance of might, U.S. imperialism is a 'paper tiger.' "[22] At the banquet given in Che's honor Chou En-lai said: "The Cuban people's struggle shows that an awakened, oppressed people, so long as they correctly assess the enemy strategically and are tactically skillful in handling the struggle against the enemy, will change from weak to strong and will certainly be able to win and consolidate victories."[23] Guevara in his address on arrival stated that "Cuba did not wish to be in the so-called free world, because Cuba did not wish to be annihilated."[24] In answering Chou En-lai he pointed out how "the great experience of the Chinese people in their 22 years of struggle in the backward countryside, which was like the countryside in the Americas, has revealed a new road for the Americas."[25]

In a communiqué published on November 30 China committed itself to buy a million tons of sugar in 1961 and granted a credit of 60 million dollars for the purchase of equipment and technical assistance. In the same communiqué the Cubans subscribed to the Chinese belief in the unchanging nature of imperialism, its basically aggressive nature, and the importance of the just struggle of the people of Asia, Africa, and Latin America. The Chinese, for their part, supported "the Revolutionary Declaration of Havana," expressed their admiration for the victory of the Cuban people, and stated their gratitude for "the brave and courageous decisions taken by the Cuban Republic in establishing diplomatic relations

[22] Editorial in *Ta-kung Pao*, November 17, 1960 (SCMP 2383, November 23, 1960).
[23] NCNA, November 18, 1960 (SCMP 2384, November 25, 1960).
[24] NCNA, November 17, 1960 (SCMP 2383, November 23, 1960).
[25] NCNA, November 18, 1960 (SCMP 2384, November 25, 1960).

with the Chinese People's Republic." In this long communiqué the Soviet Union was never mentioned.[26]

It is obvious that the trip was a success. From the ideological viewpoint, as Guevara said on leaving, "in general, there was not a single discrepancy."[27] As for economic assistance, the Soviet Union was now obliged to be more generous, since the Chinese had doubled their own commitment. For the Chinese, the conversation with Guevara cleared up something about which they had been confused. They had thought that the Cuban revolution was being undertaken "with the cooperation of the patriotic, democratic forces headed by Fidel Castro and the Cuban PSP."[28] Che corrected this error, and from the Chinese point of view his evidence was clearly corroborated by the pro-Soviet attitude of the PSP delegates at the December 1960 Moscow meeting of Communist parties. From that moment on, and already for Chou-En-lai at the banquet for Guevara, the Chinese definition of the Cuban revolution would be "the national and democratic revolution, achieved under the Cuban Revolutionary Government and its leader Premier Fidel Castro,"[29] without a reference to the PSP.

5. Now that Castro had China's backing, the Cuban leader could take one more step in his "socialist" maneuvers. The opportunity arose on December 14, when the electrical workers organized a street demonstration and marched toward the presidential palace shouting "Cuba yes, Russia no." The CTC immediately assembled to expel the leaders responsible for such "unspeakable treachery." Castro attended this assembly because his influence was needed to expel them. He said: "Do you know the most important goal, the only goal, for which the working class in a modern country should fight? . . . The conquest of political power!"[30]

6. The same day that Castro's speech was published by the press it was also reported that a Board of Coordination and Inspection (Junta de Coordinación Ejecución e Inspección — JUCEI) had been established in Oriente province. The president of the Board was Raúl Castro. Calixto García, the military chief of the province, was to be vice-president, and a certain Abilio Cortina,[31] secretary. No

26 *Hoy*, December 4, 1960.
27 *Revolución*, December 9, 1960.
28 For example, *Hung Ch'i*, September 1, 1960 (SCMP 2332, September 7, 1960), and *Ta-kung Pao*, September 1960 (SCMP 2336, September 13, 1960).
29 NCNA, November 18, 1960 (SCMP 2384, November 25, 1960).
30 *Hoy*, December 15, 1960.
31 *Revolución*, December 15, 1960.

one knew what the functions of the local JUCEI's were to be until Raúl explained them at the end of June 1961. The JUCEI was "the form that the power of the workers and poor peasants assumes in local government."[32] The first organ of this power was constituted on December 14, 1960.

7. Five days later the Soviet-Cuban communiqué was published (with admirable timing, since on December 16 President Eisenhower had set at zero the Cuban sugar quota for the first quarter of 1961). In exchange for Moscow's agreement to purchase 2,700,000 tons of sugar at the price of 4 cents per pound in 1961, the Cuban revolutionary government was willing to spell out, item for item, all its reasons for gratitude to the Soviet Union, "an independent country that is the vanguard of the nations of the socialist camp"; to underwrite all Soviet views on the international situation, in the same way that it had underwritten those of the Chinese some days earlier; and to clarify the exact nature of Khrushchev's commitment of July 9. The communiqué declared that "the third and most important aspect of the aid was the statement of Soviet Premier Nikita Khrushchev on the readiness of the Soviet Union to give Cuba complete support in maintaining its independence against unprovoked aggressions." "The atmosphere of the conversations," the communiqué went on, "was marked by the desire to preserve peace in the entire world and to struggle with every means to ensure that international disputes should be settled only by peaceful means." The communiqué ended by saying, "both parties emphatically declare that world peace will never be endangered or violated in any form by the Soviet Union or by Cuba."

It must be added that in this communiqué the Soviet government limited itself to expressing "sympathy" for the nationalization laws. These, it said, were enacted "with the purpose of creating a starting point for future economic plans that would guarantee a growing prosperity for the Cuban people." The Soviet government also reacted favorably to the urban reform laws and the Declaration of Havana — the latter not because it incited the Latin-American nations to follow the example of Cuba but, rather, because it expressed "the aspirations of the Cuban people toward new goals in its socioeconomic development."[33]

---

[32] As Raúl explained on that occasion (*ibid.*, June 5, 1961), the function of these organs was to "see that the directives given by the central government are carried through in the correct manner."

[33] The text of the communiqué was published in *Hoy*, December 20, 1960.

I think that I have thus fulfilled the promise made some pages earlier. The points enumerated reveal the existence of differences between Castro and the Soviet Union, the reaction of the Cuban leader to these conflicts of interest, and the agreement that was reached in the December communiqué. As a result of this agreement Castro was assured of selling 4 million tons of sugar in the "socialist" markets at a renumerative price.[34] In exchange, Castro did not insist that Cuba be recognized as a "socialist" country in the communiqué, and, most important, he had to agree to the reformulation of Khrushchev's rocket promise into "complete support in maintaining [Cuban] independence against unprovoked aggressions," with an added guarantee not to "violate in any form" world peace. The Soviets may have believed that with this agreement the differences were settled. Castro, as we shall see, was by no means satisfied.

Socialist Cuba

On December 18, at the congress of the sugar workers, Castro announced that he had been able to market 4 million tons of sugar and that all the cane in the fields would be ground.[35] For people accustomed to adjusting their standard of living to the yield of the sugar crop, this announcement confirmed once more their leader's clairvoyance. The final days of 1960 thus passed in an atmosphere of general lightheartedness.

Suddenly on December 31 *Revolución* came out with a banner headline "Yankee Invasion!" That same night Castro explained the situation. According to him, a North American invasion would occur before Eisenhower left the presidency on January 20. The director of the CIA at that time, Allen Dulles, had everything ready. The excuse would be the assertion that Cuba was allowing rocket pads[36] to be constructed on its territory. On the basis of this reasoning, Castro decreed a general mobilization.

On January 2, 1961, at the ceremony commemorating the second anniversary of the 1959 victory, Castro repeated these accusations and demanded that within forty-eight hours the personnel of the American embassy in Havana be reduced to eighteen members.[37]

[34] One million to China, 2.7 million to the Soviet Union, and 300,000 to the rest of the socialist countries.
[35] Castro's speech before the FNTA in *Revolución*, December 19, 1960.
[36] Castro's speech of December 31, in *ibid.*, January 2, 1961.
[37] Castro's speech of January 2 in *ibid.*, January 3, 1961.

The next day President Eisenhower severed diplomatic and consular relations with Cuba.

To my knowledge no one has alleged that a real threat of an invasion existed at that time. Guevara also did not really believe it, since a few days later he complained "we must not see ships, submarines, or shoot at shadows that do not exist."[38] Was Castro therefore the victim of an error? Or did he invent this menace for other reasons? I have not found a satisfactory answer to either of these questions. What is certain is that on January 13 Castro announced that he would demobilize as soon as the new President of the United States, John F. Kennedy, was sworn in, and on January 20 he declared, "The President who has just taken over speaks of a new beginning. Good. We also say let us begin anew. We are waiting for facts."[39]

The same attitude was taken a few days later by Guevara and the PSP. Also, it seems that Castro's march toward socialism was halted during those months. It is thus evident that the Castro regime was ready to discuss its differences with Washington. What is much more difficult to determine is why the man who at the end of November had allowed the Sino-Cuban communiqué to identify Cuba with Chinese views and in December had taken decisive steps toward "socialism," in January wanted to negotiate with "the most ferocious enemy of all the peoples," the United States.

We know that since the election of Kennedy in November, Khrushchev had been trying to re-establish the spirit of Camp David in Soviet-American relations, that is, a situation in which negotiations were intended to lead slowly but surely to the fulfillment of Soviet goals. Fidel profoundly disliked that "spirit," since he feared that an improvement of relations between the big two would be damaging to small countries like Cuba. Knowing or suspecting Khrushchev's intentions, he may have decided to make overtures to the United States so as to make it more difficult for Moscow and Washington to reach agreement behind his back. Whether for this or another reason, it is a fact that in January 1960, Castro, the PSP, and Guevara publicly expressed willingness to consider any U.S. proposal. The coincidence of attitudes between Castro and Khrushchev was bound to give the PSP great satisfaction. For as we have seen, Blas Roca and his followers[40] had com-

---

[38] Guevara's televised speech in *ibid.*, January 2, 1961.
[39] Both of Castro's speeches in *ibid.*, January 14 and 21, 1961.
[40] To the best of my knowledge the pro-Soviet reorientation of the PSP was

pletely returned to their original pro-Soviet position after the November–December 1960 Moscow meeting.

Unfortunately the Cuban Communist publications that are available give only very scanty information on the conduct of the PSP delegation, led by Aníbal Escalante, at the Moscow meetings. But, according to William E. Griffith, one of the most debated matters at the conference was the Soviet proposition making obligatory any agreement adopted by the majority. This proposition was rejected by the preparatory commission, but the Cubans and the Brazilians resubmitted it.[41] This action by the Cubans and two editorials in *Hoy* on the final Statement and on the Peace Manifesto confirm the pro-Soviet position of the PSP.

We know, in effect, that the document issued by the conference was the result of a compromise and that, in consequence, combined Soviet and Chinese points of view. *Hoy,* after pointing out the "unanimity" of the conference agreements and falsely denying "the provocative speculations of the imperialists" concerning a conflict between Russia and China, avoided all comment on those parts of the communiqué that reflected the Chinese point of view and emphatically underlined the Soviet position: the possibility of avoiding war, even though there were still parts of the world that adhered to capitalism, the necessity for peaceful coexistence, and above all, peace — which was indispensable to Cuba, because even though the revolution had had "to take power through a necessary war, it requires peace in order to construct the new . . . for production, for culture, for health. . . ." Finally, *Hoy* did not fail to emphasize the role of the CPSU as the vanguard and as "the most experienced and seasoned contingent of the international Communist movement."[42]

Given the totally pro-Soviet position of the PSP, one can understand the eagerness with which it supported Castro's friendly words for Kennedy on January 20. On January 25 a new meeting of the national party leadership took place, the last "plenum" of the PSP

carried out without any internal objections. Carlos Rafael Rodríguez, for example, was an admirer of Premier Khrushchev according to an interview by Max Frankel (*The New York Times,* November 27, 1960).

41 William E. Griffith, "The November 1960 Moscow Meeting: A Preliminary Reconstruction," *The China Quarterly,* No. 11 (July–September 1962).

42 "Nuestra Opinión: Le Declaración de los 81 guía luminosa para los pueblos del mundo" [The Declaration of the 81, Luminous Guide for the People of the World], *Hoy,* December 11, 1960; and "Nuestra Opinión: La paz vencerá a la guerra" [Peace Will Prevail over War], *ibid,* December 24, 1960.

leadership of which we have knowledge. Blas Roca, supporting his arguments with statements of Fidel Castro, Guevara, Dorticós, and Raúl Castro, Minister of the Armed Forces, declared: "It is not Cuba that is trying to negotiate, but if unconditional negotiation is offered with absolute respect for Cuban sovereignty, we would be ready to accept it."[43] As for Guevara, in his farewell speech in Peking he had completely supported the Chinese concept of imperialism, with "its aggressive and rapacious nature," adding that for him, as well as for Mao's disciples, there was no difference between Nixon and Kennedy,[44] but in January he was willing to negotiate: "We too must talk to them and explain our complaints."[45]

As far as we know, President Kennedy never decided to test the — at least verbal — willingness of the Castro regime to discuss its differences with the United States. The President had been informed on November 18 of the existence of the training camp in Guatemala and after his inauguration ordered all preparations for the invasion of Cuba to be continued, although he warned that this order could be canceled. On February 2 the plans for the invasion were approved, and Trinidad, on the southern coast of Cuba, was chosen as a landing site. On March 22 the Revolutionary Council was formed, a civilian screen that had no authority over the military forces manipulated by the CIA. About that same date the landing site was changed to the Bay of Pigs, and the day was set for April 5. This date was later changed twice, first to April 10 and later to April 17.[46]

Meanwhile the attitude of the Castro regime had hardened. This could be seen in the editorials in *Revolución*. On February 9 the headlines were "The Attacks of Kennedy and Co."; eighteen days later, "The United States, a Schizophrenic System of Government"; on March 8, "The Acrobat of Imperialism"; and on April 4, "A Dirty Paper of the State Department," referring to the White Paper published by the U.S. government that explained how the Cuban revolution had been betrayed, without revealing, however, that the mission of returning it to its true nature had been entrusted to the CIA and its docile Cuban collaborators.[47]

[43] Blas Roca's report in *Revolución*, February 3, 1961.
[44] *Hoy*, November 30, 1960.
[45] Speech by Guevara in Cabañas, *Revolución*, January 23, 1961.
[46] All the data of the April invasion are taken from Haynes Johnson, *The Bay of Pigs* (New York: W. W. Norton, 1964), pp. 65, 66, and 67.
[47] The pamphlet was entitled *Cuba*, U.S. Department of State publication No. 7171.

At the same time that Castro emphasized the struggle against "imperialism," he renewed his march toward "socialism." At that time the Schools of Revolutionary Instruction (Escuelas de Instrucción Revolucionaria), inaugurated on December 2, 1960, were already in operation. These centers of Marxist indoctrination were nominally sponsored by the July 26 Movement. However, their initial cadres were recruited almost totally from the ranks of the old Marxist-Leninist party[48] and were directed by Lionel Soto, a member of the PSP, who had been a friend of Castro's since university days.

On February 24 the cabinet was reorganized. No members of the PSP were included. Ernesto Guevara was made Minister of Industry, and Raúl Castro, besides remaining Minister of the Armed Forces, was made vice-president of the Central Planning Board so that he would have the legal powers necessary to continue organizing the JUCEI, "the local organs of workers' and peasants' power." On March 13, the anniversary of the attack made on the palace in 1957, the ambassador to the Soviet Union, Faure Chomón, referred to the revolutionary leaders as "we, the Communists."[49] *Hoy* put "Communists" in quotation marks,[50] but Chomón had not of course used the word figuratively at all. On April 6, in the presence of the President of the Republic, the radio news bulletin "Venceremos" was inaugurated under the management of Raúl Valdés Vivó, the assistant editor of *Hoy*. Anyone who listens to the Cuban radio today knows that this news broadcast is one of the official organs of "socialist Cuba." That same day *Revolución* started a new section entitled "Ideological Ammunition," in which the principal elements of Marxism were expounded.[51]

On April 8 and 16, the JUCEI for the provinces of Las Villas and Matanzas were created. In each organization the presidency was in the hands of the military chief of the province: Juan Almeida and

48 Lionel Soto, "Las Escuelas de Instrucción Revolucionaria en una nueva fase" [The Schools of Revolutionary Instruction in a New Phase], *Cuba Socialista*, February 1964.

49 *Revolución*, March 14, 1961.

50 *Hoy*, March 14, 1961. As in the case of Aguilera it would be wrong to dismiss this speech by Chomón as unimportant. After his initial anti-Communist phase, Chomón became one of the most loyal Castroites. He had been a partisan of "unity" (pro-union of all revolutionaries) since March 1959, the first ambassador to the Soviet Union, and in May 1964 he was in charge of pressing the accusation against Marcos Rodríguez.

51 Information on the first appearance of "Venceremos" in *Revolución*, April 7, 1961. The section "Parque Ideológico" appeared for the first time in *Revolución*, April 6, 1961.

Orlando Puertas, respectively. But unlike the JUCEI of Oriente, where the secretariat went to some unknown person who was not, as far as I know, a member of the PSP, in Las Villas and in Matanzas the secretariats were occupied by the district secretaries of the PSP,[52] Arnaldo Milián and Leónides Calderío.

The process of "socialization" came to a climax on April 16, the day after the air attacks in preparation for the Bay of Pigs invasion on April 17. At the funeral of those killed that day, Castro officially announced the "socialist" nature of his revolution.[53]

The PSP and Castro's "Socialism"

This study does not propose to examine the Bay of Pigs invasion. Theodore Draper, author of *Castro's Revolution*, has characterized it splendidly as "one of those rare politico-military events — a perfect failure."[54] What we are interested in is *Hoy*'s reaction to Castro's speech on April 16, to *Revolución*'s headlines, and to other subsequent developments.

Even though April 17 fell on a Monday, when *Hoy* does not come out, giving it forty-eight hours to mull over its position, its headlines on Tuesday read "The USSR Will Help Us!"; and in its editorial the far-reaching proclamation of the Cuban revolution as socialist was mentioned only at the end and in the following manner: "Long live our patriotic, democratic, and socialist revolution!"[55]

For ten days *Hoy* was content to repeat the same concepts, and only on April 28 did it make a clear statement in support of Castro. On that date it stated, in the column "A Commentary," "The people had been waiting for Fidel's statement." It went on to say that the Cuban revolution, after having "fully realized the patriotic tasks of national liberation" and having eliminated the large landed estates, "has begun the process of fulfilling a series of socialist tasks," to which the "lack of definition of the nature of the transformations" that were taking place had become an obstacle.

---

[52] With regard to organizing the JUCEI of Las Villas see *ibid.*, April 8 and 9, 1961; on that of Matanzas see *Hoy*, April 16, 1961. On March 24 the organization of the JUCEI in Camagüey was announced for the following day, but without mentioning the names of its members.

[53] Castro's speech in *Revolución*, April 17, 1961.

[54] Theodore Draper, *Castro's Revolution: Myths and Realities* (New York: Praeger, 1962), p. 59.

[55] Castro's speech declaring the revolution "socialist" was reprinted in this same issue (*Hoy*, April 18, 1961).

"Fidel, on the eve of the mercenary invasion, which was routed in seventy-two hours, defined our revolution as a socialist revolution"; hence Cuba would continue "advancing in the construction of socialism under the very nose of United States imperialism."

Hoy's delay in defining its attitude toward the declaration of April 16 requires an explanation.[56]

When Castro's "socialism" became official, it created a difficult problem for the Communists: a problem of both an ideological and a practical political nature.

When Lenin rebelled against the perspective offered by the first adaptation of Marxism to Russian reality (undertaken by Plekhanov, according to whom the workers' party would help to overthrow Tsarism only in order to let others come to power), the international Communist movement ran into a problem that has remained insoluble to this day.

Marx had maintained, in effect, that a society would not disappear until another one had matured sufficiently to succeed it, that this social dynamic was determined by the class struggle, that the conduct of classes was governed by their interests, and that these interests were determined by the place of each class in the production process. Furthermore, in his analysis of the European society of his time, which he called capitalism, Marx came to the conclusion that the social structure tended to reduce itself into two classes: the owners of the means of production, the capitalists, and those who possessed nothing but their labor power, the proletariat. He also said that the first class lived by the exploitation of the second, and while the capitalists were interested in maintaining the *status quo*, the workers were impelled inexorably to overthrow it and replace it by what the author of *Capital* called the socialist or Communist society.

Based on these assumptions, what was the situation of a Marxist in Russian society at the beginning of the century, where capitalism was just beginning to develop and did not grow with the impetuosity of English capitalism in Marx's time? Or even more difficult, what was the situation of a Marxist in the precapitalist societies of Asia, to which Lenin turned when he realized that the socialist revolution in Europe would not take place for a long time? His situation was obviously desperate. First, the possibilities of victory were practically nonexistent. In any precapitalist or semicapitalist

---

[56] "Un Comentario: Cuba defiende su revolución socialista" [Cuba Defends Its Socialist Revolution], *ibid.*, April 28, 1961.

society the working class, the only class whose interests would drive it along the path toward socialism, does not exist or is very feeble, while on the contrary, in such a society the peasant, the craftsman, the small merchant, and the like, all who own a plot of land, the instruments of their crafts, or a small commercial establishment, and are therefore potential capitalists and allergic to socialism, constitute the immense majority. Hence Marxism faces a terrible dilemma. If it hides its ideology, how is it going to compete with other political groups? How is it going to propagate its doctrine? How is it going to create the party needed to occupy a position of power? If, on the other hand, it openly declares itself socialist, how will it overcome its lack of appeal to the other groups beside the workers, who are in the minority? How will it make the "petite bourgeoisie" forget its fears? For without the support of this other social stratum the influence of a Marxist workers' party would be almost imperceptible. Second, even if Lenin did succeed, he would lack a modern industrial apparatus — the base for such a society.

From Plekhanov's time down to the "national democracy" of the 1960 Moscow Declaration the Marxists have tried different answers to these questions. They have rectified, they have confessed their "errors," they have returned to previously abandoned formulas. But to this day they have not found a viable solution.[57]

It is not necessary to mention here all of the attempted solutions to the problem. What we are interested in is the Soviet formula used by the international Communist movement in 1961,[58] which

[57] I hope the reader will forgive the audacity of trying to summarize in a few lines such a vast and complex issue; the literature dealing with this matter is too ample to enumerate here. Suffice it to mention, in dealing with Plekhanov, Samuel Baron, "Between Marx and Lenin: George Plekhanov," in Leopold Labedz, ed., *Revisionism* (New York: Praeger, 1962), and with reference to "national democracy," Richard Lowenthal, "National Democracy and the Post Colonial Revolution," in Kurt London, ed., *New Nations in a Divided World* (New York: Praeger, 1963). In general, George Lichtheim, *Marxism: An Historical and Critical Study* (New York: Praeger, 1961); Alfred G. Meyer, *Leninism* (New York: Praeger, 1962); Benjamin I. Schwartz, *Chinese Communism and the Rise of Mao* (Cambridge, Mass.: Harvard University Press, 1952); Robert E. North, *Moscow and Chinese Communists* (2nd ed.; Stanford, Calif.: Stanford University Press, 1962); Walter Z. Laqueur, *Communism and Nationalism in the Middle East* (London: Routledge and Kegan Paul, 1961); and the studies of Jane Degras, "The Communist Attitude to Colonialism," and Walter Z. Laqueur, "Neo-Colonialism, the Soviet Concept," in London, *op. cit.*

[58] See the Statement of the Communist parties of December 1960 and the new program of the CPSU approved by the Twenty Second Congress. In the next chapter we shall add a few notes on the Soviet attitude with reference to the transition from the "semifeudal" to the "socialist" phase.

was the important one for the PSP because of that party's increasingly pro-Soviet character.

According to the Soviet ideologists, countries like Cuba — "semifeudal" and under the imperialistic yoke — had to take the road to socialism by stages. The first stage would be the creation of an "independent national democracy" that would eliminate the remains of feudalism, divide up the land, and expel imperialist enterprises from the economy. After these tasks were accomplished the "construction of socialism" would begin. Transition to this second stage could well be peaceful. But, according to the doctrine still prevailing at that time, the construction of socialism presupposed the "leading role of the proletariat" and of its vanguard, the Communist party. Before Castro's Declaration of April 16 there had not been a single case of a member country of the socialist camp, whether fully socialist or in the stage of "constructing socialism," in which power was not solely or for all practical purposes in the hands of a Communist party. This was certainly not the situation in Cuba in April 1961.

The PSP was not represented in the Cuban government or in the leadership of the Rebel Army or of the mass organizations. After the arrest of David Salvador the executive committee of the CTC remained in the hands of the rest of those elected at the November 1959 congress, that is, Castroites. Rolando Cubelas was still in charge of the University Student Federation. The women's organization was "unified" in August 1960 with Vilma Espín, Raúl Castro's wife, as president.[59] In October of the same year it was the turn of the youth. In this case "unity" was accomplished under the banner of "Young Rebels" (Jóvenes Rebeldes), an organization created by the department of education of the army[60] and under the control of Joel Iglesias, an adolescent guerrilla fighter, who was introduced by Castro in one of his television appearances.[61] Rogelio Acevedo was chief of the Revolutionary Militias, and José Matar was the president of the Committees for the Defense of the Revolu-

[59] For the "unification" of the women and the presidency of Señora Espín see *Hoy*, August 24, 1960.

[60] Guevara cleared up this matter in his speech published in *Revolucion*, October 22, 1960.

[61] The creation of the Young Rebels League (Asociación de Jóvenes Rebeldes) was announced on May 10, 1960. A few days later, in a television appearance, Fidel Castro went to great lengths in praising its president, Joel Iglesias (*Hoy*, May 29, 1960). At the end of October the unification of the youth movement took place (*ibid.*, October 28, 1960) .

tion. As far as I have been able to establish, not one of these was a member of the PSP.[62]

In April 1961 only three Communists participated in Castro's regime: Lionel Soto, who was in charge of the Schools of Revolutionary Instruction and was a Castroite Communist with the same tendencies as Carlos Rafael Rodríguez, and the two men who held the posts of secretaries of the JUCEI's of Las Villas and Matanzas, both under the authority of their presidents, who were majors in the Rebel Army and faithful Castroites.

Obviously this situation was not at all satisfactory to the PSP and must have strengthened its ideological scruples. The evidence is that at least from February 1961 onward these practical political matters, especially the creation of a "unified" party, must have been a subject of discussion between Fidel and the Communists. This we deduce from the events that follow, which have no precedent as far as I know in the history of international communism.

After the January 25 plenum of the PSP leadership, the party never again made a pronouncement on any Cuban event, and not even the April invasion made it break its silence. On the other hand, there was no event, however small, in the life of a fraternal party that was not marked by a salute from the PSP. Beginning with the congress of the Venezuelan Communist Party on March 9 and ending with the anniversary of the Communist Party of the Republic of Mongolia on July 4, the PSP did not miss a single opportunity to send greetings, congratulations, or condolences.[63] In my opinion this strange behavior has the following explanation.

During the discussions between Castro and the Communists, which resulted in the creation of the Integrated Revolutionary Organization (Organizaciones Revolucionarias Integradas — ORI) in July 1961, Castro must have proposed the dissolution of the PSP, promising to establish a new revolutionary party. The Communists accepted this proposition, but knowing Fidel, they used

[62] The naming of Rogelio Acevedo as chief of the national directorate of the Revolutionary Militias was announced in *Revolución*, January 9, 1960. With reference to José Matar I must clear up two points: I am not sure that he was president of the CDR in April 1961 even though he occupies that position today; also I am not completely sure that he was not a member of the PSP, but he was not a member of the National Committee.

[63] The greetings were published in *Hoy* as follows: Communist Party of Venezuela, March 9, 1961; Norwegian Communist Party, March 18, 1961; Plenum of Young Rebels, March 18, 1961; British Communist Party, March 31, 1961; Communist Party of Israel, June 3, 1961; Communist Party of Colombia, June 25, 1961; and Communist Party of Mongolia, July 4, 1961.

every possible means to make their presence felt until Castro publicly kept his promise — that is, until he strictly fulfilled his "fraternal" obligations. The last political statement of the PSP was made at the end of January; and according to Lionel Soto the formation of the ORI did not begin until June.[64] On July 4 the last greeting, one to the Communist Party of Mongolia, was published; and in his speech on July 26 Castro, in a very vague way, as we shall see, announced "revolutionary integration."

We can easily follow the process by which the July agreement was reached, and the terms of this agreement, if we examine the documents published after April 28. On that day *Hoy* approved Castro's "socialism," making it clear, however, that the issue was the "construction of socialism."

In his speech on May 1 Castro read some paragraphs of the Declaration of Havana and affirmed: "This is the program and the essence of our socialist revolution. . . . The small industrialist, the small merchants, the craftsmen, the members of the middle class have nothing to fear from the socialist revolution."[65] Three days later *Hoy* applauded his words, explaining that "in a long process, by evolutionary methods and through discussion and persuasion," the small industrialists and merchants could "collaborate now" and step by step integrate themselves with socialism.[66]

On May 8 Aníbal Escalante, in a televised appearance, was even more explicit, "What did Fidel say?" he asked. "That our state is a socialist state? That our republic is already a socialist republic? Neither." What Fidel meant to say was that "we are entering a period of transition heading toward the accomplishment of the socialist bases of the revolution" and that "this would take a long period of time." With respect to the integrated party he was much less emphatic. He limited himself to saying that "a revolutionary vanguard is absolutely necessary."[67]

In June Guevara announced that the only thing remaining to be done was "to create the Party" and that "Fidel will be its Secretary-General."[68] Meanwhile *Hoy* applauded Raúl's report on the

[64] Soto, "Las Escuelas," *op. cit.*

[65] Castro's speech on May 1, 1961 in *Revolución,* May 2, 1961.

[66] "Nuestra Opinión: La revolución socialista y los pequeños propietarios [The Socialist Revolution and the Small Proprietors], *Hoy,* May 4, 1961.

[67] Lecture on economy and planning by Aníbal Escalante in the Universidad Popular (*Revolución,* May 8, 1961). The Universidad Popular was a popular educational program that employed television, pamphlets, and other media.

[68] Speech by Guevara at the closing ceremony of the work camps of the International Union of Students, *Revolución,* June 5, 1961.

JUCEI's, praising "the sense of collective direction" that was beginning to prevail in economic affairs. *Hoy* suggested that "this sense of discipline and organization" should be extended to "political decisions."[69]

As we have said before, it was on July 26 that Castro announced the terms of the agreement. "To declare that the revolution is socialist," he said, really meant that "the revolution is advancing toward a socialist regime, since it is not possible to establish this society without an enormous increase in production." These statements are obviously rigorously orthodox. In party matters he was not so categorical. He limited himself to saying that "revolutionary integration" was "a process" that had been taking place for some time among the people. "Integration" aims could not be declared at this moment. It was "evolving from the base," and at a given moment the process would be completed. When? He did not mention a date. He said: "When this moment comes . . . the completion of unification from the base will be announced to the people."[70]

Notwithstanding the studied vagueness of these last words, *Hoy* had to resign itself once more. It pointed out that "the decisions of the 26th of July" signified "an enormous qualitative leap." From now on, above all the mass organizations that were not controlled by the Communists, "unifying them all, directing them all," there would be the "Unified Party of the Socialist Revolution" (a term Fidel had not used in his speech), which the Communists hoped to control.

Then, "with this unity of the people, with this united revolutionary leadership," and "with a program flexibly directed toward the construction of socialism, bearing in mind not only the interests of the workers and peasants but also those of the intellectuals, the professionals, the technicians, the small merchants, and the middle class . . . ," the Cuban revolution would continue its march to victory.[71] In effect, Castro continued to govern as unilaterally as before, while the Communists threw themselves into the work of organizing the ORI in order to capture power from within.

J. P. Morray, without mentioning any source, fixes November 27, 1961, as the date on which the PSP was officially dissolved.[72]

---

[69] "Un Comentario: Avances en la organización [Advances in Organization], *Hoy*, June 6, 1961.

[70] Castro's speech in *Revolución*, July 27, 1961.

[71] "Nuestra Opinión: Las definiciones del 26 de Julio" [The Definitions of the 26th of July]," *Hoy*, July 28, 1961.

[72] J. P. Morray, *The Second Revolution in Cuba* (New York: Monthly Review Press, 1962), p. 165.

CHAPTER SIX

RUSSIA, CHINA, AND CASTRO'S SOCIALISM

Russian Reservations

On April 18, 1961, Khrushchev sent a message to President Kennedy saying that he would give "to the Cuban government and its people all the necessary assistance to repel aggression."[1] On that same day the Soviet delegate to the United Nations proposed that the United States should be declared an aggressor nation. Meanwhile, the Chinese government made a declaration of solidarity, sent messages of support, and organized demonstrations of sympathy. As the invading forces were liquidated within seventy-two hours, there is no way of knowing whether behind all these gestures there was the will to act. To celebrate the Cuban victory, a gigantic demonstration was held in Peking on April 20. It was attended by Cuba's Minister of Education, Armando Hart, who was on a visit to the Chinese capital. "This tremendous gathering," the press commented, "proves that the Chinese people are the most trusted and loyal friends of Cuba, Latin America, and all oppressed nations."[2]

The April invasion did not deter the Soviet Premier from meeting President Kennedy in Vienna in the beginning of June. *Hoy* took advantage of this occasion to restate its confidence in Khrushchev and to express its hope that the conference would produce positive results.[3] *Revolución* was more cautious. After the conference was over it explained that no agreements had been reached about Cuba because "one cannot decide a nation's destiny if that nation is not represented at such a meeting with total equality on

---

[1] *Revolución*, April 19, 1961.

[2] Text of the Chinese government declaration in *ibid.*, April 20, 1966. For message, rallies, and press comment see NCNA, April 18, 19, 20, 21, and 22, 1961 (SCMP 2483, 2484, and 2485, April 26, 27, and 28, 1961, respectively).

[3] "Un Comentario: La Conferencia en la Cumbre" [The Summit Conference], *Hoy*, June 3, 1961. On *Hoy*'s identification with the Soviets see also "Un Comentario: Un año de relaciones entre Cuba y la URSS" [One Year of Dealings Between Cuba and the USSR], *ibid.*, May 7, 1961.

its own behalf," adding, with understandable prudence, "as the Soviet Union has repeatedly declared."[4]

Meanwhile, as we already know, Castro's April Declaration had announced the socialist character of the Cuban revolution — which called for a public response from the members of the socialist bloc. As Marxist-Leninists the bloc members had the same objections as the PSP to Castro's socialism; and the Soviets, as leaders of the socialist camp, also had other reasons for not feeling very satisfied with Castro's sudden decision.

In the first place, although at the Moscow 1960 meeting the Soviet Union had renounced the title of "head" of the bloc, it was *de facto* still exercising this function in 1961, a fact that manifested itself in the hierarchic order of the member states as reflected in the greetings traditionally sent by the Communist parties of these states to the CPSU and in the slogans with which the Soviet party greeted other Communist parties at the two great Bolshevik celebrations on May 1 and November 7.

The stage through which each member of the bloc was passing was clearly illustrated in the slogans of the CPSU. Thus, for example, in October 1958 North Vietnam was still in the phase of "constructing a new life" — the same phrase that was applied to Cuba in the slogan for November 7, 1960, the first time that country was mentioned[5] — and it was only in April 1959 that Hanoi entered the "construction of socialism" phase.[6]

We have explained the origin of these stages in the preceding chapter. Now we must add that besides the reason mentioned there the Soviets had a further motive for introducing and preserving this gradation. If in the twentieth century young Communist parties — let alone neophytes like Castro — started to build socialism without the minimal and indispensable base, then, as a Soviet source puts it, such "undue haste may narrow the popular basis of socialist revolution and compromise the noble idea of socialism in the eyes of the masses."[7]

---

[4] Editorial, "Zona Rebelde: La Conferencia de Viena" [The Conference in Vienna], *Revolución,* June 6, 1961.

[5] The greetings of the CPSU on the occasion of November 7, 1960 in *Hoy,* November 6, 1960.

[6] For the order in which the parties of the bloc are mentioned in the congresses of the CPSU see Zbigniew K. Brzezinski, *The Soviet Bloc: Unity and Conflict* (rev. ed.; New York: Praeger, 1961), p. 380; and on the greetings of the CPSU see Donald S. Zagoria, *The Sino-Soviet Conflict, 1956–1961* (Princeton, N.J.: Princeton University Press, 1962), p. 112. Both works are fundamental to understanding the nature of the bloc.

[7] See G. Starushenko's article, "Through General Democratic Transformation

A second reason for the Soviets not to feel at all complacent about Castro's declaration of socialism was that it implied Soviet acceptance of military responsibility for Cuba's defense to preserve the myth of the inevitability of the final triumph of communism. This myth rests to no small degree on the fact that no nation that has abandoned "capitalism" has returned to it — even though this affirmation disregards the case of Hungary in 1919. But the acceptance of military responsibility for a new member of the camp situated only ninety miles from the coast of the leading nation of the so-called Western world rendered implausible the policy of peaceful coexistence, which aims at making the opponents of the Soviet Union diminish their vigilance and preparedness by giving them the illusion that the latter has renounced violence as a means for achieving its foreign policy aims.

We thus see that Khrushchev had every reason to think carefully before deciding to approve Castro's declaration of April 16, 1961.

Dorticós' Trip to Moscow and Peking

On the occasion of July 26 the Soviet government sent greetings to Castro, praising "the outstanding success of revolutionary Cuba in the building of a new state — democratic and free of oppressors and exploiters." The greetings from the Chinese government referred to "the development and strengthening of the revolution, and its construction."[8] The effects of two new measures taken by the U.S. government in April and June were already making themselves felt in the country. The first closed the American market totally to Cuban exports, while the second tightened the restriction of American shipments to Cuba, including fats, which comprise one of Cuba's basic foodstuffs. When President Dorticós went to Belgrade to attend the conference of nonaligned nations,[9] he was

---

to Socialist Transformation in The National Liberation Movement at the Present Stage," *Kommunist*, No. 13, September 1962 (*CDSP*, November 7, 1962). In some senses the situation was similar to that at the beginning of the nineteenth century when Bolívar and his compatriots, inspired by the ideas of the French Revolution, tried to establish democratic states in Latin America, where the necessary historical and social conditions were lacking. Thus they not only failed completely but compromised the prospects and the reputation of democracy in Latin America to this day.

8 Both greetings in *Hoy*, July 27, 1961.

9 Those who maintain that Castro is romantic, impulsive, and impetuous forget that around this time the Cuban leader simultaneously aspired to benefit from the funds of the Alliance for Progress, for which purpose Guevara attended the conference in Punta del Este in August; to figure in the Belgrade conference

also entrusted with the delicate mission of negotiating the recognition of Cuba's socialism by the two big nations of the socialist bloc; incidentally, it was hoped that this recognition would spell an increase in economic aid.

Dorticós met with Blas Roca in Moscow, and both dedicated themselves to the task of convincing the Soviet leaders that "in Cuba a true socialist regime was developing," that the term "socialist" was not used lightly, and that "the Cuban people were effectively devoting themselves to the job of "constructing socialism."[10]

The communiqué issued on the occasion of the visit shows that these efforts met with little success. Once more the Cubans stated their reasons for gratitude toward the Soviet Union and subscribed to all the Soviet points of view on the international situation. Both parties stated that "Cuba has made its revolution independently and has freely chosen the road to socialist development," but the Soviets limited themselves to "valuing highly" the "progressive economic transformations" achieved by the Cuban government and to promising their total support in the fight for the "consolidation of national independence." The reference to economic aid was limited to a promise to hold talks for the "arrangement of a long-term commercial agreement aimed at the expansion of the shipping of Cuban sugar to the Soviet Union."[11]

With these negligible results, Dorticós left for Peking, where, as far as our sources indicate, no better results were achieved either in gaining recognition for Castro's socialism or in increasing economic aid.

President Liu Shao-ch'i met Dorticós on his arrival at the airport with the words that Cuba was "the first Latin American country that had fully accomplished its national democratic revolution."[12] On the following day, at the banquet given in honor of Dorticós, Liu Shao-ch'i again repeated his statement, whereupon Dorticós, calling him "Comrade President," reminded him of the consistent attitude of the government of the Chinese People's Republic in helping and supporting "the Cuban Revolution, Cuba's sovereign destiny, and its right to choose the road of historical development

of nonaligned nations, September 1–6, 1961; to be admitted to the socialist camp; and finally not to lose all contact with Washington. Already in May he had proposed trading the Bay of Pigs prisoners for tractors, a deal that was finally concluded in December 1962.

[10] Blas Roca's appearance on Soviet television (*Revolución*, October 23, 1961).
[11] Cuban-Soviet communiqué in *ibid.*, September 21, 1961.
[12] NCNA, September 22, 1961 (SCMP 2588, September 29, 1961).

that the Cuban people had already chosen by their own decision."[13] He explained this decision by saying that Cuba had achieved its national revolution of liberation from imperialism right on the doorstep of the imperialists, and that, after obtaining its complete national sovereignty, "the Cuban people had to make a decision between two roads: capitalist or socialist development." Therefore, shortly before April 17, "Comrade Fidel Castro announced the socialist nature of our revolution." This decision increased the identification between the two nations because now "the revolution of both nations takes similar forms," "both revolutions accept the working class as their vanguard," and "both revolutions have one common enemy, Yankee imperialism."[14]

The communiqué that was finally issued showed that all this eloquence was fruitless. Both parties repeated that "American imperialism was the most ferocious enemy of all peoples" and agreed that the Cuban revolution "was a brilliant example for Latin American countries." They pointed out that with the Cuban revolution "the crumbling of United States domination" in the Western Hemisphere had begun, although it could not be expected that this imperialism "of its own free will" would abandon "the colonialist policy of controlling and enslaving Latin America. . . ." But as to Castro's "socialism," the Chinese limited themselves to stating "with satisfaction" that "the heroic Cuban people under the firm direction of the Revolutionary Government headed by its Prime Minister, Fidel Castro, has chosen the road of socialist development." Economic aid was not mentioned.[15]

The speeches marking Dorticós' departure remove any remaining doubt as to the failure of the visit. Dorticós pointed out that "our two nations will continue to be united in the struggle for world

13 Both speeches in NCNA, September 23, 1961 (SCMP 2589, October 2, 1961).

14 Dorticós' speech in NCNA, September 25, 1961 (SCMP 2590, October 3, 1961). The President had been preceded by Peng Ch'en, the mayor of Peking, who repeated, "The Cuban revolution . . . has marked a brilliant example for the national and democratic movements in Latin America."

15 Sino-Cuban communiqué in Hoy, October 3, 1961. It must be observed that Roca, who had accompanied Dorticós to Peking, was not present at the interview with Mao and did not sign the communiqué, as he had left Peking by then. His return to Moscow was so unexpected that newspapermen asked him why he had left President Dorticós, to which he answered: "I had to come to participate in negotiations concerning sugar." (Revolución, October 3, 1961.) We do not know whether this is true, but we do know that nothing was said publicly of such negotiations. In the talks with Mao, Roca was replaced by Martínez Sánchez, who had just returned from representing Cuba at a congress of the Communist Party of North Korea (NCNA, September 28, 1961 [SCMP 2592, October 5, 1961]).

peace, for the quick extinction of colonialism and neocolonialism, for the liquidation of the imperialist system, and for the freedom and progress of all nations." This time he did not salute Mao or socialism as he had done before. The Chinese President addressed Dorticós, calling him "Your Excellency," acknowledged that "the Cuban people have the right to choose their own way," and concluded by toasting "the victory of the revolutionary cause of Cuba," the "unshakable friendship between China and Cuba," "the health of his Excellency Prime Minister Fidel Castro," and "the health of his Excellency President Dorticós."[16]

From Peking Dorticós returned to Cuba. Roca, together with Emilio Aragonés, Augusto Martínez Sánchez, and Ambassador Faure Chomón, three Castroites, stayed in Moscow to represent the ORI at the Twenty-Second Congress of the CPSU.

The Twenty-Second Congress, which was convened to approve the program of the construction of communism, became the scene of the struggle against the "antiparty" group, of the differences with China, and of the attacks on Albania. When Cuba had established diplomatic relations with Albania in December 1960, *Hoy* had commented: "Well done, peasant-worker revolutionary power, to have established relations with Albania."[17] But after Khrushchev's attack on the Albanians, Roca decided to forget these words. In his speech before the congress, in the name of the Cuban delegation, Roca declared that with the Cuban revolution socialism had reached America; he affirmed the Cuban confidence in the CPSU, "headed by the Leninist Central Committee and Comrade Nikita Sergeievich Khrushchev, Cuba's great friend." He maintained that the new program was

a powerful instrument in the immediate struggle for peace and for peaceful coexistence, for the unmasking of all the lies of revisionism and dogmatism, for eliminating all the negative phenomena of the personality cult, and of violation of socialist legality, for rejection of all attempts to shake the unity, the friendship, and solidarity of the international Communist movement.

[16] Dorticós and Liu Shao-ch'i's speeches in NCNA, October 2, 1961 (SCMP 2594, October 9, 1961). It is significant that on taking leave at the airport Dorticós said that in the Cuban-Chinese friendship he noticed the vitality that resulted from "the friendly and cordial stimulus initiated by the Soviet Union." Given the state of Sino-Soviet relations this reminder seemed, at the least, indelicate. Furthermore, Dorticós again ended his speech without praising Mao.

[17] "Un Comentario: La hermandad entre dos pequeños grandes pueblos" [Brotherhood Between Two Great Small Nations], *Hoy*, December 16, 1961.

He added:

In agreement with our convictions and our experience we resolutely en-
dorse the stand taken by Comrade Khrushchev with respect to the negative
activities of the leaders of the Albanian Party of Labor.[18]

One month later it could be seen that these were not Castro's
"convictions" or "experience": on the anniversary of the liberation
of Albania and Yugoslavia Castro's government sent messages of
congratulations to both nations.[19] Roca had to change his attitude.
Although he repeated his criticism of the Albanians in a television
appearance at the end of November and in an article published in
Cuba Socialista, he omitted it in a second television appearance in
the middle of December.[20] From December 1961 onward, neither
he nor any other Cuban leader ever condemned Albania for its
behavior toward the Soviet Union.

Castro Declares Himself Marxist-Leninist

When Roca made his speech to the Twenty-Second Congress, the
slogans for November 7, the anniversary of the Bolshevik Revolution, had already been issued. In these greetings Cuba was mentioned as constructing "a new way of life," the stage preceding that
of "the construction of socialism."[21]

Another revealing incident took place before Roca's return to
Cuba. On the anniversary of the October Revolution two greetings
were sent: one from the Cuban government to the Soviet government, and the other from Fidel Castro, in the name of the leadership of the ORI, to Khrushchev as First Secretary of the CPSU. The
Soviet acknowledgments arrived at the end of November but,
although the note of the Cuban government was deemed worthy
of a direct response, the ORI's greeting was apparently included

[18] Roca's speech in *ibid.,* October 22, 1961.
[19] *Ibid.,* November 29, 1961.
[20] Roca's first television appearance in *ibid.,* December 1, 1961; the article in
Cuba Socialista, December 1961, and the second television appearance in *Hoy,*
December 16, 1961. It is amusing to see how this Stalinist of thirty years' standing
justified the attacks made on Stalin during the Twenty-Second Congress of the
CPSU, the transfer of the dictator's remains from the Mausoleum in Red Square,
and so on. He understood the anxiety that such acts caused to some "comrades."
It was a "sentimental problem." "Great feelings of admiration and affection for
Stalin were created in us." Of course, that was because "we, who were far away,
had fewer opportunities for knowing Stalin's defects. . . ." Unfortunately it had
now turned out "that the slanders of his enemies were based on some facts."
[21] *Hoy,* October 17, 1961.

among the thanks for "the many telegrams of different persons and organizations from Cuba" acknowledged by the Soviet Premier through the press.[22]

It is obvious that all these communiqués, greetings, and omissions meant, purely and simply, that the bloc did not accept Castro's "socialism." Moreover, we have no evidence that any increase of economic aid was granted in compensation for this refusal. We are thus obliged to conclude that at the end of October 1961 Castro had not made any progress along this road.

The year 1961 was not very favorable for Castro in Latin America either. It is true that the victory over the invasion forces in April considerably heightened his influence on the continent, but the ratification of the Alliance for Progress in August gave the U.S. government an effective means with which to persuade the Latin American governments to close ranks against Castroism. At the beginning of November, Venezuela broke off diplomatic relations with Cuba; Peru and Colombia were soon to follow. At the beginning of December the assembly of the OAS met in Washington and made an agreement to hold a meeting of ministers in January to consider the extracontinental threats against "American solidarity."

On the domestic front the declaration of the socialist nature of the revolution together with the shortage of supplies appeared to have nullified in a few months the favorable effects of the Bay of Pigs victory. In September the conflict with the Catholic Church came to a head with the expulsion of a bishop and more than one hundred priests. That same month an attempt to kill Carlos Rafael Rodríguez was almost successful. In October an unsuccessful attempt was made on the life of Fidel Castro.[23] A few days later the building that housed the CTC was burned.

In response to these acts of rebellion, the death penalty was established on November 30 for crimes committed by infiltrators from abroad; the regime could not admit that many of these acts

22 For the greetings see *ibid.*, November 7, 1961. The replies are in the same newspaper, December 1, 1961.

23 The attempt on Castro's life was prepared for the day of Dorticós' return from his trip to Moscow and Peking. The conspirators hid the arms in an apartment from which the palace terrace could be dominated. From this terrace Castro and the President spoke on the given date. In his speech on October 23, Castro explained all the details and added: "I do not know why they did not shoot. They must have gotten nervous!"

were the product of internal discontent (although we do not wish to deny the existence of infiltration from abroad).

We can conclude from such events that the Cuban people were slowly waking from the spell that Castro's personality had cast upon them. It is much harder to be sure of the reaction of the Castroites to the "socialist" declaration of their leader and above all to the creation of the ORI initiated in July. By October, according to Escalante, the ORI had 800 nuclei in the capital and was organized in 100 of the island's 126 municipalities. As was later revealed on the occasion of Aníbal Escalante's dismissal, the organization was completely in the hands of members of the former PSP. And Escalante himself referred to the ORI as "the backbone of the revolutionary state."[24]

Since Fidel did not raise his voice against this definition and these various activities, it seems that they had his approval. As a result the "Fidelistas" seem to have fallen into a state of frustration, following their leader's orders with indifference and resigning themselves to the prospect that the leaders of the late PSP might steal the revolution made by the Castroites under Fidel's command.

It was not only in the ORI that the Communist "old guard," or members of the former PSP, began to reap the reward of their long support of Castro. In November 1961 the CTC held a new congress. Lázaro Peña, the same Communist who had occupied the position during the period of collaboration with Batista, was elected secretary-general. The posts of administrative secretary and propaganda secretary were taken over by Communists, and at least six of the thirteen members of the new executive were members of the PSP.[25]

These successes, however, did not end the differences among the former leaders of the PSP. For example, in August, when the First National Production Meeting (Primera Reunión Nacional de la Produccíon)[26] was held to investigate the crisis in the provision of

24 For data on the organization of the ORI and Escalante's word see *Bohemia,* October 8, 1961.

25 *Revolución,* November 29, 1961. The Castroites kept the secretariats of organization, finances, labor, social and foreign relations as well as several assistant secretariats.

26 It is intriguing to read the resolutions of this meeting, which was attended by all the principal revolutionary leaders, including Fidel. It was solemnly promised that the supply of chickens to the capital would be solved in December 1961 and in all the national markets by February 1; in January 1962 the production of potatoes, squash, and bananas would surpass the needs of the national

supplies, *Hoy* did not mention the participation of Carlos Rafael Rodríguez (although he was nominally its editor) until after the meeting had taken place, at which time the statement that he had participated was preceded by the following note: "The introduction of Carlos Rafael Rodríguez, who spoke for the ORI, was made by Fidel Castro, who explained that he would give the floor to a member of the ORI who played an active role in the study and planning of these matters."[27] It is obvious that the earlier omission did not occur by chance. Moreover, there is evidence that the relations between Roca and Escalante were also not very friendly. While Roca committed errors, as in the case of Albania, Escalante, as the acting secretary of the organization of the ORI, gained power and influence day by day. It is highly significant that he never mentioned his party leader Roca in his public statements. It is clear that these differences had no ideological significance, for the debate on the "uninterrupted revolution" had already been resolved. Everyone agreed that the revolution was in the stage of "the construction of socialism," and all were equally pro-Soviet.[28] In my opinion these were purely personal conflicts encouraged by Fidel Castro, that great devourer of organizations. Having made Carlos Rafael Rodríguez subservient, he planned to enmesh Escalante so as to isolate Roca, his only important rival if Cuba was to be a "socialist" state.

At the end of 1961, then, Castro faced a situation in which Cuba's admission to the socialist bloc was denied, the economic help given to Cuba was insufficient, conditions in Latin America were not particularly favorable for revolution, and the Communist old guard, in spite of their internal differences, thought they were about to control the "backbone of the state." Castro once more decided to trust to his luck and his audacity.

In a television appearance on December 1, 1961 he disclosed

---

market; in June of that same year fish production would reach the same level; and on January 1, 1963 the restrictions on the distribution of fats and the like would be abolished. (On the National Production Meeting see *Hoy*, August 28 and 29, 1961.)

27 *Ibid.*, August 31, 1961.

28 I do not know of any leader of the PSP who has shown pro-Chinese inclinations, at least since the Moscow 1960 meeting. It was the "old guard" Communists who created the slogan that was sung in all the demonstrations: "Fidel and Khrushchev, we are with you both." I do not know what they have been saying since the ouster of the Soviet Premier. Blas Roca in an attack of tenderness attributed this theme to "the Cuban children," who wanted to show in this way their love for both leaders. (*Revolución*, November 3, 1961.)

that he had always intuitively been a Marxist-Leninist, pledged that he would continue to be one until he died, and tried to dispel any doubts or reservations that might remain concerning his real ideological position. This he evidently did to overcome the resistance of the socialist bloc, to establish himself as the leader of the Communist movement in Latin America, to maintain the initiative against the United States, and incidentally to obtain from the Soviet bloc the consumer goods he needed so desperately.

Let us see how he accomplished this.

Although he declared that he was not appearing before the television cameras to tell the story of his life, that is precisely what he did.

He said that in the university he "began to have his first contacts with the Communist Manifesto, with the works of Marx, Engels, Lenin, . . . and all that." He left unmentioned the chapters of his life when he belonged to the Revolutionary Insurrectional Union (UIR) and to the "Ortodoxo" party. His activities during both these periods, especially his membership in the UIR, would have been extremely difficult to explain in the light of Marxist dialectics. Therefore he resumed his narrative after the *coup d'état* of March 10, 1952. All his strategy, he said, was from the very beginning related to his "revolutionary concept" that "only by mobilizing the masses could power be conquered," because "revolutions do not spring from the minds of men" but advantage must be taken of "the objective conditions."

He admitted that he had made mistakes. When he attacked the Moncada barracks he had thought that "to start this kind of struggle" (the guerrilla warfare that brought him victory) "more resources were needed than was actually the case." He should have "planned the capture of the Bayamo barracks, so close to the Sierra Maestra mountains." Proving thus that he had never been a mere "putschist," he then went on to describe the war in the Sierra. He for one had always wanted a united front, but the other opposition groups insisted on "excluding the PSP"; therefore he had conceived the idea of transferring to the Sierra the united front that had been born in Caracas. There, he said, "we . . . were . . . the ones who would impose the conditions." Carlos Rafael Rodríguez was "a witness of his troubles" at this time.

He admitted that even after reading the works of Marx, Lenin, and others, and despite his efforts to achieve a united front with Communist participation, he still had "some prejudices against the

PSP" after January 1, 1959. That is why on a certain occasion (he was referring to his speech of May 21, 1959) he had verbally attacked the Communists. Today he admitted his mistake. The "divisionists" had exploited his prejudices against the PSP; and later he was able to verify that the Communists had had nothing to do with the "disorders" that he had attributed to them.

Having cleared his past, he then talked about the present: "A revolution cannot advance without a strong and disciplined revolutionary organization." Fortunately he was not born with "the vocation of a caudillo." It is true that up until then "the decisions were almost always taken because of the trust placed in the Prime Minister." But "that is wrong. The ideal system, the most perfect one found by men to govern a nation, . . . is the system of government built on the foundations of a revolutionary party, democratically organized and through collective leadership"; that would be the system established in Cuba.

Having thus provided against the eventuality that he might be charged with fostering the cult of personality, he dealt with the subject of neutralism. He said that in the revolution there had been "some who recommended the use of blackmail," that is, "a political thesis so repulsive, so cowardly, and so cheap" as to counsel taking "as much as you can from imperialism, by intimidating it and frightening it with the friendship of the Soviet Union, in other words to be a blackmailer." He never had anything to do with such despicable behavior. He always knew "that there was no half way between capitalism and socialism," that "those who try to find a third alternative fall into a false and truly utopian position."

He ended this long explanation of his behavior by stating: "I am a Marxist-Leninist, and I shall continue to be one until the last day of my life." So that there would be no doubt as to the type of Marxist-Leninist he professed to be, he recommended that his listeners "read Khrushchev's reports to the Twenty-Second Congress, which constitute a veritable texbook of politics."[29]

[29] The text of Castro's speech was published in *Hoy*, December 2, 1961. It should be added that later, in his talks with Bernard L. Collier of the *New York Herald Tribune* (*Miami Herald*, August 23, 1964), Castro slightly altered his biography. He then said that after leaving prison in 1955 "he had had contacts" with the Communists, even though they objected to the use of armed force. However, when he left Mexico and headed for Cuba, the PSP "agreed to collaborate" and "did collaborate" when "we landed." Unfortunately Castro forgets his articles, published in *Bohemia* (Havana) in July and August 1956, three months before the landing, in which he pointed out that Batista had been the presidential candidate of the Communists in 1940 and mentioned the election posters of

The Second Declaration of Havana

Given the objectives we have imputed to Castro's speech, it appears to be a masterpiece. It proved, however, to be one of his most unfortunate public appearances. In Cuba his words were received with amazement.[30] The international press misinterpreted them, reducing the whole speech to an account of a monstrous hoax perpetrated on the Cuban people from an early date — a date that each commentator fixed arbitrarily for his own convenience. The Latin American governments took it as one more argument in favor of holding a conference of ministers of state in January at which to condemn Castro.

What was even worse for Castro was that his confession of faith did not have any effect on the attitude of the members of the socialist bloc. On the fourth anniversary of the triumph of the Cuban revolution, Brezhnev and Khrushchev wished him only "success in the creation of a new society." Liu Shao-ch'i and Chou En-lai predicted victories "in the cause of the revolution and of construction," and even little Albania limited herself to congratulations on his efforts to "build a free life."[31] Not a word about his "socialism." Finally, a new round with the Soviets in the trade negotiations for 1962 ended at the beginning of January with no appreciable result.[32]

---

the dictator side by side with those of Blas Roca and Lázaro Peña; he also forgets the declaration of the National Committee of the PSP of February 28, 1957, which stated that "before November 30 [the date of the uprising in Santiago de Cuba, which was to have coincided with Fidel's arrival] our party let it be known to you, Fidel Castro and the other leaders of July 26, that we profoundly disagree with the tactics and plans elaborated by you." (This declaration was reprinted in *Bohemia Libre,* July 7, 1963.) These alterations in his biography were inspired by the situation in which he found himself in the summer of 1964. They show once more Castro's characteristic lack of veracity.

30 It is true, as was later explained, that Castro's speech was published in *Revolución*'s evening edition of December 2, 1961. But it is equally true that Castro's speeches that are first published in an evening edition of *Revolución* are invariably reprinted in the morning edition the following day. This time it was not done. Furthermore, there was no newspaper comment on such a remarkable declaration. Only Blas Roca a few days later censured the American press, which, "accustomed to lies and hypocrisies," was amazed and confused "by the sincerity of the truth." (*Hoy,* December 7, 1961.) To me this indicates the bewilderment produced by Castro's speech.

31 *Hoy,* January 3, 1962.

32 The communiqué issued on January 9 limited itself to stating the products that would be sent by the Soviet Union and the price of sugar per pound, 4 cents. It never mentioned quantity. (*Ibid.,* January 10, 1962.) But we shall see that it was only in May that a real trade agreement for 1962 was made.

It is possible that the Soviet leaders interpreted Castro's speech of December 1 as an indication that his domestication process had begun. For example, an article by Castro in the January issue of *Cuba Socialista* was reprinted by the Soviet press, but omitting the paragraphs in which the Cuban leader censured "Yankee imperialism" and referred to the countries of Central America as "fictitious" states managed from their respective "Yankee" embassies.[33] And in the course of the same month the editors of *Pravda* and *Izvestiya,* Satyukov and Adzhubei, who were in Havana attending a meeting of the International Organization of Journalists, questioned Castro on the very important matter of peaceful coexistence, which he had overlooked in his autobiographical speech of December.

According to the version published by the Soviet press, the result of this inquiry was positive. Castro was represented as saying that "Cuba's foreign policy was based on the principle of peaceful coexistence with countries of different social systems," that he did not and could not believe "that the principle of peaceful coexistence was merely a matter of tactics," and that Cuba's policy for Latin America was "a policy of peace." He declared emphatically that "without the Soviet Union, without the socialist camp" the triumph of the Cuban revolution would have been impossible.[34]

However, on January 30 the original text of the interview was published in the Havana newspapers. Here Castro started by saying, "Cuba supports the national liberation movement of all peoples colonized and subjected to imperialism." And although he did state that Cuba's Latin American policy was peaceful — blaming the aggressions on "imperialism" — and that he supported peaceful coexistence, he added:

The policy of peaceful coexistence is coexistence between states. This does not mean coexistence of classes. This policy does not mean coexistence between exploitation and the exploited. It is impossible for peaceful coexistence to exist between the exploited masses of Latin America and the Yankee monopolies. . . . As long as imperialism exists, class war will exist. As long as imperialism exists, international class war will exist between the exploited masses and the monopolies.[35]

As we can see, the two versions differ appreciably.

[33] Fidel Castro, "Tres años de Revolución" [Three Years of Revolution], *Cuba Socialista,* January 1962. Harry Schwartz in *The New York Times,* January 14, 1962, pointed out the omissions in *Pravda's* version.

[34] The *Pravda* and *Izvestiya* versions were reprinted in *Revolución,* January 29, 1962.

[35] *Revolución,* January 30, 1962.

Five days later, in response to the OAS agreement of January 31, 1962 by which Cuba was suspended from the inter-American organization, Castro proclaimed the Second Declaration of Havana, in which the growing differences between the Soviets and the Cuban leader were made even more evident. The same man who only two months before had recommended the reading of Khrushchev's reports to the congress of the CPSU now failed to mention peaceful coexistence, "national democracy," "peaceful transition," or any of the other recommended Soviet formulas for the zones of the "third world" in his words to the peoples of Latin America.

The Second Declaration of Havana reflects a mixture of the Chinese tendency to convert Marxism into the ideology of the colored races, Guevara's notions about guerrilla warfare, and the ignorance and lack of esteem of Castro and his henchmen for ideological affairs.

Since the starting point was the Chinese, racial, point of view, the writers were faced with an initial difficulty. According to them, of the 200 million inhabitants of the continent 32 million were Indians, 45 million mestizos, 15 million Negroes, and 14 million mulattoes. It was evidently not very "democratic" to identify these 106 million people — not 107 as is said further on in the Declaration — with the destiny of the entire continent. "Fidelism's" characteristic contempt for veracity helped them to solve this problem. In the rest of the document, these 106 million were referred to as "two thirds" of the population of Latin America; then, disregarding their own point of departure, the authors concentrated entirely on "the peasants."

To all — Indians, Negroes, mulattoes, mestizos, and peasants — the same example was offered — that of Cuba. To follow the Cuban example, a front consisting of the working class, the peasants, the intellectual workers, and the most progressive strata of the national bourgeoisie had to be formed. Since the peasants were the most numerous, their participation was decisive. But they could not be the leaders of the struggle. For this they needed the "revolutionary and political leadership of the workers and the revolutionary intellectuals." This leadership should never forget that "the national bourgeoisie can never lead the fight against feudalism and imperialism."

The declaration then stated that "the first and most important thing is to understand that it is not right or correct to distract the people with the vain and convenient illusion that they can conquer by legal means the power that the monopolies and oligarchies will defend with blood and fire." Once this is understood they should act accordingly; in other words, they should "follow Cuba's example," starting guerrilla warfare because "the armies structured and equipped for conventional war are totally impotent when faced with the irregular warfare of the peasants on their own terrain. . . ."

Finally, they must never forget the masses because in this fight to the death "with the most powerful imperial metropolis in the world" victory is not possible if the great majorities do not take part.[36]

The reactions of the Soviets and the Chinese to this Second Declaration dispel any doubts about the position of this document in regard to the conflict between them. The Chinese wrote long editorials and organized a huge demonstration, attended by Vice-Minister of Foreign Relations Ch'en Yi, to hail this "solemn proclamation before the whole world."[37] In the message of congratulations that was sent to the revolutionary government, emphasis was put on the way in which the declaration rejected "all illusions about Yankee imperialism and its lackeys."[38] The Soviets on the other hand, saw in this document, which called for racial war, guerrilla warfare, and a fight to the death with "imperialism," an expression of the "peaceful and humane purpose" that inspired the Cuban people. They also saw "the will of the republic of Cuba to base its relations with all nations on the principles of peaceful coexistence and nonintervention."[39]

The Ousting of Escalante

On February 10, 1962 the pilot of the U-2 plane that had been shot down on Soviet soil in 1960 was returned to the United States. Two days later Khrushchev proposed that the heads of state attend the conference on disarmament that was to start on March 14 in Geneva. And on March 18 the Kremlin at last issued a statement condemning the exclusion of Cuba from the inter-American system, pointing out that Washington's policy toward Cuba created "a

---

[36] *Ibid.,* February 5, 1962.

[37] Title of the editorial in *Jen-min Jih-pao,* February 10, 1962 (SCMP 2679, February 15, 1962).

[38] For rally and message see NCNA, February 12, 1962 (SCMP 2680, February 16, 1962).

[39] Soviet communiqué giving support to Cuba in *Revolución,* February 19, 1962.

serious threat to the security and peace of the world." It repeated
its "well-known warning" to the enemies of the Cuban people —
a rather enigmatic reference to the promise of symbolic missiles
made by Khrushchev in July 1960.[40]

Neither the tone of the Soviet statement nor the events indicating
a Soviet-American *rapprochement* (almost simultaneously with the
announcement of new U.S. restrictions against trade with Cuba)
could have been agreeable to Castro.[41] On February 25 the revolutionary government gave thanks for "the repeated offers" (not the
actual provision) "of Soviet help in facing economic aggression"
and for Soviet solidarity and good wishes. But it also suggested that
something else was needed. A warning should be given to "the
imperialists" that "a crime" committed against Cuba "would not
go unpunished." It should be made clear that the Cuban people
did not count "solely on its own strength" to defend itself but also
on the strength "of the nations that defend peace, peaceful coexistence, the right of self-determination, and liberty of all nations."
The statement ended by saying: "Cuba will not fail" — as if it
feared that someone else would.[42]

Cuban doubts about Soviet conduct — as revealed in this document — arose at a time when Castro already knew that the regime
would be unable to keep its promises either for production or for
supplies. The 1962 plan for sugar production had set a goal of
5,820,000 tons,[43] and at the end of the sugar season the crop was
only 4,800,000 tons. Instead of the improvements in supplies promised in August 1961, rice, beans, soap, detergents, toothpaste, meat,
chicken, fish, eggs, milk, and potatoes had to be rationed at the
beginning of March 1962, in addition to fats which were already
rationed.[44]

Moreover, it had also become clear that Escalante had willfully
misinterpreted Castro's intentions for the ORI. It was not just that
the secretaries-general of the six provincial committees were former
members of the PSP; that had of course been known and approved

40 *Ibid.*

41 On February 4, invoking the resolutions of the OAS, the U.S. government
imposed a total embargo on trade with Cuba.

42 *Revolución*, February 26, 1962.

43 According to the résumé of the economic plan for 1962 published in *ibid.*,
October 21, 1961.

44 This rationing was established when the National Board for the Distribution of Supplies (Junta Nacional para la Distribución de los Abastecimientos)
was created (*ibid.*, March 13, 1962).

by Fidel.[45] The trouble lay in Escalante's great haste in organizing the ORI at the same time that the Soviet leaders failed to recognize Cuban "socialism," defaulted on their promise to increase economic aid, and were friendly with the Americans.

In December 1961, general provincial assemblies of the ORI were staged in three provinces. In one of these general assemblies Escalante pointed out the advantage of organizing the party within the ranks of the army. At the end of December he announced that there was no difference between the ORI and the future United Party of the Socialist Revolution (Partido Unido de La Revolución Socialista — PURS); that "the ORI will become the PURS"; and that the only thing still needed to bring this about was "Comrade Fidel's[46] official announcement."

All this must have shown Castro that if things continued the way they were, his socialist declarations and his vows of loyalty to Marxism-Leninism would serve no purpose other than to deliver him into the hands of the old *apparatchiki* of the PSP, which would probably mean that Cuba would become a Soviet pawn in negotiations with the United States. Neither the Soviets nor the former leaders of the PSP paid sufficient attention to Castro's dissatisfaction, the first open expression of which had been the publication late in January of the original text of the interview with Satyukov and Adzhubei by the Cuban press. Castro, therefore, went over to the offensive, which culminated in the crushing of Aníbal Escalante on March 26.

On February 13 it was announced that Carlos Rafael Rodríguez would replace Castro as president of the INRA (National Institute of Agrarian Reform). Two days later the National Directorate of the ORI, whose composition was still unannounced, set up an economic commission headed by Dorticós, Guevara, and Carlos Rafael Rodríguez and organized a department of inspection under the direction of Rafael Francia Mestre, a Communist leader from Las Villas province.

Castro later stated that Carlos Rafael Rodríguez had been his

---

[45] I have not been able to establish the name of the secretary-general of the provincial committee of the ORI in Camagüey province at that time. But those in the other five provinces, José L. G. Carvajal, Silvio Quintana, Leónides Calderío, Arnaldo Milián, and Ladislao González Carvajal, came from the ranks of the PSP.

[46] On the ORI and the army see Escalante's report to the general assembly of Oriente province in *Revolución*, December 9, 1961; and on the ORI identification with the PURS see *Hoy*, December 30, 1961.

personal choice for president of the INRA.[47] I am inclined to believe him. Whether Castro decided to abandon the presidency of the INRA because of its failure in agricultural production or whether the change was imposed on him by the National Directorate of the ORI, Carlos Rafael was an adequate successor from Castro's point of view both because of his intellectual qualifications and because of his attachment to Castro; above all, because his succession would accentuate the differences that existed among the leaders of the PSP. *Hoy* immediately demonstrated the accuracy of this assumption. The former party newspaper responded to the nomination of its editor-in-chief to the first position of importance in the revolutionary government to be given to any member of the PSP merely by registering the event and wishing the new president of the INRA "useful work and success."[48] Whatever the reason for replacing Castro in the presidency of INRA, there is no doubt that this affected his prestige, indicated by the fact that *Revolución* used his appearance at a baseball game as a pretext to deny the "rumors started by the UPI" about a crisis concerning "the great Chief and respected Leader."[49]

On March 9 the composition of the National Directorate of the ORI was officially announced. It was made up of thirteen members chosen from the July 26 Movement, ten ex-leaders of the PSP, a representative of the Revolutionary Student Directorate, and President Dorticós, who, as we know, had once been a member of the PSP but had retired from political activities until chosen by Castro to be President.[50] *Revolución* applauded the formation of

[47] In his television appearance on March 12, Castro, referring to the appointment of Carlos Rafael, said: "This caused some intrigues by the enemies of the revolution. . . . It was quite simply my decision." (*Revolución,* March 13, 1962.)

[48] *Hoy,* February 14, 1962.

[49] "Con el fusil o el bate ¡Cuba no fallará!" [With a Rifle or a Bat Cuba Will Not Fail!], *Revolución,* February 26, 1962.

[50] From the "26": Fidel, Raúl, Guevara, Aragonés, Martínez Sánchez, Ramiro Valdés, Juan Almeida, Armando Hart, Sergio del Valle, Guillermo García, Osmani Cienfuegos, Raúl Curbelo, and Haydée Santamaría. Of these only the two Castro brothers, Ramiro Valdés, Almeida, Hart, and Haydée Santamaría were founders. Guevara, del Valle, and García won their stripes in the guerrilla war. Aragonés, Curbelo, Osmani Cienfuegos, and Martínez Sánchez owed their promotions to the sagacity with which they had guessed Castro's wishes after the victory.

The ex-leaders of the PSP were Blas Roca, Carlos Rafael Rodríguez, Aníbal Escalante, Severo Aguirre, Flavio Bravo, César Escalante, Joaquín Ordoqui, Lázaro Peña, Manuel Luzardo, and Ramón Calcines. It is remarkable that among the twenty-five leaders of this Marxist-Leninist party the only one who had ever been a labor leader was Lázaro Peña.

the organization with an editorial entitled "With Marxism-Leninism and with Collective Leadership."[51] Castro praised the appointments three days later;[52] but in the following years the National
Directorate played no part in Cuban policymaking. And though in
his speech of March 26 the Prime Minister announced that the
National Directorate would be enlarged by "all the historical
names," this promise was not kept. Above all, it is extraordinarily
significant that Castro began his attacks on Escalante the day after
the composition of the National Directorate of the ORI had been
announced. These first words of criticism, still deliberately vague
and enigmatic, were spoken during a carnival parade on March 10
and reported by *Revolución* on March 12. Some days later the newspaper specifically pointed out their pertinence to the campaign
that was by then in full swing.[53]

We must conclude that the announcement of the composition of
the National Directorate was the last straw for Castro's patience.

On March 12, when he appeared on television to announce the
food rationing already mentioned, Castro was apparently still
doubtful about the accusation he was preparing against those who
intended to limit his powers and also about the nature of the
ideological deviation he would attribute to them. According to him
the revolutionary leaders had not kept the promises they had made
to the First National Reunion of Producers, in August 1961, because they were victims of "subjectivism" — which meant that they
had not made "an objective analysis of the circumstances." But
though he referred in passing to the necessity of improving the
organization and "starting to revise" the "nuclei," as the basic
organs of the ORI were called, he did not go into detail. Escalante,
who attended the television appearance and applauded Castro, was
apparently still unaware of the maximum leader's intentions.[54]

The following night Castro announced in a speech at the celebration of the anniversary of the 1957 attack on the presidential
palace that he had now suddenly realized both the extent and the
true nature of the threat. He said that while he had been waiting
for his turn to speak he had noticed to his horror that one of the

---

[51] " Con el marxismo-leninismo y la dirección colectiva," *Revolución*, March
10, 1962.
[52] In his appearance on March 12 already cited (*ibid.*, March 13, 1962).
[53] In the *Revolución* editorial of March 19, 1962.
[54] *Ibid.*, March 13, 1962. The same issue had photographs of those who had
listened to Fidel in the television studio from which these words were transmitted. Escalante can be seen among them applauding.

speakers, in reading the testament of José Antonio Echeverría, a noted student leader killed in the attack, had left out the name of God invoked in the martyr's document. Of course the same sin of omitting the name of God had been committed in the constitutional text that had been promulgated in the first months of the revolutionary government, which was based on the letter of the 1940 constitution; and at that time Castro had not voiced any objection. But in March 1962, allegedly, although the offense this time was only that of an almost anonymous orator, it revealed to Castro that the revolution was threatened by "sectarianism," by a "miserable, cowardly, mutilated tendency" of those without faith "in Marxism, nor in its ideas, nor in the revolution." He now realized that "sectarianism" had captured the party machine, and he promised to work tirelessly until it had been eliminated, so that "the best men and women in the country would be gathered together in the United Party of the Revolution."[55]

From that moment on Castro kept harping on these same themes: the struggle against "sectarianism," the need to purge the ORI, and the importance of maintaining the link with the masses.[56] But the events foreshadowed by his words began to take shape only on March 22. On that day the National Directorate of the ORI named a secretariat consisting of Castro as first secretary, his brother Raúl as second secretary, and Guevara, Dorticós, Aragonés, and Roca. It also created an organization commission presided over by Dorticós and a labor commission under Augusto Martínez Sánchez and entrusted Blas Roca with the editorship of Hoy. Twenty-four hours later a reorganization of the Council of Ministers took place. Among other changes Faure Chomón, the ambassador to the Soviet Union, was named Minister of Communications, although for the moment no new ambassador was appointed, and Manuel Luzardo took over as Minister of Domestic Trade. On March 25 it was made known that Raúl Castro, besides occupying the post of second secretary of the ORI, was to be Vice-Prime Minister.

The appointments had these results: First, in the Secretariat, one of the decisive organs in every Marxist-Leninist *apparat*, the Communist "old guard" had only one representative, Roca. Second, two principal leaders of the PSP, Rodríguez and Luzardo, held

---

55 *Ibid.*, March 14, 1962.

56 See his speeches made on the graduation ceremony of three hundred revolutionary instructors (*ibid.*, March 17, 1962) and on receiving the Lenin Peace Prize (*ibid.*, March 22, 1962).

executive positions, while Roca, the head of the party, was banished to the mere editorship of a newspaper. Since Aníbal Escalante was ousted immediately after this, the former secretary-general of the PSP was left without his most important assistants.[57] Lastly, Cuba was left with no ambassador in the Soviet Union.

On March 26, using his favorite instrument of execution, the television camera, Castro ended the political career of Aníbal Escalante; he accused the latter of organizing not a revolutionary party but "a straitjacket," a "yoke," a "counterrevolutionary monstrosity." He charged him with wanting to make of the ORI "a machine for personal aims." He indicated that with this "machine" Escalante had tried to seize control of the administration. He denounced the fact that the ORI had been taken over by former members of the PSP and that numerous veterans of the Sierra were not allowed to command troops because "of their low political level." After dwelling on these and other accusations at length, he finished by saying that he would enlarge the National Directorate by "all the historical names" and recommended that the same be done on all levels of the organization.[58]

The ferocity of Castro's charges and the extent of his exasperation persuaded *Hoy* on March 28 to support all the accusations against its former managing editor, who had been the second figure of the PSP, and with utter abjection to go even further by affirming that "the conduct of Aníbal Escalante had its roots in the past, in his thirty years of party activities."[59]

On the other hand, as far as we know, not one Castroite leader raised his voice in public condemnation of Escalante or demanded sanctions against his former party comrades.[60] This was not the case in the lower echelons of the ORI. Castro was forced to prohibit the purging of nuclei except through the National Directorate, for in many localities meetings had already been called for that purpose.[61]

March ended without either the Soviets or the Chinese expressing

[57] As may be recalled, in 1959 the Secretariat of the PSP was formed by Roca, Escalante, and Luzardo. The last two, since his return from the Soviet Union in 1935 or 1936, had been Roca's main instruments in maintaining his personal control of Cuban communism.

[58] *Revolución*, March 27, 1962.

[59] *Hoy*, March 28, 1962.

[60] *Revolución*'s headlines on March 27 said: ¡Ni una pulgada atrás!" [Not One Inch Back!], and next day the editorial was entitled "Ni un paso atrás, dos pasos adelante" [Not One Step Back, Two Steps Forward]. The apparent intention was to diminish the importance of the event.

[61] *Hoy*, March 30, 1962.

an opinion on Castro's speech of the 26th. Thus relations between Cuba and the two great powers of the socialist bloc remained unchanged. That is, toward the first anniversary of Castro's declaration on April 16, 1961, his "socialism" had not been officially recognized. The commercial agreements for 1962 with both countries had not been signed; and, as we have tried to show, there were grave differences of opinion with the Soviet Union on such matters as general strategy and the extent of the protection that the Soviets should give to Cuba.

CHAPTER SEVEN

THE CRISIS OF OCTOBER 1962 AND CASTRO'S ENTRY INTO THE SOVIET BLOC

The Missile Agreement

On April 11, 1962 *Pravda* published an editorial on the Cuban revolution. Referring to Castro as "Comrade," it explained the difficulties in the organization of a Marxist-Leninist party in Cuba; the task consisted not in a mechanical merger of the Revolutionary Student Directorate, the July 26 Movement, and the PSP but in the establishment "of a monolithic Marxist-Leninist party theoretically and organizationally united." It approved the measures taken against Escalante, repeating Castro's accusation of "sectarianism" and adding to this the charge of "dogmatism," both vices habitually attributed by the Soviets to the Chinese. Although it recommended placing "the veterans of the revolution," that is, the former members of the PSP, in positions of responsibility, it also acknowledged the importance of bestowing "responsible political positions on the youthful leaders who had been hardened in the revolutionary struggle." Finally, it referred to the nature of the phase through which the revolution was going as "the construction of a new life" but added that the revolutionary movement "carried inscribed on its banners the slogan of the construction of socialism."[1]

Four days later the May 1 slogans of the Communist Party of the Soviet Union were published. Cuba was listed after the eleven socialist republics that, together with the Soviet Union, form the socialist bloc, but before Yugoslavia. It was referred to with the following expressions: "Fraternal greetings to the heroic people of Cuba, who have embarked on the path of building socialism"; and even though this was not the phrase used for the other countries — "fraternal greetings to the working people of . . . who are building

[1] "The Cuban Revolution's Forces Are Rallying," *Pravda*, April 11, 1962.

154

socialism"[2] — it is obvious that the Cubans had been promoted a step in the rigorous hierarchy that had been established by the Russians. A few days later, on the anniversary of Lenin's birth, Leonid F. Ilyichev, a member of the Presidium of the Communist Party of the Soviet Union, confirmed this description of Cuba by referring to it as a country "that has taken the path of the construction of socialism."[3]

This time the Soviets went beyond mere verbal acknowledgments. At the time the *Pravda* editorial was published on April 11, Soviet Vice-Minister of Foreign Trade Kuzmin had already arrived in Cuba. And on May 14 a definitive commercial treaty for 1962 was signed in Moscow — the treaty Cuba had been negotiating from the time of Dorticós' visit to the Soviet Union in September of the preceding year. As a result of this new treaty, according to the report of the Cuban Ministry of Foreign Trade, the commercial exchange between the two countries would rise from 540 million pesos in 1961 to 750 million in 1962; the report also listed the various products that would be exported by the Soviet Union.[4] Nothing was said about Cuban exports. However, it seems that either at this time or earlier the Soviets had promised to buy 3,200,000 tons of sugar, half a million more than in 1961, even though, owing to a poor sugar crop in Cuba, only 2,800,000 tons could be sent.[5]

An editorial in *Revolución* emphasized *Pravda*'s unconditional support of Castro's ouster of Escalante.[6] *Hoy,* now under the direction of Blas Roca (who had already condemned Escalante's conduct), took one more step along the path of absolute submission with the statement: "Of all the leaders of our revolution it is Fidel Castro who is most imbued with the revolutionary spirit of Lenin; he is the best and the most effective Marxist-Leninist of our country. . . ."[7]

2 *Ibid.*, April 15, 1962, quoted from *CDSP,* Vol. XIV, No. 15 (May 9, 1962), pp. 9–12, at p. 10.

3 *Hoy,* April 24, 1962.

4 The signing of the agreement was announced in *Revolución,* May 15, 1962, and the report of the Ministry of Foreign Trade was printed in *Hoy,* May 31, 1962.

5 According to Jacinto Torras, "Dos años de relaciones fraternales entre Cuba y la Unión Soviética" [Two Years of Fraternal Relations Between Cuba and the Soviet Union], *Cuba Socialista,* June 1962.

6 "Ratifica 'Pravda' la correcta posición marxista-leninista de Fidel y las ORI" [*Pravda* Approves the Correct Marxist-Leninist Position of Fidel and of the ORI], *Revolución,* April 12, 1962.

7 "Un Comentario: Lenin," *Hoy,* April 22, 1962.

The day after the *Pravda* editorial was published, Chinese Vice-Premier Ch'en Yi hastened to draw the sting out of its oblique attack on China by also approving the ouster of Escalante: "We give our complete support to the struggle of Prime Minister Fidel Castro to fortify revolutionary unity against sectarianism," adding that such a struggle "was very beneficial to the Cuban socialist revolution."[8] In the following days *Jen-min Jih-pao* and *Ta-kung Pao* devoted editorials to the Cuban revolution, saying that "it had entered on the path of socialism."[9] On April 25, three weeks before the signing of a Cuban-Soviet trade treaty, a trade agreement between China and Cuba was signed for 1962.[10] However, Chinese approval did not arouse the same echo in Cuba as had Soviet approval. Neither *Revolución* nor *Hoy* said a word about Ch'en Yi's statement or the editorials in the Chinese press.

Castro should have been satisfied. The ORI was being reorganized in accordance with a procedure invented by himself — unprecedented in the international Communist movement — by virtue of which the workers in every enterprise were to elect "model workers" from among whom, in turn, the future members of the party would be selected.[11] This procedure would prolong the actual formation of the ORI indefinitely. Blas Roca had acknowledged Castro as the leading Marxist-Leninist in the country, so that in the future ideology in Cuba would be whatever Castro wanted it to be. The Soviets and the Chinese were beginning to acknowledge his "socialism" officially; and both, especially the first, were rushing to assist him in pulling himself out of the economic morass into which he had waded through his spectacular ignorance of administration and economics and through his insatiable ambition, as a result of which he was willing to sacrifice everything to the prospect of heading the Latin American revolutionary movement. In spite of all this, however, Castro was apparently not satisfied.

---

8 NCNA, April 17, 1962 (SCMP 2724, April 25, 1962).

9 Editorials by *Jen-min Jih-pao* and *Ta-kung-pao*, April 18 and 19, 1962 (SCMP 2725, April 26, 1962).

10 *Revolución*, April 26, 1962. The newspaper limited itself to saying that trade between the two countries would be greater than in the preceding year.

11 To the best of my knowledge the new procedure was first put into practice at the end of May, at a meeting of the electric workers. (See *ibid.*, May 30, 1962.) That Castro was "its inspirer and guide" was said in the May 1962 issue of *Cuba Socialista*, where the method is explained in the section "Vida de la Organización Revolucionaria" [Life of the Revolutionary Organization].

The delegation of the ORI to the May 1 celebrations in Moscow consisted of Joaquín Ordoqui and Osmani Cienfuegos, two subordinate figures in the revolutionary leadership. The message sent by Castro on this occasion was addressed to the Soviet people and made no mention of either the government or Khrushchev. Among the leaders who headed the May 1 parade in Havana there was not one of the former leaders of the PSP. On May 5 Cuban Ambassador Chomón said goodbye to Brezhnev; his successor, Carlos Olivares, was appointed twelve days later but remained in Cuba. At the end of May Soviet Ambassador Kudryavtsev took leave of President Dorticós and returned to Russia. Thus both diplomatic posts were left without their respective occupants.[12]

That this sequence of events had some meaning is confirmed by the arrival almost coincidentally with the departure of Kudryavtsev of S. R. Rashidov, candidate member of the Presidium of the CPSU.[13] Nothing is known of the purpose or the results of this visit, but we do know that Rashidov's departure was followed by the arrival of Adam Rapacki, the Polish Minister of Foreign Affairs. If Castro had been hoping to become a party to the Warsaw Pact, and if the Russians did not wish or were unable to satisfy his hopes, then one of the persons best qualified to explain their objections was the Polish Foreign Minister. It is significant that in his lecture at the University of Havana Rapacki considered it appropriate to remind his listeners that "Cuba was not a signatory of the Warsaw Pact"; "the political affinities and sympathies that arose out of the socialist character of the Cuban revolution" had nothing to do with "the independent position of the revolutionary government of Cuba in international affairs"; and he pleaded for peaceful coexistence between the United States and Cuba.[14]

Whatever the conclusion to be drawn from both visits, one thing is certain: After they had taken place Castro did not modify his dissatisfaction; on the contrary, he made it more obvious. On the other hand *Hoy*, which ever since May had been insisting on the "necessity for unity, for collaboration, and for mutual aid between socialist countries," while fighting "national communism" and

12 It may be added that May 16, 1962, the anniversary of the founding of *Hoy*, was commemorated by nothing more than a short note on the last page of the issue for that day.

13 Rashidov came as chairman of a commission of "hydraulic technicians" (*Hoy*, May 30, 1962).

14 Rapacki's speech is in *Revolución*, June 14, 1962.

"leftism" and expatiating on "revisionism,"[15] suddenly, on June 16, discovered a new theme, "Trotskyism."

Let us see what this meant. On June 15, 1962, after Rashidov's and Rapacki's visits, Castro "rose up," that is, he once again took up his knapsack and his telescopic-sight rifle and set out for the Sierra Maestra. To emphasize the significance of this gesture he said to the journalists who accompanied him, "Gentlemen, I have once more raised the banner of rebellion."[16] He did not, of course, explain against whom this unexpected action was directed; but in view of the situation one may interpret this "rebellion" as a demonstration of his dissatisfaction with the conversations with the Soviet functionary and the Polish Foreign Minister. Another indication of tension may be seen in the *Hoy* articles just cited. On June 15 Castro started his tour of the Sierra; on June 16 *Hoy*, in the column "Aclaraciones" edited by Blas Roca, opened fire with a polemic against "Trotskyism." Apparently there was no question of Cuban disciples of Leon Trotsky. The polemic was motivated by an article published in a Uruguayan periodical. Roca, however, devoted at least eight successive columns to this remote manifestation of the "Trotskyite" heresy. The followers of the Soviet ex-Commissar were blamed for every kind of error and deviation but were especially castigated for having maintained that "our revolution will not go well" until it is permitted "to speak in every possible way against the Communist Party of the Soviet Union and the Soviet government, led by the great friend of Cuba and distinguished Leninist, Nikita S. Khrushchev."[17]

Suddenly the tensions and differences reflected in these gestures and articles vanished. On June 24 the series in *Hoy* against Trotskyism was broken off. The following day Raúl Castro recalled the "heroism" of the "old" Communists in preventing, for instance, a single Cuban soldier from being sent off to the "imperialist" war in Korea — a service that no one up to that point had even dreamed

15 In the "Aclaraciones" [Explanations] column, *Hoy*, May 10, 1962; "¿Qué es el extremismo?" [What is Extremism?], *ibid.*, May 12, 1962; and "Breve nota sobre el revisionismo y los revisionistas" [A Short Note on Revisionism and the Revisionists], *ibid.*, June 6, 1962. See also "Sobre el discurso de Kruschev" [On Khrushchev's Speech], *ibid.*, June 8, 1962.

16 The "diary" of this trip to the Sierra was published in *Revolución*, June 26, 27, 28, 29, and 30, 1962. Castro's statement was in the issue of June 28. The "diary" explains that the first day of the trip was June 15 and that it lasted eight days.

17 The series against Trotskyism in *Hoy*, June 16–24, 1962.

of ascribing to the PSP — stressing, however, that during the phase of the struggle against Batista it was "Comrade Fidel who had the great vision to conceive, plan, and implement the correct methods of struggle demanded in Cuba in order to come to power."[18] On June 26 Carlos Olivares finally left for Moscow to take up his post as ambassador. On June 27 Castro himself acknowledged that the "spirit" with which the errors introduced by Escalante in the creation of the ORI had been rectified had been "a genuinely revolutionary spirit, genuinely Marxist"; he made fun of those who "believed that the rectification of errors was the justification of other errors," attempting to "disguise their anti-Marxism as anti-sectarianism"; he also reaffirmed that when he spoke of political science he was referring to the "only true political science and the only true revolutionary science, which is Marxism."[19] Two days later, after bidding farewell to a group of Soviet technicians who were returning to their country, Castro found words of praise for "the Soviet people, led by the thousand-times glorious Communist Party of the Soviet Union . . . and by that great and dearly beloved friend of Cuba, Nikita Khrushchev," ending with a stentorian shout: "Long live the great friend of Cuba, Nikita Khrushchev!"[20]

Blas Roca, who had gone to Uruguay to represent the ORI at the Eighth Congress of the Uruguayan Communist Party, humbly acknowledged that the "old Marxist-Leninists, those who had fought in the PSP," were guilty of not having seen, as Fidel had, that guerrilla war was the correct means of struggle against the Batista tyranny, so that "as a party we made a late and feeble entry into the war." He confirmed that Fidel was not only the first secretary and the chief and the leader of the ORI but also "the most capable and the firmest Marxist-Leninist in Cuba."[21]

Finally, on July 3, it was announced that Raúl Castro, accompanied by a delegation of Cuban army officers, was in Moscow and had been received by Marshal Malinovsky, the Soviet minister of defense.[22]

18 Raúl Castro's speech in commemoration of the beginning of the Korean War (*Revolución*, June 26, 1962).
19 Fidel Castro's speech to the directors and staff of the Schools of Revolutionary Instruction (*ibid.*, June 30, 1962).
20 *Hoy*, July 1, 1962.
21 Roca's speech in *Cuba Socialista*, July 1962.
22 *Hoy* and *Revolución*, July 3, 1962.

All this obviously meant that the double crisis of Cuban-Soviet relations and of Castro's relations with the "old" Communists had been overcome. Some form of agreement must have been reached shortly before June 25, the day on which the atmosphere suddenly cleared. It is perhaps correct to assume that the decision to station missiles in Cuba formed part of the agreement, since Raúl's appearance in Moscow in the first days of July was obviously connected with this decision. It is unthinkable that the younger Castro could have made the decision on his own responsibility while in Moscow, and, indeed, Fidel Castro later, in a speech on April 19, 1963, stated that "conversations" on the subject were begun as early as June.[23]

Conversations on such an important matter must obviously have been conducted on a very high level. A high-ranking Soviet dignitary, Rashidov, was in Cuba in the early days of June. We may thus conclude that missiles were a subject of conversation between him and Castro, that the result was indecisive, and that some time later during Castro's "rebellion" word came through from Moscow that made the agreement and the subsequent clearing of the atmosphere possible.[24] It would appear that Blas Roca was already informed of the missile agreement when he made his speech to the congress of the Communist Party of Uruguay. There he said: "If the mercenaries return . . . we shall rout them. If they come with the OAS we shall rout them. If they come directly with Yankee marines" — *nota bene!* — "we are strong enough to hold them and gain enough time for the solidarity of the socialist camp headed by the U.S.S.R. to stop them once and for all. . . ."[25] This cautious *apparatchik* of more than thirty years would hardly have shown such assurance if he had been ignorant of the Soviet promise.

We may further surmise that the terms of the agreement included Soviet acceptance of Castro as the supreme representative of Marxism-Leninism in Cuba and the relegation of their own agents, the "old Communists," to a secondary role. On June 25 Raúl had

[23] See Castro's speech of April 19, 1963 in *Revolución,* April 20, 1963.

[24] The Soviet reply accepting Castro's terms and agreeing to place missiles in Cuba may have arrived on June 18. When *Hoy* on July 1 began to publish a daily column under the heading "Registro de violaciones del espacio aéreo y aguas jurisdiccionales" [A Register of the Violations of Air Space and of the Waters under Cuban Jurisdiction], the date taken as a starting point was June 18. Later, on a date that I have been unable to ascertain, the same column took as its point of departure July 1. The purpose of this column may well have been to justify the possession of the missiles by these "violations," even though it was impossible openly to admit possession.

[25] Roca's speech in *Cuba Socialista,* July 1962.

stressed that it was his brother Fidel, not the PSP, who had provided leadership in the struggle against Batista; and shortly afterward Blas Roca had demonstrated his acceptance of this by his self-criticism, renouncing all claims that the PSP had played an important role during the struggle, and thereby for all practical purposes renouncing also any claim to share the leadership of "Cuban socialism" with Castro.

Let us now compare this with the various, frequently contradictory accounts of how the missile decision came about that were later given by the two chief protagonists of the affair, Khrushchev and Castro. In his letter to Kennedy of October 27 and then in his report to the Supreme Soviet on December 12, Khrushchev attributed the installation of the missiles to a request from Cuba. He surely did this on the strength of a Soviet-Cuban agreement reached at the end of August and announced in a communiqué on September 2.[26] The communiqué stated that because of the "imperialist" threats against Cuba "the Government of the Cuban Republic addressed the Soviet Government with a request for help by delivering armaments and sending technical specialists for training Cuban servicemen," and that "the Soviet Government attentively considered this request . . . and agreement was reached on this question." This, however, cannot have been the original missile agreement, since at least conventional arms and specialists were already in Cuba at the time it was published.[27]

Castro gave his first version in a speech on January 2, 1963, denying that Cuba had ever made a request and stating that the introduction of "strategic arms" had been decided in a mutual agreement between the two governments.[28] In his interview with Claude Julien of *Le Monde* on March 22, 1963, he had revised his story: "Moscow offered them to us. . . . Such is the truth even if other explanations are provided elsewhere."[29] In spite of this statement, which sounds so definite, he seemed to return to the thesis of "common accord" in his speech of April 19, and on May 23, in the Moscow Lenin Stadium, he categorically stated: "In the middle of last year the governments of Cuba and of the U.S.S.R. decided

26 The communiqué was published in *The New York Times* on September 3, 1962.

27 The missiles too were either already in Cuba or on their way. According to U.S. sources the first missiles arrived on September 8.

28 *Revolución*, January 3, 1963.

29 The original version of the interview was published in *Le Monde*, March 22, 1963. I am using the version in *The Sunday Star* (Washington), April 7, 1963.

to adopt appropriate measures to halt the attack that was being plotted against our country."[30] Meanwhile Khrushchev had revised his own version by accepting Castro's thesis of "common accord," as can be seen in his speech to the Sixth Congress of the East German Communists. This version seems to have been accepted as definitive by the Soviets since it was repeated in the Soviet Communist Party letter of July 14, 1963 to the Chinese Communist Party.[31] Castro nevertheless preserved his flexibility. He told Herbert L. Matthews "flatly . . . that the idea of installing the nuclear weapons was his, not the Russians."[32] A few weeks later he said to Jean Daniel that the proposal, "which surprised us at first and gave us great pause," came from the Soviets.[33] Finally, when C. L. Sulzberger confronted him with the two contradictory versions, "Castro never did give a precise answer but said: 'I told both Daniel and Matthews that Cuba took the responsibility for the presence of missiles here . . . both Russia and Cuba participated.' "[34]

Castro has been just as tortuous in explaining his motives in this respect as in others. In his January 1963 speech he said that the missiles had been brought to Cuba in order to fulfill "two obligations: one to the fatherland . . . and the other . . . an international proletarian duty." In his conversation with Julien he had already forgotten the first obligation and referred only to the need to "strengthen the socialist camp on a world scale," adding that for him Khrushchev's intentions were "a mystery." I do not wish to bore the reader by reproducing all the remaining versions put out by Castro. I only mention what he told Sulzberger: "We aspired to get an effective guarantee to ward off the possibility of a U.S. attack on Cuba . . . and Russia had its own position."

My own belief is that from the moment Khrushchev first mentioned the missiles in July 1960 Castro saw in them ideal instru-

[30] *Revolución*, May 24, 1963. Contrary to his custom Castro read this speech.

[31] "The Soviet government and the government of Cuba reached agreement on the delivery of missiles to Cuba. . . ." See "Open Letter from the CPSU Central Committee to Party Organizations and All Communists of the Soviet Union, July 14, 1963," *Pravda*, July 14, 1963; reprinted in full in William E. Griffith, *The Sino-Soviet Rift* (Cambridge, Mass.: The M.I.T. Press, 1964), pp. 289–325, quotation at p. 302.

[32] Herbert L. Matthews, *Return to Cuba*, special issue of *Hispanic-American Report* (Stanford, Calif.: Stanford University, Institute of Hispanic-American and Luzo-Brazilian Studies, n.d.), p. 16.

[33] See Jean Daniel, "Unofficial Envoy," *The New Republic*, December 14, 1963, and "Further Clarification," *ibid.*, December 21, 1963.

[34] C. L. Sulzberger interview with Castro in *The New York Times*, November 8, 1964.

ments for the realization of his own plans: to secure Soviet protection and thus enable him to obtain the leadership of the Latin American "anti-imperialist" movement, while at the same time guaranteeing his Cuban base. By mid-1962 Cuba had been suspended from the OAS; the majority of Latin American countries had broken diplomatic relations with Castro; his internal situation was deteriorating; and the prospects for a revolutionary movement on the continent were highly doubtful. At such a time it is futile to conjecture whether defensive considerations — the defense of the Cuban base — or offensive ones — to step up revolutionary activities on the continent — were decisive for him. But I do feel justified in saying that Castro was desperately anxious to get the missiles and that mankind can breathe a little easier because they are no longer within his reach.

As for Khrushchev, he has always maintained that his sole aim was to defend "little Cuba" from the "imperialist monster."[35] But it is obvious that his real motives had little or nothing to do with this aim, which he could have achieved much more effectively by associating Cuba with the Warsaw Pact or by signing a defense treaty similar to the June 1964 treaty with East Germany (which specified that any armed attack against one of the contracting parties would oblige the other to give immediate assistance). He must have had other reasons. In the first place, Cuba was the only tangible gain to which he could point in the field of foreign policy. Thus when Castro, as we believe, confronted him with the alternatives, the treaty or the missiles, Khrushchev must have felt obligated to give him something and chose the missiles as the more advantageous alternative. In the second place, the Chinese were hammering out their criticism against the policy of peaceful coexistence, while Khrushchev's repeated missile threats had finally ceased to make any impression on the Western powers. By placing nuclear arms ninety miles from the coast of the United States he would be making these threats more plausible. He, peaceful Khrushchev, would thus demonstrate audacity and resolution while the warlike Mao limited himself to the declaration that the United States was only a "paper tiger." Finally, James Reston — who saw President Kennedy at the American Embassy in Vienna in 1961 after the President's encounter with Khrushchev — has described Kennedy's irritation and annoyance at the fact that owing to the Bay of Pigs

[35] For instance, in his report to the Supreme Soviet on December 12 (Hoy, December 13 and 14, 1962).

fiasco "Khrushchev decided he was dealing with an inexperienced young leader who could be intimidated and blackmailed." Reston continues: "The Communist decision to put offensive missiles into Cuba was the final gamble of this assumption."[36] We may thus assume that under the pressure of Castro's rebelliousness and Chinese criticisms, and at the same time believing that he had correctly gauged the caliber of his chief adversary, Khrushchev decided to place his nuclear arms in Cuba on the assumption that a demoralized United States, faced with a *fait accompli*, would allow him to chalk up the victories he needed to preserve his own prominence in the Soviet Union and in the international Communist movement.

Today we know he made a mistake. Before relating the events that made this clear to him, we must deal with the internal situation in Cuba and the way in which it was affected by the missile agreement.

The Internal Situation

By the summer of 1962 Cuba was in a serious economic crisis. The trade agreements with the Soviet Union and China prevented a complete breakdown but failed to bring about any visible improvement. Consequently, popular discontent increased. Guanajay in Pinar del Río province, El Cano in Havana province, and various localities of Matanzas province, especially Cárdenas, were scenes of disturbances. The President of the republic personally had to go to Cárdenas, guarded by tanks, to get the situation under control.[37]

---

[36] James Reston, "What Was Killed Was Not Only the President," *The New York Times*, November 15, 1964.

[37] *Revolución*, June 18, 1962, gives an account of the Dorticós speech in Cárdenas. For the rumors of disturbances in Guanajay, which were answered by "a meeting to reaffirm loyalty to the revolution," and for a similar meeting in Matanzas province with the same purpose, see *Hoy*, July 10, 1962. An idea of the seriousness of the supply situation is given in the "Aclaraciones" column in *ibid.*, June 8, 1962, devoted to a reply to a citizen who had proposed that the works of art in the National Museum be sold in order to buy cows. The importance of popular dissatisfaction can be seen in the headings of the editorials for these months. For instance: *Hoy*, on June 15, "La revolución tiene que estar a la ofensiva" [The Revolution Must Be on the Offensive], on June 27, "¡ A la ofensiva obreros y campesinos!" [Workers and Peasants to the Offensive!], and on June 28, "Los Comités de Defensa en su Puesto" [Defense Committees at Their Posts]; and *Revolución*, on July 14, "Golpear al enemigo, conocer al enemigo" [Strike the Enemy, Know the Enemy], and on July 18, "Bienvenida la lucha

The discontent spread to the militia, which was still an authentic armed force of the people. As a result, it was purged. Those who were most trustworthy and capable were incorporated into the Army; many resigned; the others were reorganized, renamed "People's Defense," and divided into two branches: the Active People's Defense, of those below forty, which was a sort of military reserve force, and the Passive People's Defense, of those who were more than forty years old and were used to guard factories and other buildings.[38] Thus began a process by which, within the next year and a half, the Castro regime acquired a growing military profile.

Before the missile agreement the revolutionary leadership appears to have been uncertain what road to take to stop the decline in agricultural production. There were those who proposed a temporary retreat in the manner of the New Economic Policy (NEP) inaugurated by Lenin in Russia in 1921. *Hoy* favored such a policy.[39] The Soviets evidently also took this line: Khrushchev in his farewell speech to the Cuban scholarship students in the Soviet Union explained to them at length what the NEP had been.[40] Castro's own position is difficult to determine. In his speech to the National Association of Small Farmers (Asociación Nacional de Agricultores Pequeños — ANAP) on May 17 he promised "absolute respect for the liberty, freedom of decision, and desires of the peasants"; but at the same time he said that he was turning over in his mind the idea of turning the sugarcane cooperatives — "a phase that is intermediate between what in the Soviet Union has become the rural artel and the state farm" (in the words of Carlos Rafael Rodríguez) into state farms — "equivalent to the sovkhozes"[41] — undoubtedly a radicalization of policy.[42] On the same day,

---

que nos hace mas fuertes" [Welcome to the Struggle That Will Make Us Still Stronger].

38 See "Información gráfica sobre batallones de las Milicias Nacionales que entran a formar parte del Ejército" [A Graphic Account of the Battalions of the National Militias That Form Part of the Army] *Bohemia,* June 1, 1962. The organization of the People's Defense is described in *Hoy,* November 4, 1962.

39 See, for instance, "La gran alianza en bien de los obreros y campesinos" [The Great Alliance of the Workers and Peasants] *ibid.,* June 20, 1962, and "Reparar arbitrariedades es parte de la ofensiva contra la contra-revolución" [The Restriction of Arbitrariness Is Part of the Offensive Against the Counter-revolution], *ibid.,* June 24, 1962.

40 Khrushchev's speech in *La Tarde,* June 4, 1962.

41 An article, "Cuba hacia 1962" [Cuba until 1962], in *Verde Olivo,* January 28, 1962, in which Carlos Rafael uses the expressions quoted in the text to define the cooperatives and the state farms.

42 *Hoy,* May 18, 1962.

Carlos Rafael Rodríguez expressly rejected any idea of a Cuban NEP.[43] However, the return of fifty-five estates in Matanzas to their owners and *Hoy*'s enthusiastic approval of this measure show that in mid-June no definite decision had as yet been reached.[44]

The missile agreement ended all vacillations. Now that the Soviet Union had acknowledged that Cuba was entering on the path of the "construction of socialism" and was demonstrating its good faith by promising to send missiles, Castro determined to sail full speed ahead toward "socialism."

On August 1 that great achievement of the socialist countries, the "labor book," was introduced in Cuba. This is a document containing the worker's employment record without which, once the system is organized, he cannot obtain work. In the middle of the same month the sugarcane cooperatives were transformed into state farms, or sovkhozes, as Carlos Rafael Rodríguez had put it.[45]

As late as the beginning of 1962 Carlos Rafael Rodríguez had explained to the Soviets how the sugarcane cooperatives, which had been colonies devoted to the production of sugarcane under "capitalism," were "formed by one-time farm workers with a high degree of political conscience and with splendid traditions of struggle."[46] But only a few months later it was admitted that "the sugarcane cooperatives had produced less cane in 1962 than in 1961 and still less than had been taken from the same land in 1960."[47] Or, which is the same thing, that from its very inception the whole thing had been no more than a vulgar swindle.

Lastly, the official entry into the phase of the "construction of socialism" was marked by the initial attempts to establish "work norms," a minimum production schedule for each worker in a fixed unit of time. At the end of August the Ministry of Labor enacted laws prohibiting raises in wages, authorizing the transfer of workers

[43] In an interview on the anniversary of the agrarian reform law, *La Tarde*, May 17, 1962.

[44] "Reparar arbitrariedades," *op. cit.*

[45] In his speech to the sixth meeting of representatives of the Schools of Revolutionary Instruction, Castro had explained how the idea for introducing the concept of cooperatives into the agrarian reform law — directed and administered by the INRA in accordance with Article 43 — had come to him "in the airplane" on his way to the Sierra to sign the law. See *Revolución*, December 22, 1961.

[46] In an article in *Verde Olivo*, January 28, 1962, reprinted from the Soviet press.

[47] "Las nuevas granjas cañeras y la producción de azúcar" [The New Sugarcane Farms and the Production of Sugar], *Hoy*, September 21, 1962.

from one production center to another without their consent, and setting fines for absences or delays in coming to work. At the beginning of October the Law of Socialist Emulation was passed.

It is easy to see that all this legislation to restore working habits and productivity through coercion was bound to reduce mass support for the regime even more. But for several reasons the regime was not shaken: First, it went easy on strict compliance with the laws and disregarded infractions of their most repressive aspects, which, of course, also had the negative effect of maintaining absenteeism, lack of discipline in work, and low productivity. Second, the wasteful policy was maintained of paying wages and salaries with no corresponding service or with insufficient or unnecessary services. (A particularly telling example of this is the case of the "scholarship students," 80,000 young people lodged in the best houses, fed and clothed by the state, who continue to prepare for careers, for instance, in diplomatic law.)[48] Finally, the missile agreement, a new triumph for Castro, convinced the Castroites that he would continue to maintain the upper hand over the "old" Communists of the former PSP and made them rally behind him. Thus old fighters like Faustino Pérez, Marcelo Fernández, and Efigenio Ameijeiras, who had disappeared from view in preceding years, now reappeared in government posts. To this may be added the fact that neither Washington nor the majority of the groups of Cuban exiles had the slightest understanding of what was going on in Cuba and were thus unable to exploit the weaknesses and inner conflicts of Castroism. It was for all the reasons mentioned that a regime sure of itself and full of confidence moved toward the confrontation of October.

The Confrontation

At the end of July and the beginning of August substantial quantities of arms and Soviet troops began arriving in Cuba. On August 29, U.S. reconnaissance plans discovered ground-to-air mis-

---

[48] "Do you know how many have been trying to enter the diplomatic service at the University of Havana? Three thousand students! And do you know how many wanted to study economics? Not even one hundred!" (Castro's speech, in *ibid.,* July 2, 1963.) In his speeches on September 19 and 28 and October 21, 25, and 31, 1964, Castro launched a campaign against "bureaucratism," that is, against the excess number of employees in the administration, which he himself had been promoting until then. On October 31, 1964 it was still impossible to determine how many employees there were in public administration.

sile bases in Cuba. On September 4, Washington accepted the "defensive" fortification of Cuba — rejecting the invasion that had been suggested by more impatient circles — and laid down the conditions that would raise "the gravest issues": an organized combat force in Cuba from any Soviet bloc country, Soviet military bases in Cuba, violation of the 1934 treaty relating to Guantánamo, the presence of offensive ground-to-ground missiles or "other significant offensive capacity either in Cuban hands or under Soviet direction or guidance."[49] Three days later the President requested authorization from Congress to call up 150,000 reservists. On September 8, according to Secretary McNamara,[50] the first offensive missiles, as described in Washington, arrived in Cuba. On September 11, the Soviet government replied to the American statement distinguishing between defensive and offensive capability by stating that the arms and "specialists" sent to Cuba would serve "exclusively defensive purposes"; but at the same time it declared that "there is no need for the Soviet Union to set up in any other country (Cuba for instance) the weapons it has for repelling aggression" and warned that "one cannot now attack Cuba and expect that the aggressor will be free from punishment. . . . If this attack is made, this will be the beginning of the unleashing of war."[51] At that time and, indeed until October 14, when, as we know, the first photographs of the launching pads were obtained, Washington was not convinced of the existence of offensive missiles in Cuba even though an attentive reading of the speeches of the Castro brothers would have helped to confirm the suspicions already held by some, among them, the director of the CIA. On September 12, Raúl, for instance, had shouted: "If they shoot, it will be the end of imperialism!" A few days later Fidel warned that "if the imperialists underestimate the solidarity of the Soviet Union, if they make a mistake — and let us hope they do not — if they do not believe, if they do not know, we, for our part, do know just how far that support will go!"[52]

[49] Kennedy's statement on Cuba, *The New York Times*, September 5, 1962.

[50] For example, Secretary McNamara has testified that "available evidence" indicated that the first landing of mobile MRBM's occurred on that date; Roberta Wohstetter, "Cuba and Pearl Harbor: Hindsight and Foresight," *Foreign Affairs*, Vol. 43, No. 4 (July 1965), p. 696. See also Arnold L. Horelick (Memorandum RM-3779-PP of the RAND Corporation), and Roger Hilsman, "The Cuban Crisis," *Look*, August 25, 1964.

[51] The statement of the Soviet government in *The New York Times*, September 12, 1962, and in the Cuban press of the same day. The Chinese government also offered its support in a statement signed by the Minister of Foreign Affairs (*Hoy*, September 20, 1962).

[52] Raúl Castro's speech at the graduation of the Matanzas officers (*Revolución*,

On October 22 President Kennedy initiated the confrontation: he denounced the presence of ballistic missiles on Cuban territory, called upon Khrushchev to remove this threat to world peace under the inspection of the United Nations, ordered a blockade of all shipments of offensive military equipment to Cuba, and warned that any nuclear missile launched from Cuba would be countered by one directed at the Soviet Union. The following day the Soviet government rejected the American President's demands and declared that his insistence on the withdrawal of the military equipment "necessary" for Cuba's "defense" constituted a demand that "of course no state that respects its independence can satisfy." However, instead of making the customary threats, the Soviet government limited itself to announcing that Moscow had instructed its representative in the U.N. Security Council to accuse the United States of endangering peace.

Castro, who had put his country on a war footing at 5:40 in the afternoon of October 22, that is, before President Kennedy made his speech, also responded during the night of October 23. He insisted on Cuba's right to possess all the arms it thought necessary and rejected any attempt at supervision or inspection. He demonstrated his determination in the following words: "It calms us to know that the aggressors will be exterminated. It calms us to know this." Even though he was not especially effusive about the attitude of the Soviets, he did not show any lack of confidence, describing it as "serene . . . exemplary," a "genuine lesson to imperialism, firm, serene, laden with arguments, with correct thinking."[53]

A *Pravda* editorial of October 24 revealed that the Soviet leaders did not contemplate with the same "calmness" the grim fate that would also be that of their own people in the event of a nuclear war. *Pravda* clung almost desperately to the hope of the United Nations. "In the situation that has arisen," it said, "a special responsibility falls on the U.N. . . . The question is whether it will show itself capable of fulfilling the mission to which it has been called . . . or whether there will be reserved for it the fate that befell the League of Nations. . . . There is no third solution."[54]

On that same date U Thant initiated his mediation. On October 26 Khrushchev gave orders for the Soviet ships on their way to

September 13, 1962), and Fidel's on the second anniversary of the CDR (*Bohemia*, October 5, 1962).

[53] *Revolución*, October 24, 1962.

[54] "Foil the Criminal Schemes of the Enemies of Peace," *Pravda*, October 24, 1962, quoted from *CDSP*, Vol. XIV No. 43 (November 21, 1962), pp. 4–5.

Cuba to turn back, and U Thant addressed a letter to Castro requesting suspension of the work on the launching pads, which, as aerial observation showed, had been continuing. On this same day at 1:30 P.M. John Scali, an American Broadcasting Company correspondent in Washington, received a telephone call from "a senior Soviet official" urgently requesting an immediate meeting. Shortly afterward he heard from the official's own lips the Soviet proposal for the solution of the crisis: withdrawal of the missiles under U.N. inspection, a Soviet promise not to reintroduce them, and a U.S. promise not to invade Cuba.

At 7:30 P.M. Scali had another interview with the Soviet official to tell him that the U.S. government saw "real possibilities" in this offer;[55] at the same hour Kennedy received a telegraphed letter from Khrushchev, the text of which we do not know but which according to American sources "indicated a willingness to negotiate."[56] Everything seemed to be on the road to a solution.

On October 27, however, the scene changed. That day Castro rejected U Thant's request, insisting again on Cuba's right to possess all the arms it thought necessary; he warned that any combat plane that invaded Cuban air space would be met with "our defensive fire."[57] Following this warning a U-2 airplane was shot down and others were fired upon. That the Cubans and not the Soviets were responsible for the shooting down of the U-2 was later publicly admitted by Castro in his speech of May 1, 1964.[58] And at 10:17 on the morning of October 27 a new letter from Khrushchev came in by broadcast. It set the withdrawal of American missiles from Turkey as the condition for the withdrawal of Soviet missiles from Cuba.

Why did Khrushchev thus go back on the much milder proposal that had been communicated to Scali? Scali's Soviet contact later explained this change of position by saying that his communication reporting the favorable reaction of the American government had arrived in Moscow only after Khrushchev's second, stiffer, letter had already been sent off. Henry Pachter, in his book *Collision Course*,[59] supposes that the stiffer letter, though received later, had

[55] The entire Scali episode is related in Hilsman, *op. cit.*

[56] *Ibid.*

[57] On October 29 *Revolución* published all the documents, beginning with U Thant's appeal on October 24 and including Fidel Castro's letter of October 27 to U Thant and the order of the same date concerning the airplanes.

[58] *Hoy*, May 2, 1964.

[59] Henry M. Pachter, *Collision Course: The Cuban Missile Crisis and Coexistence* (New York, and London: Praeger, 1963), p. 68.

been written earlier than that of October 26 which was more in line with the proposal to Scali.

To me, a more logical explanation would seem to be that late on October 26 Khrushchev communicated to Castro his willingness to negotiate on the basis of the proposals to Scali, that Castro's reaction was violently negative, as is reflected in his refusal to accept U Thant's request and in his order to shoot down American planes, and that this caused Khrushchev to change his mind and adopt a stiffer attitude.[60]

Whatever the true reason for Khrushchev's change of attitude in his second letter, President Kennedy decided to disregard it and answer the first in the affirmative. On October 28 at 9:00 A.M., Radio Moscow broadcast a third letter by Khrushchev in which it was made known that the Soviet government had given orders for the missiles placed in Cuba to be dismantled, packed up, and sent back to their place of origin. This ended the first confrontation of the atomic age.

Castro, Khrushchev, and Mao

The same day that Khrushchev sent his capitulation to President Kennedy, Castro drew up his five conditions for ending the crisis: The United States must end the blockade and all measures of economic pressure, cease all subversive activities in Cuba, stop the "piratical" attacks by exile groups, terminate the overflights, and withdraw from the Guantánamo naval base.[61]

Until October 27 *Hoy* and *Revolución* had continued to praise the "serenity" of the Soviet Union. On October 28, a Sunday, the former organ of the July 26 Movement did not come out but *Hoy*, in the same issue that made public Castro's order to fire upon airplanes violating Cuban air space, hailed "the sensible, realistic, and fairminded acts and proposals" of "Comrade Khrushchev."[62] On October 29 *Hoy* did not come out, so it fell to *Revolución* to tell the Cuban people of the Soviet decision to withdraw the "equipment necessary for its defense" — the demand for which the Soviets

[60] In May 1966, referring to the October crisis, Raúl Castro said: "Our Commander-in-Chief warned that the flights over Cuba must stop, and when different persons from different places were asking us not to obstruct the negotiations, we gave the order to fire against every airplane. And they disappeared from our skies." (Speech of May 23, 1966 in *Verde Olivo*, May 28, 1966.)

[61] *Revolución*, October 29, 1962.

[62] "Un Commentario: Camilo está con nosostros" [Camilo Is with Us], *Hoy*, October 28, 1962.

five days before had declared as one that "of course no state that respects its independence can satisfy."

It is obvious that, properly speaking, the five conditions were not a part of the actual confrontation. The cause of the crisis had been the placing of nuclear weapons in Cuba by the Soviets. On October 28 Khrushchev not only sent his letter of capitulation to Kennedy but asked the United Nations to send a team to Cuba to verify the dismantling. U Thant had to remind him that before this "the most important thing was to obtain the prior consent of the Cuban government."[63] Castro never accepted inspection. But the withdrawal itself was a foregone conclusion, and all he could do with his five conditions was to create difficulties for Khrushchev. It was now up to Khrushchev to calm Castro with concessions.

In this new round of difficulties with the Soviets, Castro could count on the sympathy of the Chinese. On October 25 the Chinese had supported the Soviet declaration of the day before, and *Ta-kung Pao,* after repeating that "imperialism" was no more than a "paper tiger," recommended that "to deal with U.S. imperialism the most important thing is to wage a resolute and blow-for-blow struggle against it."[64] When Khrushchev clearly yielded on October 28, the Chinese remained silent for two days; but on October 31 an editorial in *Jen-min Jih-pao,* entitled "The Cry of the People Is: Defend the Cuban Revolution!" (which was reprinted in *Revolución* the following day), reiterated Castro's five conditions, declaring that they were "completely justified and were absolutely necessary."[65]

By contrast, that same day *Pravda* said only that Castro's demands were "finding wide support among peace-loving forces," and it was not until November 1 that *Izvestiya* stated that the Soviet Union, "together with peace-loving countries, heartily supports the recent announcement of Premier Fidel Castro."[66]

While these divergences between the Soviets and the Chinese were manifesting themselves, a rift appeared between *Revolución* and *Hoy.* On October 30 and 31 *Hoy* ignored the five conditions,

[63] According to the conversation between U Thant and the Cuban government, the text of which was read by Castro at his press appearance of November 1, 1962 (*Revolución,* November 2, 1962).

[64] Statement and editorial by *Ta-kung Pao* in SCMP 2849, October 30, 1962.

[65] *Revolución,* November 1, 1962.

[66] V. Borovsky, "Ensure the Security of Cuba," *Pravda,* October 31, 1962, and N. Polyanov, "Not a Test of Strength but Negotiations," *Izvestiya,* November 1, 1962 (both in *CDSP,* Vol. XIV, No. 43 [November 21, 1962], pp. 14–15).

and it was only after the *Izvestiya* article of November 1 and the announcement of Mikoyan's departure for Cuba on the same day that its support for Castro's five points, "clamored for by the whole nation," was announced.[67]

The existence of a rift was confirmed by the different reactions of the two newspapers to Castro's television appearance on November 1 when he reported on the latest developments. In this appearance Castro stressed his confidence "in the principled policy of the Soviet Union," in its "principled leadership," "that is, in the government and in the ruling party of the Soviet Union," and he declared: "We are Marxist-Leninists; there will be no breach between the Soviet Union and Cuba!" But he also referred to a "certain displeasure" that had manifested itself due to "the misunderstandings and differences" with the Soviets and added, "all the differences will be discussed on the governmental and on the party level."[68]

These words merited an editorial in *Revolución* signed by Carlos Franqui, the editor-in-chief, entitled "The Speech of the Commander of the Victory." In a typically "Fidelista" enthusiastic tone this editorial ascribed to Cuba "the sling of David, the fury of Robespierre, the wisdom of Marx, the audacity of Lenin, the dream of Martí, and Fidel's invincible beard."[69] The *Hoy* editorial, entitled "Peace with Dignity," was probably written by Carlos Rafael Rodríguez[70] (who now initiated his return to the side of his old PSP comrades, which culminated in March during the trial of Marcos Rodríguez) and constituted an intelligent attempt to further Cuban-Soviet reconciliation. Invoking the danger of division in the revolutionary ranks, alluding to the "intrigue-mongers" who were still working in the country in the service of Washington (a snide attack on the rival newspaper), and insisting on the gratitude due the Soviet Union, the ex-editor of *Hoy* recommended "serenity and reason," expressing his confidence that in the discussions "on the governmental and on the Party level" all divergences

---

[67] The *Hoy* editorial of October 31 was entitled "Gloria a los héroes del trabajo," [Glory to the Heroes of Labor], dedicated at the time to the "model workers." However, in the same number Blas Roca, speaking in Berlin, gave his support to the five points.

[68] *Revolución*, November 2, 1962.

[69] *Ibid.*, November 3, 1962.

[70] Blas Roca was not in Cuba when the crisis broke out, as we know by his letter from Bulgaria (*Hoy*, November 22, 1962). He said he had been in Germany when the "crisis occurred," and he mentioned "mass meetings, interviews," as reasons for not having opened his mouth.

would disappear, and Cuban-Soviet friendship would be restored firmer than ever before.[71]

On November 2 Mikoyan arrived, very interested to know whether the Cubans were aware of his statements in New York in support of Castro's five conditions.[72] Mikoyan stayed in Cuba until November 26. Castro seems to have found an adversary worthy of his mettle in the Soviet functionary. The missiles were removed from Cuba without any difficulties. Although Castro on November 15 addressed himself to the United Nations to protest the U-2 flights, which were still going on, and repeated his threats of October 27, he had to agree four days later to the withdrawal of the IL-28 bombers stationed in Cuba, which had also been classified as offensive weapons.

On November 22 he appears to have tried a new maneuver: Havana issued an energetic denial of "the speculations of the American agencies concerning the supposed signature of a new treaty of economic aid between the Soviet Union and Cuba," asserting that "during the development of the current crisis Cuba has not signed any treaty with the government of the U.S.S.R."[73] If this was a hint to Mikoyan, he did not take it up; he left Havana offering only the statement that "in this noble struggle" Cuba had "the complete support of the Soviet Union."[74] But Castro was not the man to be satisfied by mere words. This was shown by the joint declaration of the revolutionary government and the ORI of November 26. It stated that Cuba did not believe "in simple promises of nonaggression" but required fulfillment of the five conditions, and reserved "the right to buy arms of any type whatever for its own defense." The "imperialists" ought not to confuse a "principled position with weakness in the face of their aggression." In contradiction to the assurances of the Soviet government that its behavior had served to

---

71 "Un Commentario: Paz con dignidad" [Peace with Dignity], *Hoy*, November 3, 1962. In reading this editorial it is difficult to establish whether *Hoy* supported the five conditions at this time. Carlos Rafael Rodríguez mentions them, calling them "just" and "reasonable," but immediately afterward he says that Castro, when presenting them to U Thant, had said: "We shall never put obstacles in the path of a genuine solution." Later, again repeating Castro's words, he demanded "deeds and not words," thus revealing the difficult equilibrium that the whole article is at pains to maintain—to further the conciliation with the Soviets without falling afoul of Castro.

72 In Mikoyan's interview published in *Hoy*, November 3, 1962.

73 *Ibid.*, November 22, 1962.

74 Mikoyan's letter to the President and the Prime Minister on leaving Cuba (*ibid.*, November 27, 1962).

maintain peace, the Cuban declaration repeated: "An armed conflict has been avoided, but peace has not been achieved."[75]

In spite of all these threats and resounding statements, Castro seems to have resigned himself to remaining without strategic weapons. Because the year was about to end, the imbalance of trade between Cuba and the Soviet Union had grown in favor of the Soviets, and the thorny question of a trade agreement for the following year was on the agenda, he concentrated on forcing the Soviets to make up for his lack of weapons by new economic concessions. At the beginning of December a mission headed by Carlos Rafael Rodríguez left for Moscow. On December 20 a communiqué was published. The two parties had only reached an agreement to go on talking.[76] Even though on his return Rodríguez declared that the results could not be more satisfactory, it is obvious that Cuba was faced with the same situation as at the end of 1961 (and a solution to that problem had been found only in May of the following year).

However, Castro now had at his disposal a new factor that he could not count on in 1961 — the deepening Sino-Soviet schism. After the *Jen-min Jih-pao* editorial of October 31, Mao and his followers rarely let a day go by without reaffirming their solidarity with Cuba.[77] On November 15 the same periodical published the first basic document in the new polemic phase of the Sino-Soviet rift: "Carrying Forward the Revolutionary Spirit of the Moscow Declaration and the Moscow Statement." On November 29, after the declaration of the Cuban government and the ORI, *Jen-min Jih-pao,* "with matchless admiration," sent the "loftiest revolutionary greetings" of the Chinese people "to the heroic Cuban people and to its great leader Comrade Castro." The following day the Chinese government issued a formal declaration in support of the Cuban statements. On December 15 the second basic document of

75 The statement is in *Revolución,* November 26, 1962. See also Carlos Franqui, "La posición de Cuba" [The Position of Cuba], an editorial on the same date.

76 *Hoy* and *Revolución,* December 20, 1962.

77 See, for instance, the *Hung Ch'i* editorial, November 1, 1962, in *Selections from China Mainland Magazines* (SCMM) 341, "The Heroic Cuban People Will Surely Win," November 26, 1962; the mass meetings and demonstrations of November 2 and 3 in support of the five points in SCMP 2855, November 7, 1962; the statements of Chou En-lai on November 5, supporting the same five points, in *ibid.;* the editorial in *Jen-min Jih-pao,* November 5, 1962, "The Fearless Cuban People Are the Most Powerful Strategic Weapon" (SCMP 2856, November 8, 1962).

the new polemic phase appeared: "Proletarians of All Countries Unite to Struggle Against the Common Enemy." It was reprinted in the Havana press.[78] On the same day Chou Yang, deputy director of the propaganda department of the Central Committee of the Chinese Communist Party, who headed the Chinese delegation attending the First National Cultural Congress in Havana, said to the audience: "The Cuban people deserves the name of courageous people, and Comrade Fidel Castro deserves to be called a firm revolutionary champion of Marxism-Leninism."[79]

Thus Chinese admiration for Cuba kept growing as the Sino-Soviet rift deepened. China, however, did not have the resources necessary to solve Cuba's serious economic problems — as was shown when the Cuban trade mission headed by Faustino Pérez returned from Peking in December empty handed.[80] If Castro was to exploit the Sino-Soviet rift he would have to move with great caution.

It was in his speech on the fourth anniversary of his accession to power that Castro began to feel his way into the near-impenetrable thickets of the Sino-Soviet dispute with the prudence necessitated by the circumstances. Contradicting Khrushchev's speech to the Supreme Soviet, Castro declared that it was not because of a request from Cuba but because of a common agreement that the missiles were installed in Cuba, and that it was not merely a question of defending "little Cuba" but also an "international proletarian duty." After repeating his desire to remain within the "great socialist family . . . which is our camp, which is and always will be our family!" Castro alluded to "the serious problems that preoccupy us all in the struggle against the common enemy." He ended by saying that the task of the Cubans was to eliminate everything that divided the camp to which they all belonged and to struggle

78 The editorial, "Long Live the Cuban Revolution," *Jen-min Jih-pao,* November 29, 1962 (SCMP 2871, December 3, 1962); statement of the Chinese government in *Hoy,* November 30, 1962; the editorial of December 15 was reprinted, as far as I know, in *Hoy,* on December 16, 1962 and in *Bohemia,* on December 23, 1962.

79 NCNA, December 16, 1962 (SCMP 2884, December 20, 1962).

80 For the arrival of the Cuban trade mission in Peking see NCNA, December 12, 1962 (SCMP 2881, December 17, 1962). Its failure to obtain any results is proven by the fact that the 1963 treaty was signed on February 22, 1963. The Chinese granted long-term credits with no interest in return for the balance in 1962 being in their favor, as well as what was expected in 1963 (*Hoy,* February 26, 1963).

for its unity, but always in accordance with the principles — "Unity in accordance with the principles is our line!"[81]

That these brief and somewhat enigmatic allusions to the Sino-Soviet rift were understood by the Soviets and the Chinese is demonstrated by the fact that the Soviets omitted any reference to them, whereas the Chinese reproduced the entire speech verbatim.[82]

Since the Soviets maintained their silence, Castro became more explicit. Thirteen days later, on January 15, 1963, at the Inter-American Women's Congress, he assailed "experts in figures," when "what was needed was experts in changing the situation." He attacked "tired-out theoreticians" who claimed that "Cuba had had a peaceful transition," when these "false interpretations of history did not square with the situation of the immense majority of the Latin American countries." He railed against the revolutionary organizations of Latin America — obviously the Communist parties — that had given the Second Declaration of Havana the "honors of the trash can," and in a very clear reference to the Soviet Communists he expressed his hope "that in 40 years we shall not have to meet again, our grandchildren and yours, to deal with the same problems." Then he referred to "the divisions, or the differences, or however you want to call them, more or less optimistically." He was not, of course, going to "throw any more wood on the fire." He was going to devote all his energies to unity. But he was going to do this in a way "all his own," since he was far from ready to renounce his right to think for himself.[83]

The following day Castro's delegate to the congress of the Communist Party of East Germany (SED) insisted on the need for unity in accordance with "the principles of proletarian internationalism."[84] Shortly before Blas Roca had been the Cuban delegate at the congresses of the Bulgarian, Italian, and Czechoslovak parties, however, at the East German party congress Cuba was not represented by an "old" Communist but by a young Castroite, Armando Hart, and this must be interpreted as one more indication of Castro's dissatisfaction with Soviet-Cuban relations. The reactions

[81] Castro's speech in *Revolución*, January 3, 1963.
[82] See, for instance, "Demonstration of Unbreakable Unity: A Holiday in Havana," by the correspondent Timur Gaidar, *Pravda*, January 4, 1963 (*CDSP*, Vol. XV, No. 1 [January 30, 1963]). Castro's speech was reprinted in *Jen-min Jih-pao* January 6, 1963 (SCMP 2962, April 19, 1963).
[83] *Hoy*, January 16, 1963.
[84] Hart's speech in *Revolución*, January 26, 1963.

of *Hoy* and *Revolución* to Castro's speech to the Women's Congress show that the split between the Castroites and the Communists, which had been reopened by the October crisis, was still in existence. *Hoy* insisted that "no more wood was to be thrown on the fire of the differences" and that "neither the recriminations . . . nor the materials for stimulating the polemic should be spread"; it expressed satisfaction with the speech made by Khrushchev to the East German party congress proposing that public discussion should be suspended.[85] *Revolución* devoted seven successive editorials to Castro's speech. Their titles are revealing: "How to Bring the Masses to the Struggle," "The Caribbean Crisis Has Not Been Resolved," "Unity in Accordance with Principles Is the Line," "Latin America: The Creation of Subjective Conditions," "The Declaration of Havana Is a Path," "The Yankee Alliance: A Plan for Exploitation," and "Unity in Order to Resist and Unity in Order to Win."[86]

Two days after Castro's speech of January 15 there appeared the first indications that his campaign for "unity in accordance with the principles" was beginning to have the desired results. On that date an agreement with the Soviet Union for irrigation and drainage works was announced, Cuba receiving "a long-range credit under favorable conditions."[87] That same day Soviet Deputy Foreign Minister Kuznetsov arrived in Havana and was received by Castro. On February 8 the trade agreement for 1963 was published. It was as terse as usual but it showed that the Soviet Union was granting another credit, "long-range, with favorable conditions" for "the imbalance in the trade with Cuba" for 1961 and 1962 and for the prospective imbalance in 1963.[88] Nor was this all.

<hr />

85 In its editorial of January 13, 1963, "Por la unidad dentro y fuera" [For Unity Inside and Out], *Hoy* had said: "We must abstain from venting our polemics abroad." On January 18 Roca wrote on the theme that "the unity and cohesion of the socialist camp and of the Communist movement is essential for us," commenting on Castro's speech of January 2, not on the speech of January 15.

86 *Revolución*, January 18, 21, 23, 24, 25, 26, and 28, 1963.

87 *Ibid.*, January 17, 1963.

88 The agreement is given in *Hoy*, February 8, 1963. On January 22 the signing of a commercial agreement with Albania was announced, and on February 26, as I have already pointed out, with China.

On the difficulties in Cuban-Soviet trade relations it should be enough to say that by September 1963 all the products the Soviet Union had promised to send for 1962 had not yet arrived in Cuba. According to *Hoy*, September 8, 1963, p. 7 (JPRS 21,309, October 3, 1963), "the basic reason" for this was the shortage of shipping. The article lists the quantities and kinds of goods exchanged

It seems that the Soviets permitted Castro to take a million tons of sugar from the annual quota assigned to Moscow and sell it in the world market, thus obtaining dollars and better prices.[89] Furthermore, when the trade agreement signed on February 6, 1963 was ratified, it was announced that the Soviet government had proposed that "a change be introduced into the agreement in order to raise the price of the Cuban sugar that was to be bought in 1963."[90] It thus appears that this "impulsive," "romantic" young rebel was capable of negotiating with the skill of the proverbial horse trader.

It is possible that the reconciliation illustrated by these economic agreements also had a political content. On February 10, 1963 *Pravda* for the first time mentioned fourteen socialist countries, including Albania, Yugoslavia, and Cuba.[91] When the CPSU slogans for May 1 were published, although in October of the previous year the slogan only mentioned the "heroic people of Cuba, who have entered on a path of socialist construction," Cuba was put on the same level as the other members of the bloc, "building socialism."[92]

Sixteen days after signing the trade agreement for 1963, Castro gave a talk "on the United Party of the Socialist Revolution of Cuba (PURS)."

The background of this event is significant. After Escalante's removal the task was begun of holding meetings among the workers for the election of "model workers" (the raw material of the future ORI) and for the purging of the "nuclei" already constituted. But this program of gigantic dimensions moved ahead with a sluggishness that may have been deliberate on Castro's part. In March 1963

---

in 1962. According to the same source the total value was 992 million pesos in that year.

89 See Tad Szulc's report in *The New York Times*, June 2, 1963. According to him Cuba was to receive for this million tons an average of 7.22 cents per pound of sugar. He added that Cuba had sold some 500,000 tons the year before in various markets, also with the permission of the Soviets. Szulc believed that the permission for 1963 had been conceded during Rodríguez' trip to Moscow in December 1962. In my opinion, however, on the basis of the facts given, it was in February 1963.

90 See the Cuban government note in *Hoy*, December 27, 1963.

91 See Griffith, *The Sino-Soviet Rift, op. cit.*, p. 107; in a footnote on the same page Griffith mentions that the integration of Cuba into the socialist camp was reiterated in a *Pravda* article on February 20, 1963.

92 The slogans for November 7, 1962 were published in *Pravda*, October 14, 1962, (*CDSP*, Vol. XIV, No. 41 [November 7, 1962], pp. 3-5); those for May Day 1963 in *Pravda*, April 8, 1963 (CDSP, Vol. XV, No. 13 [April 24, 1963], pp. 3-5).

the party organ had only 16,000 members throughout Cuba[93] although in October 1961 it had had 800 active nuclei in the province of Havana alone. Only two traces remain of the participation of the ORI in government decisions: the signatures of Guevara and Aragonés as representatives of the ORI on the communiqué signed in Moscow at the beginning of September 1962, and the joint declaration of the government and of the ORI on November 25 of the same year when Mikoyan was in Cuba. It is highly probable that in the second case the ORI was included by Castro only in order to compromise the ex-members of the PSP who were ORI members and who, as I have said, were expressing a more or less marked resistance to the progressive hardening of Castro's position vis-à-vis Soviet policy. Since Castro called the organization to which he devoted his talk of February 22 the "United Party of the Socialist Revolution," and the *Hoy* editorial of the following day was entitled "Long Live the PURS," we have to conclude that in the same mysterious manner as with the July 26 Movement, the Revolutionary Student Directorate, and the PSP, it was decided to bury the ORI and invent a new phantom, the PURS. We may assume then that the Cuban-Soviet discussions that preceded the trade agreement of February 6, 1963 also dealt with these two other questions: the official recognition of "socialist" Cuba by the Soviets, and the solemn, formal promise by Castro to form the type of party that characterizes all Communist states.

If this commitment did in fact exist, the talk by Castro was a clear indication of how he proposed to fulfill his part of the agreement. Castro stretched the talk out to great length so that eventually it comprised seventeen single-spaced mimeographed pages without saying anything concrete. The only thing that can be extracted with any clarity from this verbal flood was that in the municipality of Güines, near Havana, an experiment at "local government" was being planned under party direction, and afterward, "we shall go and apply the experience we gain to other regions."[94] As can be seen, after two years of Cuban "socialism" Castro was intending to go back to something very much like the JUCEI's that had been set up in December 1960.

If we may assume that the official entry of Castroite "socialism" into the socialist camp took place in these months, any remaining

[93] According to the data of the National Directorate of the PURS (*Cuba Socialista,* April 1963).
[94] Stenographic version of this speech taken from the Radio Cuba broadcast.

doubt on the status of Castroist Cuba in relation to the bloc was dispelled by the joint Cuban-Soviet declaration of May 23 on the occasion of Castro's first visit to the Soviet Union. This was signed by Khrushchev, both as First Secretary of the CPSU and as Premier, and by Fidel Castro both as Secretary-General of the PURS and as Prime Minister of Cuba.[95] This meant that the CPSU now formally accepted the PURS as a "fraternal party," a true Communist party, and Cuba as a state ruled by such a party, that is, a member of the "socialist camp."[96]

The joint Cuban-Soviet declaration of May 23 did not clarify who had had the idea of installing the missiles in Cuba or whether that measure was taken in order to defend "little Cuba" or to fulfill "an international proletarian duty." The solution of the October crisis was depicted in the following way: "The firm position of the Soviet Union and of other countries in the defense of revolutionary Cuba, the firmness and the good sense shown by the responsible statesmen of Cuba and the Soviet Union with respect to the understanding of the situation, and the support lent Cuba by all the peace-loving states, forestalled a thermonuclear war." As for the situation in the Caribbean, where existing tensions were still acknowledged, the declaration noted that the acceptance of Castro's five conditions "could" help alleviate them, Castro having to accept the Soviet promise that in case of any U.S. aggression Russian power would fulfill "its international duty" — a promise accompanied by the warning that "the organizers of aggression must take note that any intervention in Cuba will place mankind in the face of a destructive thermonuclear and missile war."

On the ideological level Castro accepted in general the Soviet point of view, including the mention of the triumph of "socialism" in Cuba as an instance of the benefits produced by the policy of peaceful coexistence. But it was also pointed out that this policy by no means implied "the cessation or the weakening of the ideological struggle against imperialism." And with respect to the "roads of transition," that is, the roads to victory, both parties

[95] Text of the declaration in *Hoy*, May 25, 1963. It is significant that neither Blas Roca nor Carlos Rafael Rodríguez nor any other member of the former PSP leadership formed part of the group chosen by Fidel to accompany him on his first trip to the Soviet Union. The Cuban party representatives participating in the "fraternal" talks with the CPSU were all Castroites, that is, besides Castro himself, Emilio Aragonés, Sergio del Valle, Guillermo García, Regino Boti, and Raúl Curbelo.

[96] Report of his trip to the Soviet Union in *Revolución*, June 5, 1963.

agreed "that the question as to the peaceful or nonpeaceful road to socialism in any given country will definitely be settled by the peoples themselves."

Finally, on the economic plane, the Soviet government "on its own initiative" offered to buy Cuban sugar in 1963 at a price harmonizing with the "levels reached in the world market," apparently 6 cents a pound. Everything indicates, however, that this "generosity" was obtained only in exchange for promises from Castro that were not shown in the document and that would have damaged his propaganda image as a "romantic" and "impetuous youth."

It must be admitted that Castro's position in the economic negotiations with the Soviets was far from easy. As he himself said later, the trade imbalance with the Soviet Union at that time amounted to $150–$200 million; and as early as May it could be seen that the failure of the sugar crop in 1963 would be even more disastrous than the year before. The crop in fact came to only 3,800,000 tons. Castro therefore had to make two compromises: first, to reduce gasoline consumption in order to save on Soviet oil, the price of which was doubled at the beginning of June, and second, to abandon the dreams of rapid industrialization, going back to the straitjacket that "capitalism" had imposed — reliance on the cultivation of sugarcane. In the same speech in which he announced the rise in the price of gasoline, Castro stated that "sugar is the basis of our economy and of our development,"[97] thus launching the present course of the Cuban economy.

In spite of this it was clear that the Prime Minister came back from his trip very satisfied.

When Castro reported his Moscow visit to the Cuban people on June 4, he called Khrushchev an "extraordinarily human person," "a very simple man," "one of the most luminous intelligences I've ever met," and assured the Cubans that the Soviet Premier was "a serious adversary of imperialism . . . a great leader, and a formidable adversary of imperialism." It is possible that the satisfaction revealed by these phrases had something to do with secret military agreements. It is highly significant that this man, to whom the war materials at his disposal have never appeared sufficient, said that as a result of his trip "the maintenance of our armed forces in the

[97] Speech at the announcement of the results of the third people's sugar crop (*Hoy*, June 28, 1963). The way the price of gasoline was doubled is very characteristic of the regime. Castro spoke about the appropriateness of the measure, and the next day gasoline was selling at $0.60 a gallon.

best possible combat condition" had been guaranteed; he repeated several times that from the military point of view the situation was one of "complete security."[98]

The Soviets were also satisfied, as is shown by the reprinting in both *Pravda* and *Izvestiya* of Castro's complete speech, even though it took up four and a half pages of each of their June 6 and 7 issues.[99]

The Chinese printed the joint Cuban-Soviet statement but not Castro's subsequent speech. At the beginning of February, when the Cuban leader had not yet consummated his reconciliation with Khrushchev, the Chinese had managed to get the third conference of the Afro-Asian People's Solidarity Organization, which was being held in Tanganyika, to accept Castro's invitation to hold a further meeting in Havana with the participation of Latin American delegates.[100] But almost at once the intimacy that had been increasing between the Chinese and the Cubans since the October crisis began to cool off at the same time that the growing cordiality between the Cubans and the Soviets became more and more evident. The best proof of this is the fact that Castro was in Moscow for May 1 whereas the celebration in Peking was attended only by José Matar, president of the Defense Committees.[101] Later, the Chinese disregarded the October crisis in their letter to the Communist Party of the Soviet Union on June 14, and the Soviets, in their answer of July 14, asked with obvious irony, "Why then do the Chinese comrades stubbornly ignore the assessment which the leaders of the Cuban revolution themselves give to the policy of the government of the Soviet Union, which they call a policy of fraternal solidarity and genuine internationalism?"

This by no means implies that Castro had adopted a completely pro-Soviet position in the Sino-Soviet dispute. He continued his role as a partisan of "unity." He had now forgotten about the "principles." But this did not make him neglect his relations with the Chinese, as is proved by the fact that immediately after his trip

98 "Our present situation is one of security." This was, moreover, the title of one of the three editorials devoted by *Hoy*, June 6–8, 1963, to Castro's report.

99 According to *CDSP*, Vol. XV, No. 21 (July 23, 1963), in which Castro's speech is translated from the Russian.

100 Griffith, *The Sino-Soviet Rift, op. cit.*, p. 125. Such a conference took place in January 1966, but Castro and the Soviets, not the Chinese, predominated at it.

101 See SCMP 2962, April 19, 1963; 2964, April 23, 1963; and 2972, May 6, 1963, among others.

to Moscow Castro sent Antonio Núñez Jiménez, one of the men he has always made use of for confidential affairs,[102] to visit Peking. At the banquet given for him, which was attended by Vice-Premier Nieh Jung-chen and Kuo Mo-jo, Núñez Jiménez stated: "Geographically we are friends from afar; ideologically we are very close friends." Then they all clasped hands and sang in Spanish, "Cuba yes, Yankees no."[103]

Inside Cuba the Castro-Soviet cordiality led to an intensification of the activities leading to the organization of the PURS, especially during Castro's absence from the end of April to the beginning of June, with the help of his younger brother Raúl, Minister of the Armed Forces. On May 16, at the celebration of one more anniversary of the foundation of *Hoy*, Raúl congratulated Blas Roca, expressing the hope that, "as Fidel said to me," the former newspaper of the PSP, *Hoy*, would be "the official organ of the PURS." That same day, at the celebration that took place with the participation of the President and of the ministers of the cabinet, Dorticós also called *Hoy* "the most faithful exponent of the National Directorate of the Cuban revolution and of the PURS." But in the congratulations sent by Castro from Moscow, even though they were very cordial and laudatory, nothing similar was said,[104] and after his return Castro never spoke of the matter again; so those who went on ascribing to *Hoy* the status of the official organ of the PURS and of the government were doing so without authority.

On May 29 a general assembly of the members of the PURS of Havana was held under the joint chairmanship of Raúl Castro and Blas Roca. At this meeting it was agreed to submit a proposal to the National Directorate to consider the "possibility" of holding a national assembly in July to discuss such matters as the methods of building the party and the functioning of the "nuclei."[105] The content of the proposal gives some idea of the backward stage of the party organization at this time. Naturally, after Castro's return no further mention was made of this suggestion.

---

[102] It will be remembered that it was Núñez who in June 1960 traveled to Moscow to invite Khrushchev to Havana, as was reported in the press. In my opinion the real aim here was to prepare for Raúl Castro's trip to Prague in order to acquire from the socialist camp the first arms that arrived in Cuba.

[103] NCNA, June 13, 1963 (SCMP 3001, June 18, 1963).

[104] *Hoy*, May 16 and 17, 1963, and an editorial in *Revolución*, May 16, 1963, which hailed *Hoy's* anniversary with a "brother's jubilation," and Raúl's speech was reprinted.

[105] *Revolución*, May 30, 1963.

Thus in June 1963, one year after Khrushchev had promised the missiles, Castro had managed to get his "socialism" formally accepted by the socialist bloc, so that his claims on military and economic protection from the Soviet Union were strengthened. It is difficult to believe, however, that this consoled him for the loss of the "strategic" arms he was still longing for. Even though it depended on Soviet protection, Cuba was not a "satellite"; inside Cuba Castro went on governing in the same manner as he had ever since he made himself Prime Minister, that is, absolutely by himself. He had also managed to make some advances in the reduction of shortages and poverty, although he had failed completely to solve the economic problems confronting him by bringing production back at least to former levels. Lastly, the "revolutionary unity" between the "old" Communists and the "Fidelistas" seemed to have been restored once again. If Castro recalled the critical days of October and those that followed, he had good reason to feel satisfied. However, imperceptibly perhaps, the universal and continental conditions that had made the installation and continuation of the Castro regime possible were disappearing or about to disappear, thus creating new and growing difficulties.

CHAPTER EIGHT

PEACEFUL COEXISTENCE AND INTERNAL CONFLICTS[1]

Castro made skillful use of the following external circumstances in obtaining his initial foreign policy successes. First, prior to the 1962 missile crisis the West vastly overestimated the Soviet Union's admittedly formidable nuclear strength. Second, the attention of the United States was fixed on the Soviet challenge in the other parts of the world, to the neglect of Latin America, which was assumed to be safe. Consequently Washington had allowed its position in the area to deteriorate to the point where the machinery designed to protect the continent — the Organization of American States — had become almost totally ineffective. Finally, the so-called "Latin American Democratic Left" — Venezuelan Democratic Action, Colombian Liberals, and similar movements — proved incapable of guiding the mighty wave of rebellion that had begun to manifest itself with the overthrow of Rojas Pinilla in Colombia in mid-1957, had continued with the Venezuelan revolution of the following January, and had culminated in the victory of January 1959 in Cuba. Because of this failure Castro was offered the opportunity to exploit the genuine discontent against the United States.

The International Situation and Castro's Policy

Castro's early successes, however, were not decisive, because they created new difficulties for him. By becoming more radical and entering the Communist bloc, Castro deprived himself of the element of surprise that had been crucial for his first successes. Faced with Soviet activity in the Caribbean, Washington was shaken

---

[1] It should be noted that this chapter was completed in March 1965.

out of its indifference. With the Act of Bogota in September 1960, and especially with the "Alliance for Progress," approved in August 1961, it put into practice a program that restored some effectiveness to the OAS. Today the Alliance seems to be just one more bureaucratic project, and there are some who have already pronounced it dead.[2] But in 1961, if it did not arouse the enthusiasm of the Latin American masses, it at least provided some stimulus and justification for the majority of their rulers to respond to the Castroist challenge in the most convenient and the cheapest way — by collaboration with Washington.

Moreover, the propertied classes of the continent, and above all the armed forces, were able to witness in Cuba just what would be lying in wait for them if Castro ever set foot on the mainland. As early as 1962 the military in both Argentina and Peru deposed the elected presidents. Their example was followed the next year by their colleagues in Guatemala, Ecuador, Santo Domingo, and Honduras, while in Venezuela only Rómulo Betancourt's skill saved him from an end similar to that of the presidents of these countries. It may well be that in the long run these events will have favorable consequences for Castroism, but until today, except in Guatemala, there are no guerrilla nuclei in any country where the military has taken power. Since the Castroist elements in the countries concerned were repressed, each one of these events constituted a defeat for them — which does not mean that I approve of or defend such methods.

Lastly, the October 1962 missile crisis demonstrated that in this hemisphere Soviet military power could not stand up to the United States. The Chinese, who harass the Soviets from the "left," were not likely to be exposed to nuclear warfare, and had nothing to lose in Latin America, could pretend to ignore the obvious lesson of the confrontation. But the Soviets could not afford the luxury of such a pretense. This is shown by the attitude of their Brazilian spokesman, Luis Carlos Prestes, who from Havana rejected the idea of an armed struggle and recommended "the peaceful road" to power.[3] And the Soviet ideological organ Kommunist chose Enrique Rodríguez, a secretary of the Communist Party of Uruguay, to censure "the unjustifiable conclusions" that "disoriented and feverish individuals" had extracted from "the special character of the Cuban

[2] Victor Alba, "The Alliance for Progress Is Dead," The New Republic, September 5, 1964.
[3] Prestes' interview with José Manuel Fortuny, Hoy, March 9, 1963.

revolution."[4] That is, the Latin American "comrades" were informed that the Soviets had no intention of repeating their Cuban adventure, and if anyone were to provoke "imperialism" he alone would be responsible for the consequences. That this warning was understood is indicated by the fact that the majority of the Communist parties in the hemisphere made a public display of their allegiance to the Soviet line and condemned China.[5]

One would have assumed that this unfavorable situation would have induced Castro to renounce at least temporarily the pursuit of continental revolution and for the first time to go over to the defensive. In fact, however, he behaved quite differently. This could hardly have been due solely to his natural reluctance to abandon the strategy that had led him to all his victories. Rather, it is probable that certain factors in the international situation made him feel that a new crisis was imminent, one he could face only by maintaining an attitude of rigid defiance.

It is true that in March and April 1963, on the eve of Castro's first visit to Moscow, the situation did not appear to be serious. Differences between the U.S. Department of State and the Cuban Revolutionary Council, which represented the anti-Castro exile groups, led to the resignation of that council's president, Dr. Miró. And on May 4 the *Diario las Américas* announced that on the order of the U.S. State Department representative in Miami the removal of "the furniture and office equipment from the council's rooms had begun," thus practically terminating this stormy center. It is not unlikely that this news played some role in the "feeling of security" displayed by Castro upon his return from Moscow.

In July, however, the picture changed. On July 3 the OAS agreed to recommend to its members measures to reinforce the isolation of Cuba; on July 8 Washington seized the funds of the Cuban government in America; on July 17 the U.S. President declared that the United States would not and could not accept peaceful coexistence "with a Soviet satellite in the Caribbean"; and at the end of the month it became known that Manuel Artime, the so-called "Civil Chief" of the Bay of Pigs invading force, Brigade 2506,

---

4 *Kommunist,* No. 16, November 1963 (JPRS 22, 368, December 19, 1963).

5 Branko Lazitch, "Le communisme latino-américain et le conflict Moscou-Pékin," *Est & Ouest,* No. 306 (October 1963) (JPRS 21, 765, November 7, 1963). On Uruguay and Costa Rica, not mentioned in this article, see *La Epoca* (Montevideo), August 5, 1963 (JPRS 20, 930, September 5, 1963), and *La Nación,* August 9, 1963 (JPRS 21,077, September 13, 1963).

had resumed his belligerent activities, this time from Nicaragua with the protection of the despot Somoza.[6]

That same month the Sino-Soviet conversations in Moscow ended in an absolute failure, whereas the Soviet negotiations with Washington and London led to the nuclear test ban treaty. All of this must have exacerbated Castro's habitual suspicions to the highest degree. Castro once more demonstrated his disregard for "objective conditions." He responded to the seizure of Cuban funds by announcing the expropriation of the U.S. embassy in Havana (thus establishing a precedent that was later imitated by Albania with respect to the Soviet embassy in Tirana). Thereupon, in his speech of July 26, 1963, he inaugurated a new stage of disagreement with the Soviets, of coincidence of views with the Chinese, and of extremism in his domestic policy — in brief, revolutionary radicalism. In this speech he praised the test ban treaty, "a victory for peace of the world conscience and a victory for the Soviet Union's peace policy." But he did not say that he would sign it, hinting instead at his later arguments justifying abstention: continuation of tension in the Caribbean where the "imperialists" had not stopped their economic aggression and were transporting "mercenaries to Nicaragua." The rest of his speech was devoted to a reiteration of the lessons to be learned from the Cuban example, inciting the Latin Americans to imitate it, and even a promise that "the people who will do what the Cuban people has done will have the firm support of the Soviet Union and of the whole socialist camp."[7]

In August *Cuba Socialista* published the Chinese platform of June 14, 1963 in its entirety.[8] This action was unique among the countries of the Soviet camp, since even the Rumanians had published only a condensation. That same month Guevara gave an interview in which he recalled that the PSP, trained in loyalty to the Soviet Union, had not been among the leaders in the struggle

---

6 *The Washington Post*, July 26, 1963.

7 For Castro's speech see *Hoy*, July 27, 1963.

8 "A Proposal Concerning the General Line of the International Communist Movement — The Letter from the Central Committee of the Communist Party of China in Reply to the Letter from the Central Committee of the Communist Party of the Soviet Union of March 30, 1963," *Jen-min Jih-pao*, June 17, 1963, and *Peking Review*, Vol. VI, No. 25 (June 21, 1963), pp. 6–22; complete text in William E. Griffith, *The Sino-Soviet Rift* (Cambridge, Mass.: The M.I.T. Press, 1964), pp. 259–288. The same issue of *Cuba Socialista* carried the Soviet reply to the Chinese, "Open Letter from the CPSU Central Committee to Party Organizations and All Communists of the Soviet Union, July 14, 1963," *Pravda*, July 14, 1963; complete text in Griffith, *op. cit.*, pp. 289–325.

against Batista but had deplorably mistaken the characteristics of the situation and had recommended a wrong method of struggle: "mass struggle."[9] In September Guevara expounded anew the principles of the correct method, guerrilla warfare, in an article that was reprinted on January 15, 1964 by *Peking Review*.[10] On October 3 the second agrarian reform was promulgated, nationalizing all rural estates with an area of more than five caballerías (67 hectares and 1,000 square meters). Lastly, the arms cache discovered by the Venezuelan police in November of that year surely constituted a manifestation of increased revolutionary activity.

It is obvious that such behavior was bound to provoke Soviet displeasure and Chinese sympathy. The Soviets reacted with indifference to the sporadic attacks that were being made during these months against the Cuban shores. The Chinese, on the other hand, denounced them vigorously and pointed out that they constituted "a slap in the face for those who were trying to present the arch-imperialist as a sensible statesman."[11]

Developments and events later in the year must have suggested a more prudent course to Castro. The Soviet-American *rapprochement* was making little progress, while it became clear that American aid to Artime was of very limited scope. Moreover, in October hurricane "Flora" devastated Cuba, leaving more than 1,200 casualties and ruining the crops. The destruction was so great that Castro himself used it as a reason for asking Washington to stop its boycott.[12] In its October Revolution anniversary slogans the Soviet Communist Party stated that there could be "no real relaxation in international tension" unless "the United States stopped supporting the counterrevolutionary elements in Cuba."[13] Khrushchev, Malinovsky, and Podgorny solemnly affirmed Soviet solidarity with Cuba.[14]

9 *Revolución*, August 21, 1963 (JPRS 21,174, September 20, 1963).

10 This work, entitled "Guerra de guerrillas: Un método" [Guerrilla Warfare: A Method], originally appeared in *Cuba Socialista*, September 1963.

11 "Statement by the Spokesman of the Chinese Government," *Peking Review*, Vol. VI, No. 36 (September 6, 1963), pp. 7–16, at p. 14.

12 For Castro's October 21 television appearance see *Cuba Socialista*, November 1963.

13 *Pravda*, October 17, 1963, quoted from *CDSP*, Vol. XV, No. 41 (November 6, 1963).

14 Khrushchev, in a conversation with "21 heads of large American companies," *The New York Times*, November 7, 1963; Malinovsky in his speech at the parade, *Pravda*, November 8, 1963 (*CDSP*, Vol. XV, No. 45 [December 4, 1963]); and Podgorny in a report at the Palace of the Congresses, *CDSP, ibid.*

One may assume that all these declarations helped to reassure Castro and persuaded him to moderate his course.

A Stage of Moderation

Castro's policy evolves through alternate stages. In order to distinguish between them we may speak of radical or leftist periods, like the one we have just described, and moderate or rightist periods, like the one that began at the end of 1963. It is relatively easy to determine when the regime moves from one stage into the other. When Cuba's relations with the Soviet Union are cordial and little effort is devoted to subversion on the continent, while the major emphasis at home is placed on the organization of the party and the development of the economy, then Castro's policy is passing through a moderate stage. It is no accident that such features occur together. The policy of peaceful coexistence, reaffirmed and accentuated by the Soviets after the missile crisis of October 1962, did not encourage such provocations against "imperialism" as subversion directed from Cuba. As for the party and the economy, these are of major concern to the CPSU: first, because by definition a state of the Communist type presupposes the existence of a Communist party;[15] second, because in Cuba it is in the party, not in the state, that the "old" Communists, conditioned in loyalty to the Soviet Union, still retain some influence; and finally, because it is the Soviet state that with its resources makes up for Castro's incapacity to provide for the economic independence of Cuba.

With these criteria in mind we can affirm that the final months of 1963 saw the initiation of such a stage.

After the threats of the summer of 1963 the United States moved hesitantly toward a position that did not change with the death of President Kennedy and was formulated with clarity, months later, by Undersecretary of State George Ball. According to this interpretation, Cuba did not constitute a direct military threat to any country on the continent but did represent a danger of subversion

15 In December *Kommunist* repeated: "The key process in the development of the Cuban Revolution is the establishment of the vanguard which is leading and guarding this revolution. . . . The expansion of the PURS is currently the priority task." Then it castigated "certain theoreticians outside of Cuba" who had denied "the existence of a proletarian vanguard during the preparation and implementation of the Socialist Revolution." The refutation is so feeble that it can only underline the nonexistence of this "vanguard." *Kommunist*, No. 18, December 1963 (JPRS 22,923, January 27, 1964).

in the southern half. For Washington two elements in the Cuban situation were not negotiable: Cuba's "military, economic, and political dependence" on the Soviet Union, and the issue of subversive activities. On the other hand Washington did not intend to commit an "act of war." Short of war, "all the available instruments of force" would be used to prevent Cuba from continuing subversive activities, and the policy of isolating Cuba economically — a highly successful one, in the opinion of this State Department official — would be continued.[16]

If Castro were forced by circumstances to seek a *rapprochement* with the United States, he would obviously have to begin by eliminating the second of these "nonnegotiable" elements, that is, subversion. He would have to trust that en route a compromise might be reached with respect to the invitation to suicide that constituted the first element, that is, giving up Soviet support. As early as the end of November 1963 the French journalist Jean Daniel, who was in Cuba and had conversations with Castro, concluded that the reasoning of a number of revolutionary leaders was as follows: "It will certainly be necessary for the United States to come to an agreement" (with Cuba); so why not give up "Cuban subversion" in exchange for "the United States giving up aid to the counterrevolution?"[17]

Castro did not go so far in his speech of January 2, 1964, but he did indicate the existence of "a universal anxiety about peace." He explained his proposals that would contribute toward peace, especially in his relations with Washington. He declared that he was ready to consider compensations for the U.S. properties that had been nationalized if trade was restored with Cuba. He maintained that the only things that could not be expected of him were "ideological concessions," suggesting he would be willing to talk about giving up subversion. This impression is confirmed by Castro's answer when someone indiscreetly reminded him of one of his favorite targets, President Betancourt of Venezuela: "That is a problem for the Venezuelan people, not a problem of ours."[18]

The anti-American riots in Panama, which began a few days

[16] Undersecretary of State George W. Ball's speech at the convention of the Omicron Delta Kappa society at Roanoke, Virginia, on April 22, 1964. The Spanish translation of his speech appeared in *Diario las Américas*, May 24, 1964.

[17] Jean Daniel, "Boycotting Cuba," *The New Republic*, December 28, 1963.

[18] The speech was printed in *Revolución*, January 3, 1964.

later, gave Castro an excellent opportunity to show in practice that his words were meant seriously. His reaction to the riots was restricted to an announcement that his government was ready to set up, in conjunction with the other Latin American nations, a common fund to assist the Panamanians.[19]

The communiqué issued on the occasion of his second visit to Moscow, on January 22, 1964, served to confirm Castro's new policy of moderation. Khrushchev repeated the Soviet promise to come to the aid of Cuba in case of aggression, and "fully" supported the familiar five points that had been made public at the time of the October 1962 crisis. For his part, Castro recognized that the test ban treaty was "a step forward in favor of peace" and declared that his government was ready to "do everything necessary to re-establish good-neighbor relations between Cuba and the United States," with no condition other than that Cuba's "socialism" be accepted. Further, he condemned "the factionalist and sectarian activity in the ranks of the Communist and workers' parties" — clearly a slap at the Chinese — and he stated his agreement "with the steps that had been taken by the Central Committee of the CPSU" with the aim of doing "away with the existing differences and of fortifying the unity and cohesion of the ranks of the international Communist movement."[20]

Apparently Cuban-Soviet intimacy reached new levels as a result of this visit, since on his return Castro said, among other things, "at no time has the friendship" between the two peoples "been more lofty, more firm, and more solid."[21] By now the reader will not be so trusting as to believe everything that Castro says. A list of his companions in the negotiations shows that Castro's "trust" did not go far enough for him to include any "old" Communists or indeed anyone who was not completely under his spell. Not one was a member of the National Directorate of the PURS. One, Pedro Miret, was an old crony of his student days whom Castro had elevated to the office of head of the artillery; another, Aldo Santamaría, belonged to a family that was utterly devoted to the "maxi-

19 In his speech on his return from Moscow (*Sierra Maestra*, January 25, 1964). Since no one paid any attention to this, he did not speak of the matter again. The investigating committee appointed by the OAS to ascertain the origin of the riots came to the conclusion that "Castro-communism" played a negligible role in them (*The New York Times*, February 17, 1964).

20 Text of the communiqué in *Hoy*, January 23, 1964.

21 Castro's speech in *Sierra Maestra*, January 25, 1964.

mum leader";[22] a third, René Vallejo, has been something like Castro's personal physician ever since the Sierra days; and the last, Captain Bienvenido Pérez, as far as I have been able to ascertain, was the chief of Castro's bodyguard at the time. It was these four nonentities, who owed everything to Castro and were spiritually subject to him, who confronted Khrushchev, Brezhnev, Kosygin, Mikoyan, and Malinovsky to work out the terms of the communiqué of January 22, 1964. It is needless to add that the agreements with the "brotherly and beloved Soviet Union" were received with immense joy by *Hoy*,[23] and that all revolutionary leaders approved of them, even though without quite so much enthusiasm.

However, there were signs that the policy of seeking a *rapprochement* with the United States, at the cost of sacrificing — even if only verbally — the Latin American comrades, aroused some discontent. According to Guevara, "there can be no bargaining, no half measures, no partial guarantees of a country's stability. The victory must be total."[24] And throughout these months, whenever he had the chance, Guevara insisted on recalling that the Cuban movement was bound up "intimately with the struggle for the liberation of the oppressed peoples."[25] It does not seem that Raúl was very much in agreement with his brother. In January Raúl condemned the repeated television appearances, evidently alluding to Fidel. He announced his own intention of "submerging himself," a promise he carried out during the following months, and he blurted out, "We must never establish peaceful coexistence with our enemies."[26]

Similar divergences among the revolutionary leaders could be noted in the domestic field — in cultural activities, in the organization of the PURS, and in the army.

[22] A brother of Aldo's died at the Moncada barracks, and a sister, one of the founders of the July 26 Movement, is the present wife of the Minister of Education (1964).

[23] "Bienvenida a Fidel y a los acuerdos" [Welcome to Fidel and to the Agreements], editorial in *Hoy*, January 24, 1964.

[24] Speech at the closing of the celebration of the solidarity with South Vietnam week (*El Mundo*, December 22, 1963).

[25] For this attitude of Guevara's see his speech at the Forum for Electrical Energy (*Revolución*, November 25, 1963); his speech on January 12, 1964 (*ibid.*, January 13, 1964); and his speech on March 14, 1964 (*Hoy*, March 15, 1964), which includes the words we quote in the text.

[26] Speech at the Cuban Institute of Geodesics and Cartography (*Revolución*, January 6, 1964).

Internal Dissensions

In November 1963 the PURS had 28,000 members,[27] but, except in the field of revolutionary education, the influence of this *apparat* was almost imperceptible. The sole aspect of national life in which the party had made certain progress up to this time was culture, with the creation of the Commission for Revolutionary Orientation (Comisión de Orientación Revolucionaria — COR), headed by César Escalante, the brother of the PSP leader who was purged on March 26, 1962. Escalante was clearly hoping to get all cultural activities into his own hands. In December, however, these ambitions suffered a serious setback. When "La Dolce Vita" and similar films were being shown in Havana, Blas Roca said he had not seen them himself but that he knew of "workers who had seen them and thought they should not be shown to the public."[28] The director of the Institute of Cinematography, Alfredo Guevara (not related to Che), himself from the ranks of the PSP, lost no time in disagreeing publicly with the criterion of the editor of *Hoy*. He denied that Roca's opinions represented the cultural policy of the regime; he attributed such value only to Castro's statements. He maintained that the institute's decisions were guided by them, and he made a sarcastic reference to the partisans of "socialist realism," like Roca, according to whom "the work of art must be replaced by propaganda sugar coated with certain formulas, and the public will be reduced to a vast mass of babies who, by their nurses, will be fed perfectly prepared and sterilized 'ideological pap.' "[29] Confronted with his former subordinate's aggressive language, Roca acknowledged the unofficial status of his own opinions. He denied the possibility of any differences between him "and the First Secretary of our party, Comrade Fidel Castro," and he reproduced a great many statements of the Prime Minister that in his opinion supported his own criticisms.[30]

Meanwhile about four hundred intellectuals and artists had composed a statement of support for Guevara; it was not published

27 According to *The New York Times*, December 2, 1963, in a dispatch taken from *The Times* (London). I use this source because, in the first place, its information, which comes from Havana, shows familiarity with the situation despite its brevity, and then because the facts about the PURS have since appeared in a publication called *Construyendo el Partido* [Building the Party], which I have been unable to find in the United States.

28 "Aclaraciones," *Hoy*, December 12, 1963 (JPRS 22,821, January 20, 1964).

29 *Hoy*, December 17 and 21, 1963.

30 "Aclaraciones," *ibid.*, December 24, 1963.

because the President of the Republic, Osvaldo Dorticós, repeated the contention of the director of the Institute of Cinematography that Roca's opinion was not that of the government.[31] Since Castro himself never made clear which of these two analysts was giving the correct interpretation of his thinking, and since the controversial films continued to be shown, Roca could do nothing but end his polemic, promising to continue on some other occasion and declaring that he respected and esteemed all the honored artists and intellectuals even if they were neither revolutionary nor socialist.[32]

It is obvious that after this mishap suffered by the chief representative of the Soviet viewpoint in Cuba, the tasks of COR became far more difficult. This does not mean that Roca or his followers were giving up their ambitions, which were to turn Cuba into a copy of the Soviet model. On the contrary, they took advantage of the growing cordiality between Cuba and the Soviets — reaffirmed at the beginning of January by the signing of the commercial treaty for 1964 and by Castro's second visit to Moscow — and made it clear that they were directing their efforts toward organizing the party within the armed forces.

In a Communist state it is not enough for the majority of the cadres of the armed forces to be party members. It is also necessary to give them a party organization that will enable the leadership to impose its will on them. Before January 1964 there had been talk at various times about following this example in Cuba,[33] but it was not until after Castro's second visit to Moscow that a serious

[31] See an excellent article on this by Angel Rama, "En Cuba se polemiza" [Polemics in Cuba], *Marcha* (Montevideo), March 6, 1964. According to Rama, when summaries of Ilyichev's and Khrushchev's remarks at the Soviet Communist Party Central Committee session of June 18–21 concerning questions of ideology were published in *Cuba Socialista*, August 1963, "there were a great many intellectuals who were alarmed . . . and tried to express their opposition. . . . When the politicians in charge were consulted, they requested that since it involved the head of state of a friendly country there should be no discussion of opinions."

[32] "Final de respuesta a Alfredo Guevara" [Final Reply to Alfredo Guevara], *Hoy*, December 27, 1963.

[33] Escalante did this in his report to the plenum of the ORI in Oriente (*Revolución*, December 11, 1961), and we know what happened. Raúl Castro returned to the theme in July 1963 (*Hoy*, July 21, 1963). On December 7 it was announced that the setting up of the PURS in the FAR would soon begin (*Verde Olivo*, September 27, 1964), and one unit was in fact set up in the middle of that month (*Hoy*, January 5, 1964). But the task was not seriously embarked upon until the January 25, 1964 speech of Raúl Castro (fragments of which appeared in *Cuba Socialista*, March 1964), that is after Castro's return, as it says in the text.

attempt was made to organize the PURS within the Revolutionary Armed Forces. This in itself indicates very convincingly that the decision was one result of his trip.[34]

By the autumn of 1964 the organization of the party in the Eastern Army had been completed, and it had been begun in the Central Army. All this conformed to the Soviet model, modified, with respect to recruiting, by Castro's innovations. The soldiers of every unit selected "model fighters."[35] Then, through meetings, self-criticism, and analysis, the party cell was formed and elected its Bureau. All the cells depend on the political department of the armed forces, composed of the political chiefs of the three army corps and headed by a chief. Finally, the political department is subordinated to the military department of the National Directorate of the PURS.

In spite of the party organization, the army is ruled on the principle of a single chain of command, which means that orders from superiors are obligatory. However, if an order has been dictated by a member of the party it may be subjected to criticism from the superior political organ. Members of cells at the same level must submit criticism in writing and only to the secretary of the cell, and they are forbidden to raise such questions in the meetings. Finally, once the state of combat alarm is announced, all the party organs cease to function, and the military chain of command stands alone.

Two things must be explained. First, Castro, in spite of his title of Commander-in-Chief, was never present at any of the numerous meetings held during the organization of the party in the Revolutionary Armed Forces, nor, as far as I have been able to ascertain, has he ever referred to this activity, whereas his brother Raúl and Blas Roca participated in it and identified themselves with it. It is difficult not to see in this differing opinions concerning the task to be accomplished. Second, in spite of the Prime Minister's disinterest, it seems significant that at the end of 1964 neither the chief of the political department nor the two political chiefs of the army corps were people who had belonged to the ranks of the PSP.[36] Hence it

34 It is significant in this connection that *Hoy* waited until January 31, 1964 to devote an editorial to "the building of the party in the armed forces."

35 For what follows see Justina Alvarez' report in *Hoy*, March 27, 1964, based on the "Constitutional Draft for the PURS Organizations in the FAR."

36 At the time mentioned, José N. Cause was the chief of the National Political Department, Julio Camacho was the chief of the Central Army (Matanzas and Las Villas provinces), and Walfrido de la O. Estrada was the

would be excessive to conclude that the "old" Communists had been given a prize worthy of their patience and their efforts.

In addition to this extremely important extension of the PURS's activities, it was announced in December that the mass organizations had been restructured to adapt them to the organization of the PURS, and in January the Union of Communist Youth was reorganized, removing Castro's protégé Joel Iglesias as secretary-general.[37] All this indicates that the period of Cuban-Soviet cordiality initiated at the end of 1963 was being well exploited by those who wanted to adapt Castro's "socialism" to the Soviet model. But a considerable distance still remained between the two models. There is no evidence whatsoever that the decisions taken during this period were made by the National Directorate of the PURS or by its Secretariat. In reality we do not even know whether either one of these two organs ever made any decisions at all.[38] Moreover, the Prime Minister kept administration of the state in his own hands. Even in the local sphere the "experiment" of establishing an administrative organ in the municipality of Güines had not been completed even after one whole trial year.[39] And in the Council of Ministers, even though Carlos Rafael Rodríguez became a member, the two other changes that were made gave cabinet rank to two Fidelistas of the oldest vintage — Marcelo Fernández and Jesús Montané.[40]

As for the economy, the objectives outlined by Castro on his return from Moscow remained unchanged, that is, the building of a type of socialism not foreseen by Marx based on the cultivation of sugarcane and the breeding of livestock. This total revision in

chief of the Eastern Army (Camagüey and Oriente provinces). The statement in the text is unqualified with respect to the first two, and with some reservations about the last.

Since this was written the organization of the party within the army has been completed. It would seem that the army too is going through some kind of reorganization. For example, there is now an "Armored Army Corps, Reserve of the Commander in Chief" (Castro), which had never been mentioned before (*Granma*, February 3, 1967).

[37] The restructuring of the mass organizations was announced in *El Mundo*, December 19, 1963. For the removal of Joel Iglesias see *ibid.*, January 7, 1964.

[38] The Cuban press never mentioned the meetings of the National Directorate of the PURS or its resolutions, if there were any.

[39] See *Hoy*, February 23, 1964, according to which the "constitution of the party organs" had not yet been completed at the local level.

[40] Carlos Rafael Rodríguez acquired the title of Minister in November 1963, when Article 48 of the agrarian reform law was modified; Marcelo Fernández as president of the National Bank had been one since August. Montané replaced Chomón in communications in December, the latter becoming the Minister for transport. Omar Fernández was left outside of the cabinet.

his initial intentions — namely, to shake off the yoke of mono-culture and to industrialize the country — and his persistent in-ablity to get back to the economic levels that preceded socialization called for an explanation; but Castro, as was his habit, did not give one or at least did not do so in a coherent fashion. Carlos Rafael Rodríguez and Ernesto Guevara undertook this painful task. Mistakes, they said, had been made, but these had been so numerous that they could not even begin to give an account of them.[41] Correction of the mistakes was favored by the following cir-cumstances: First, sugar had reached exceptionally high prices in the world market during these months. Second, the Soviet Union agreed to let Cuba take advantage of this trade situation by selling more sugar on the world market, so that although the imbalance of trade between the two countries came to $240 million in 1963 and was estimated at $159 for 1964, Castro found some foreign exchange in order to buy, for instance, buses from Great Britain.[42] Finally, dur-ing his stay in the Soviet Union in January Castro signed a treaty whereby the Soviets agreed to take 2,100,000 tons of sugar in 1965 and one million more tons each successive year until the figure of 5 million was reached in 1968; all this was at the price of 6 cents a pound, which was lower than the world market price at that par-ticular time but was nevertheless very profitable for the Cubans.[43]

As I have said, all this was bound to encourage correction of the errors that had been committed. But here two differences emerged between the revolutionary leaders. Guevara, for instance, stated that as far as he was concerned "economic socialism without Com-munist morality" had no interest for him, and he defended very energetically "the development of a feeling of work consciousness" as a much more effective means by and large than "the whole com-plex system of material incentives" to increase productivity.[44] Con-

41 The interested reader can find them in Carlos Rafael Rodríguez' speech in *Revolución*, November 8, 1963 (JPRS 22,302, December 16, 1963), and in his article "El nuevo camino de la agricultura Cubana" [The New Road of Cuban Agriculture], *Cuba Socialista*, November 1963. As for Guevara see, among others, his interview with the Mexican periodical *Siempre* (*Hoy*, June 19, 1963), his Algerian address (*Revolución*, July 15, 1963), his speech at the Forum for Electrical Energy (*ibid.*, November 25, 1963).

42 Data concerning 1963 have been taken from an article by Harry Schwartz based on Soviet statistics (*The New York Times*, September 20, 1964), and the estimates for 1964 from the statements by a member of the Soviet delegation who signed the agreement for 1964 (*El Mundo*, January 19, 1964).

43 In accordance with the agreement the Soviet Union was also to buy 5 million tons in 1969 and 1970. For the text see *Hoy*, January 23, 1964.

44 For instance, in his interview with Jean Daniel, reproduced in *Marcha*,

sequently, in the businesses that were subjected to the authority of the Ministry of Industries, piece-work wages were rejected and "voluntary" labor was insisted on; the establishment of what is called "wages for standard time with bonuses" was initiated. Each class of work was assigned a minimum production goal within a given unit of time. If the worker failed to accomplish the work indicated, his salary was cut proportionately. If he went above the production goal, he was paid a bonus.[45] Carlos Rafael Rodríguez, on the other hand, proposed to generalize the piece-work wage system by extending it to agriculture.[46] "Material incentive" was the basis of the system that was established for the sugarcane producers until 1970.[47]

Nor did the differences stop there. Even though Guevara accepted as a matter of discipline Castro's decision to concentrate on the production of sugar, he lost no opportunity of reminding the "comrades" that there could not be "any vanguard country that did not develop its industry."[48] He clashed openly with the director of the National Bank over the best method to finance nationalized enterprises. Marcelo Fernández defended the system called "economic autonomy," "self-financing," or "financial autonomy" that was, he said, used "in the Soviet Union and in almost all the socialist countries." In this system the goals were laid down by the state economic plan but the enterprises retained relative autonomy in their realization: they had the right to handle the resources entrusted to them, to establish direct relations of interchange with the other enterprises, to measure the results of their activity in monetary terms, and to have recourse to banking credit to supplement their needs.[49] As against this, Guevara came out "energetically, on all fronts," for "the principle of centralized organization of the economy in accordance with Cuban conditions" and for "the principle

---

August 2, 1963; his speech at a graduation held in December (*Revolución*, December 18, 1963); and his speech at the giving of awards to the winners of the "emulation" contest in 1963 (*Hoy*, March 15, 1964).

[45] See Augusto Martínez Sánchez, "La implantación del nuevo sistema salarial en las industrias de Cuba" [The Introduction of the New Wage System in Cuban Industries], *Cuba Socialista*, October 1963, and the various comments made at the television round table presented on the occasion of the introduction of the wage scale, *El Mundo*, December 28, 1963. According to this, 247 factories and 44,000 workers were "experimenting with the norms."

[46] In his "El nuevo camino," *op. cit.*

[47] See the text of Law No. 1143, published in the press on February 2, 1964.

[48] In his speech published in *Hoy*, March 15, 1964.

[49] Marcelo Fernández' article in *Cuba Socialista*, February 1964.

of the budgetary system of financing," which he himself had established when he took over the Department of Industrialization of the INRA. Once the plan was approved, the resources assigned each enterprise for a fixed period of time were laid down in the budget and also the amount consumed. As a consequence, there was never any need to call on bank credit, but profitability was measured by means of "cost control."[50] It is obvious that under this system subordination to the plan was far more strict, but it is also obvious that, as Fernández objected, the enterprises would lack any incentive to demand payment for the goods and services they were producing, so that the deficits kept getting bigger all the time.[51]

The Trial of Marcos Rodriguez

Toward the spring of 1964, Castro, with the approval of the Soviet Union, attempted to reach an understanding with the United States, which he assumed was strenuously trying to persuade Khrushchev to withdraw from Cuba of his own volition.[52] Under these conditions the Cuban leader obviously had to take great pains not to displease the Soviets, for instance, by raising obstacles to the extension of party activities. But in the long run this meant the limitation of his personal power. In the short run it accentuated the misgivings and the alienation of the Fidelistas who were not ready to share with others the revolutionary booty, which kept getting more and more meager all the time. They had not been trained in loyalty to the party but believed simply in the charismatic qualities of their chief. They lacked the ideological education, the dedication, and the discipline that would have been indispensable both for opposing the Communist challenge within the PURS and for preserving their own cohesion under the leadership of Castro. Hence Castro needed to produce some event similar to, though far more subtle than, the Escalante affair of March 26, 1962 that would cool off the organizational ardor of the "old" Communists, restore the

50 Guevara's answer in *ibid.*, March 1964, under the title "La banca, el crédito, y el socialismo" [Bank, Credit, and Socialism].

51 See Marcelo Fernández' article in *ibid.*, February 1964, and Guevara's television appearance, reproduced in *Revolución*, February 26, 1964, where he gave figures both on the failure to fulfill the plan for 1963 and for the sums that the enterprises had failed to collect.

52 In a conversation with some foreign journalists Castro said that Washington's objectives were "war against us and peace with the Soviet Union" (*Bohemia*, August 7, 1964).

confidence of his followers, and once again remind everyone that he alone was in command.

In my opinion this is the significance of the trial of Marcos Rodríguez, which began on March 14, 1964. Since it sheds much light on the history of the Cuban revolution, we shall consider it in some detail. Castro later maintained that he had been one of those taken by surprise by this trial,[53] but the evidence indicates just the opposite.

On February 21, 1964 a mass demonstration was held to welcome a number of fishermen who had been detained by the American authorities and later released. Castro was present and, as always, was close to a television camera; however, instead of joining in the national rejoicing, he castigated the journalists, accusing them of incompetence and mendacity and berating them for not telling the truth in much of their reporting.[54] Seven days later one of the most widely read Cuban commentators, Segundo Casáliz, who used the pseudonym "Siquitrilla," headed his column "The Press in the Revolution." He thanked Fidel for his "criticism" and reproduced his remarks. After alluding to the times in which "sectarianism" — a term used to refer to the stage that preceded Escalante's expulsion — had "reared its ugly head," he summed up the duty of the revolutionary journalist: "to demand more and more access to news, . . . to speak the truth more and more, . . . to print the news as it was":[55] that is, let us add, to disregard the existence of the Commission for Revolutionary Orientation (COR), among whose duties was to determine the publishing policy of the revolutionary press.

It was surely in fulfillment of this "duty" stipulated by Casáliz that on March 16 *Revolución* informed its readers on the front page that the preceding Saturday the trial of Marcos Rodríguez had begun. Rodríguez had been accused of being the informer responsible for the assassination of four revolutionaries during the struggle against Batista. The newspaper reproduced some excerpts from his confession. In them Marcos Rodríguez stated that he had been a member of the Socialist Youth, that is, the youth organization of the PSP, at the time of the betrayal, which he explained as the result of "differences about the methods of struggle"; he, as a

[53] In his statement to the Supreme Court during the review of Rodríguez' appeal (*ibid.*, April 3, 1964).

[54] Castro attributed his annoyance to certain false reports put out by the press in connection with the building of fishing boats (*Revolución*, February 22, 1964).

[55] *Ibid.*, February 25, 1964.

socialist, had been a partisan of "mass struggle," whereas the victims, who were members of the Revolutionary Student Directorate, had been for violence of the type of the July 26 Movement.[56] If this background is further filled in by the fact that the principal witness for the prosecution was Faure Chomón, whom we know as one of Castro's favorites for carrying out his maneuvers, and that his mimeographed statement was widely circulated in Havana[57] — the only case in which it had been possible to "mock" police vigilance in this way — Castro's alleged ignorance in the matter appears implausible. The obvious conclusion is that the whole spectacle was staged under his direction and for very precise purposes: to demoralize the Communists and encourage his own followers.

Who was the accused?

In 1955 Marcos Rodríguez was eighteen years old. He worked in the cultural group "Our Times," which was controlled by the Communists. He was enrolled at the University Theater, had Marxist ideas, and was involved in some way with the PSP.[58] However, he did not behave as a Communist while at the university but collaborated with the Revolutionary Student Directorate in some of its clandestine activities and informed the PSP about them. The members of the Student Directorate did not trust Rodríguez — even without knowing of the services he was performing for the PSP — because of his relations with the Communists, his efforts to introduce anti-imperialist slogans into the demonstrations, and his opposition to "direct action."[59] Hence when the attack on the palace that was carried out on March 13, 1957 was being planned, not even Rodríguez' best friend in the Directorate, Joe Westbrook, told him a word of what was under way.

After the failure of the attack the survivors hid out wherever they could. Westbrook finally took refuge in an apartment rented by

56 On Sunday, March 15, *Hoy*, did not carry one word on the beginning of the trial; *Revolución* did not come out that day.

57 On March 19 Casáliz wrote that "Chomón's statement might be said to be on everyone's lips" (*Revolución*, March 19, 1964).

58 All the data concerning Rodríguez' life, as well as those dealing with the trial in general, are based on Chomón's statement at the hearing as revised and published by him, not the original document that was circulated in Havana, and on the stenographic version of the appeal session, both published in *Bohemia*, March 27 and April 3, 1964.

59 In addition they believed him to be a homosexual because he always carried a yellow coat, wore sandals, and walked about with a book under his arm. It has always been very difficult to convince Cuban "men of action" that someone who is seen with books does not have something homosexual about him.

another friend of Rodríguez'. There, on the night of April 19, he was joined by three of the most redoubtable fighters of the Directorate: Pedro Carbó, Fructuoso Rodríguez, and José Machado. A little later Marcos arrived for a meeting with Westbrook. When he found Westbrook in such company, he could not conceal his anxiety; he knew that both he and his friend were lost if the police found them there. The new arrivals noticed his fear, reproached him for it, and made coarse fun of him. Rodríguez left feeling humiliated, thirsting for revenge, and knowing that Westbrook would no longer be in the apartment the next day.

On the morning of April 20 Rodríguez telephoned Ventura, one of the most notorious of Batista's police officers, and made an appointment with him for three o'clock that afternoon. He then ascertained that Westbrook would not return to the apartment, saw Ventura, gave the address of the hideout, took a bath, and went to the movies. When he came out of the theatre he already saw the results of his betrayal in the press. They were all dead. But he had two surprises. According to the press report there were four, not three, corpses — he soon learned that the fourth was that of his friend Westbrook, who had unexpectedly gone back to the hiding place — and for reasons that are still unknown, the police had named Marcos Rodríguez as the only one who had escaped. Terrified, Rodríguez took asylum in an embassy and a little later left Cuba.

In 1958 Marcos arrived in Mexico, where he met Joaquín Ordoqui, who later became Vice-Minister of Defense, and his wife, Edith García Buchaca, two eminent leaders of the PSP. One afternoon he confessed his treachery to Señora Buchaca,[60] in what terms we do not know. But the manner in which he justified himself can easily be surmised. He had been giving the PSP information on the

---

[60] Señora Buchaca, of course, always denied hearing such a confession. In his confrontation with her, Rodríguez retracted his statement, claiming that it had been suggested to him by the interrogator. On being confronted with this official, however, he did not maintain this new version. Nevertheless, at the hearing and at the appeal session, he again accused the interrogator. For various reasons, I am inclined to believe that Señora Buchaca did indeed hear a confession from Rodríguez and withheld this information from the authorities after the triumph of the revolution, thus making herself an accessory after the fact to Rodríguez' crime. It seems significant that she has completely disappeared from public view since the trial. Without the confession, one of the fundamental elements of Communist implication in the case would have been lacking, and the idea of using the trial against the "old" Communists probably would not have come up.

activities of the Revolutionary Directorate, as Señora Buchaca doubtless knew. He had ascertained that this was an "action group" without ideology or principles, against "unity," accepting money from the tyrant Trujillo as well as from the Auténticos — in brief a new "revolutionary mafia," which like its predecessors would end up assassinating Communists. From the party's point of view, accordingly, his sin was not irredeemable. It is not known whether Señora Buchaca approved of his conduct. But Rodríguez relates that she told him of an episode in Chinese party history in which certain comrades — Tang Ling and Lin Tang — who had fallen into similar "errors" later obtained absolution by a life consecrated to the party. Rodríguez promised to redeem himself in the same manner, applied for party membership, and was admitted. But instead of going into the underground or to the Sierra, he used his new membership to apply for a scholarship in Czechoslovakia.

Before he was granted the scholarship, Batista fled, and Rodríguez decided to return to Cuba. The members of the Revolutionary Directorate, among others the widow of one of the dead men, Fructuoso Rodríguez, had suspected him ever since the police had indiscreetly mentioned him as the one who had escaped at the time of the shooting. How could the police authorities know him if he had never been arrested, and how could they identify him with the Directorate? Rodríguez naturally avoided the members of the Directorate but was finally tracked down working in the cultural department of the Rebel Army. They managed to have him arrested but could not prove the crime. Two of Ventura's henchmen who knew the informer were shot before a confrontation could be arranged, in spite of Fructuoso's widow's request that the executions be postponed. A third one did not recognize Rodríguez when the latter was brought before him; furthermore, the PSP demanded that the Student Directorate should make its accusations concrete. But now the Directorate was "unitary" and was interested in eliminating any friction with the Communists. Hence it made little effort to prove the accusation, and in any case did not convince the representatives of the PSP. Rodríguez was released and sent to Prague to take up his scholarship.

At the beginning of 1961 the government Department of Security suspected that Rodríguez, who was performing a great many services for the Cuban embassy in Czechoslovakia, was providing some foreign power with reports. The department had him arrested, taken to Cuba, and imprisoned. At his trial nothing appeared to confirm the charge, but the accusation that he had been a police informer turned up again, we do not know how or when. In September 1962 Rodríguez managed to send a letter to Ordoqui from prison. He reminded Ordoqui of the services he had performed for the PSP in the ranks of the Student Directorate, denied the betrayal, emphasized the distinction between informing one's party and informing the police, invoked the principles of "socialist law" that had been violated in his case, and made a threat: "This game may turn out to be dangerous, like exploding a nuclear weapon in the bosom of mankind."

Under the "petit-bourgeois" regime of the first few months of the revolution, the PSP had been able to protect its comrades, but in Castro's "socialist Cuba" a member of the National Directorate of the PURS was apparently unable to do anything. Ordoqui ignored the letter. Then friends and acquaintances of Rodríguez made copies of it and sent them to well-known revolutionary figures.[61]

Early in 1963, at the time Castro was getting ready for his trip to Moscow, Rodríguez finally confessed his crime. When Castro was told of the confession, he informed his brother Raúl and Dorticós but not the Secretariat or the Directorate of the PURS, gave them strict orders to keep silent, and reserved the handling of the whole question to himself.[62] Finally Ordoqui, who must have heard of the circulation of Rodríguez' letter, decided to visit the Minister of the Interior, who passed him on to the President. Dorticós gave him an appointment for the following day and, after getting permission from Castro, told him in the presence of Blas Roca about the accused's confession. The result was a confrontation between the "contemptible traitor" and the "distinguished" wife of one of the vice-ministers of defense. Dorticós was left with the impression that all those present had been convinced of Señora Buchaca's innocence, but he was mistaken. At the trial the accusation against her was repeated.[63]

Now that we have this background, which sheds so much light on the character of the forces that finally imposed themselves on the process of the Cuban revolution, on the conflict that divides them,

61 Including Castro, who in his statement at the 1964 trial maintained that the copy had failed to reach him; he gave a confused explanation.

62 This is what Castro said at the trial. However, it must be remarked that Ordoqui was appointed one of the vice-ministers of defense on April 25, 1963, that is, when Castro was about to leave for Moscow. Hence it appears that at that time he did not ascribe much importance to Rodríguez' confession.

63 Castro was not present at the confrontation.

and on the internal mechanisms of power in Cuba and its monopolization by Castro, we can resume the account of the trial itself.

On March 18 Rodríguez was condemned to death, but on March 16 the ex-members of the PSP had already gone into action,[64] so effectively that on March 20 Castro himself announced that the sentence had been appealed and that there would be no limitation whatever to the calling of witnesses before the Supreme Court.[65]

This was the first indication that things were not going according to plan. The disappearance of the accused would have made it virtually impossible for the Communists to explain the part they had played in the events.

Soon there were other indications. At the first session of the appeals court Chomón disavowed the mimeographed version of his statement at the hearing and deplored its use by "counterrevolutionary elements" to spread "an antisectarianism that was nothing but another sectarianism." The same day, March 23, Blas Roca attended a meeting of the PURS, accompanied — significantly — by a secretary of the Soviet embassy, and announced that the trial would end with "a victory of the revolution," that is, that the PSP would be exonerated.[66] The next day Roca himself started a series of articles entitled "Trotsky Sabotaged the Peace Negotiations."[67]

It is true that the other two Fidelistas most compromised in the operation — Enrique de la Osa, who had replaced Franqui in the editorship of *Revolución,* and Casáliz — continued with the offensive,[68] but the successive court sessions confirmed what Castro's letter had already made likely in any case, that the original plan had to be abandoned and that the most to be hoped for was an orderly retreat.

[64] Carlos Rafael Rodríguez said at the trial that the moment he read the report in *Revolución* he began to make arrangements for the Communists to be heard. According to Blas Roca, when Chomón's statement began to be circulated "the situation was taken under consideration by the National Directorate of the PURS." Roca continued, "with the letter of Comrade Fidel and with the decisions that were announced, the leadership of the revolution, the PURS, took the situation in hand." (*Cuba Socialista,* May 1964.) This is one of the very rare occasions on which, as far as we know, the National Directorate of the PURS took anything "in hand."

[65] Castro's letter to Blas Roca was published in *Hoy,* March 21, 1964.

[66] *Revolución* and *Hoy,* March 24, 1964.

[67] Continued the following day in *Hoy,* March 25, 1964.

[68] An editorial, "Decir siempre la verdad" [Always Tell the Truth], in *Revolución,* March 26, 1964, and Casáliz' column in the same issue, "¿Informar, confunde o aclara?" [Does Information Confuse or Clarify?].

In fact, even though Rodríguez confirmed his original confession, the witnesses of "Castroite" origin avoided political exploitation of it against the Communists, while the latter displayed an unusual aggressiveness. Señora Buchaca denounced the "campaign of slander and calumny" against the ex-members of the PSP. César Escalante even defended his brother Aníbal. And Carlos Rafael Rodríguez took advantage of the occasion to demonstrate publicly his return to the ranks from which he had come: "I am an old Communist, and proud of it," he said, "proud of my whole life, and proud of the life of the PSP."

Castro made his appearance on the last day. His statement simply confirmed the failure of the whole operation. In spite of the confession of the accused, he maintained that Rodríguez had not been a member of the Socialist Youth in 1957, that he had informed the Communists about the activities of the Student Directorate on his own accord, and that his activities had been justified, because he himself, Castro, had infiltrated some of his men into other revolutionary organizations during the struggle against Batista. He exonerated the PSP of any responsibility for the events that had taken place in 1959 and had enabled Rodríguez to make a mock of revolutionary justice. He proclaimed the innocence of Edith García Buchaca and displayed his admiration for the statement of César Escalante, "who was on a lofty height, incredible, and humane" and "very fair and very valiant in the defense of his brother Aníbal." He even attempted to explain why he had not brought the matter to the attention of the National Directorate of the PURS after he had been told of the accused's confession. He was critical only of Ordoqui for having allowed Rodríguez to enter the PSP in 1958 and for having hidden from the Revolutionary Student Directorate the letter that Rodríguez had sent him in September 1962.

After making all these concessions, Castro could extend his protection to Chomón and the editor of *Revolución,* for whom he had some slight criticism but whose conduct he defended, sacrificing only the most insignificant, Segundo Casáliz, who disappeared from the pages of the revolutionary press.[69]

69 The disappearance was temporary, since a few months later his byline reappeared in *Bohemia,* for instance, on October 23, 1964. At the beginning of 1966 Casáliz broke with Castro. He has since published, in Venezuela, a book titled *Significación real del caso Marcos Rodríguez* [The Real Meaning of the Trial Against Marcos Rodriguez] (Ediciones Isla Sola, 1966). Although he does not say very much he does write that Castro himself "authorized" the opening of the trial with the purpose of condemning Ordoqui, his wife, and Raúl Valdés Vivó, the assistant editor of *Hoy.*

The response of the two parties involved, the Fidelistas and the "Communists," to the result of the trial shows both its peculiar characteristics and the meaning of the event. While Chomón, de la Osa, and Casáliz kept absolute silence, Ordoqui hastened to thank Castro for his criticism and to acknowledge "fully" his errors.[70]

Blas Roca, who had never been touched personally by the affair, possibly because he enjoyed some special — Soviet — protection, expounded the lessons to be drawn from these events: The trial had resulted in a triumph over "the divisionists," "the schemers," "the new breed of sectarians," "and even over the defenders of" the freedom of artistic creation — showing that he had not forgotten Alfredo Guevara's attacks on "socialist realism." Even though the damage that could still be caused by such elements must not be underestimated, the innocence of the PSP had emerged so resplendently from the ordeal and Castro's posture had been so unequivocally "unitary" that the whole affair offered an excellent opportunity to end once and for all the "factional spirit," replacing it with "the reality of a single party" and the "acceptance of a leadership, headed by our chief and guide . . . Comrade Fidel. . . ."[71]

As for Marcos Rodríguez himself, after the sentence against him had been confirmed, he was shot.

The Climax of the Moderate Phase

The adverse result of the Marcos Rodríguez trial does not seem to have changed Castro's foreign policy. When Senator Fulbright made his famous speech, in which he recommended abandoning "the myth that Cuban communism . . . is going to collapse or disappear in the immediate future" and accepting that it would stay on as "a disagreeable reality,"[72] Castro hastened to express his approval and once again offered to restore trade relations between the two countries and to consider the possibility of paying indemnity for the confiscated U.S. properties.[73] But the overthrow of President Goulart of Brazil by a military coup on April 1, 1964 was a rude blow for him. Goulart's government had been one of the five in Latin America that still maintained relations with Cuba. Moreover,

[70] "Self-criticism" by Comrade Joaquín Ordoqui (*Hoy,* March 29, 1964).

[71] An editorial in *ibid.,* March 29, 1964, and Roca's article in *Cuba Socialista,* May 1964, *op. cit.*

[72] Senator Fulbright's speech in *The New York Times,* March 26, 1964.

[73] A telephone conversation with a correspondent of the American Broadcasting Company (*ibid.,* April 3, 1964).

Washington's delight at the coup and the openly pro-U.S. attitude of the new Brazilian government was bound to arouse in Castro the fear that his formidable opponent would soon try to exploit the worsening of Cuba's international position. Consequently Castro for a brief period abandoned his moderate line.

Once more he warned world public opinion of the danger for peace of the flights of U.S. U-2 planes over Cuba, although these had been going on for many months without his mentioning them. Rather than accept any principle, theory, or doctrine that would oblige him to endure these violations, he would prefer to "disappear as a revolution, as a people, and even as an island." He vowed that he would never betray "the faith put in us by the exploited peoples of this continent."[74] But once he saw that the only result of the coup was the rupture of Brazilian relations with Cuba and some new OAS decisions against him, while the Soviets copiously reiterated their solidarity,[75] he recovered his composure.

At the beginning of July, in an interview with Richard Eder of *The New York Times,* Castro revealed with complete clarity all the objectives he had been pursuing since the end of the previous year. He said that since the revolutionary leaders were now more mature, and the United States had been demonstrating, with the Alliance for Progress, that it was ready to accept a certain degree of social change in Latin America, there was now the possibility of a reconciliation. To this end "Cuba would commit herself to withhold material support from Latin American revolutionaries if the United States and its American allies would agree to cease their material support of subversive activity against Cuba." The resumption of trade relations could begin appropriately with discussions over compensations for the confiscated properties, and if the friendship proceeded, as many as 90 per cent of the political prisoners — whom he conservatively estimated at 15,000 — would be released, just as other measures of liberalization would be taken until a constitutional government was established — not later than June 1, 1969.[76]

74 The April 19 speech in *Hoy,* April 21, 1964, and the May 1 speech in the Cuban Press the following day.

75 For example, in the May 1 greetings of the Soviet Communist Party in *Pravda,* April 14, 1964 (*CDSP,* Vol. XVI, No. 15 [May 6, 1964]); an editorial in *Izvestiya* [*Hoy,* April 26, 1964]. Khrushchev's speech in the Kremlin in the presence of Ben Bella (*The New York Times,* May 2, 1964); the communiqué issued on this occasion (*Revolución,* May 7, 1964); the statements of the Soviet ambassador in Cuba, Alexeyev (*Bohemia,* May 15, 1964); the communiqué on the occasion of Khrushchev's visit to Egypt (*The New York Times,* May 25, 1964).

76 *The New York Times,* July 6, 1964.

Although this interview was not printed verbatim in Cuba, the proposal to sacrifice Latin American "comrades" in exchange for anti-Castro fighters seems to have been received badly in revolutionary circles.[77] Castro thus deemed it necessary to clarify the matter: The journalist had not rendered his thought correctly. What he had in fact said was as follows: "Could there be any international relations if countries did not carry out their promises? Of course not. And if Cuba's neighbors promised not to meddle in its internal affairs, could the revolutionary government betray their confidence by fomenting subversion on their territory? There could be no question of that."[78] Thus, "dialectically," the offer was confirmed.

In his interview with Eder, Castro avoided reference to the other "nonnegotiable element" — an agreement with Washington concerning his dependence on Russia. However, there are certain signs that he had not lost sight of this obstacle and was preparing to circumvent it. Cuba was planning to take part in the conference of nonaligned countries, announced for October in Cairo, in spite of the presence of Venezuela, its accuser at the OAS. It is true that he responded in the negative when asked, "Is neutralization an adequate description of your goal?"[79] But one must not always believe Castro's words, especially when, as in the present case, acceptance of his neutrality by the United States would permit him to continue doing as he wished in Cuba.

In my opinion the offers and counteroffers made in July brought to a head the moderate phase that had been initiated at the end of 1963. It is obvious that there are many people who will think that the whole thing was merely one more pretense and that in his innermost heart Castro continued to be an intransigent revolutionary. This may be so, but I should like to make three points.

First of all, even if it were a mere pretense, the fact that Castro had to resort to it would be a sign of the deterioration in his position. Second, this deterioration imposed precisely the sort of

77 Raúl Castro, who had already reappeared around this time and seemed to have been integrated with the "peaceful" line, mentioned the interview with his brother, advising his listeners to be "very, very careful of prefabricated clichés" in the analysis of the international situation. See his speech of July 20, 1964 in *Revolución*, July 27, 1964.

78 Speech made on July 26, 1964 in Santiago de Cuba (radio version) and a news conference with foreign journalists (*Bohemia*, August 7, 1964).

79 It is a meaningful coincidence that *Le Monde* should have published on April 29, 1964 a plan drawn up by "a group of Cuban revolutionaries living on the island . . . for the neutralization of Cuba."

policy that was adopted by Castro. Third, since his offer was rejected, explicitly by the United States and implicitly by the OAS, we shall never be absolutely sure that it was nothing but a deception.[80]

In the terminology of the Sino-Soviet conflict this policy was a manifestation of peaceful coexistence aimed at an agreement with "Yankee imperialism," "the most ferocious enemy of all nations," as the Chinese put it, in the very year 1964 that the Sino-Soviet conflict reached new heights. Furthermore, even though Castro never signed the nuclear test ban treaty, he always insisted that it was because this "victory of the Soviet Union's peace policy" was contradicted by U.S. conduct in the Caribbean — whereas the Chinese considered the nuclear treaty unspeakable treachery. At the numerous international meetings, such as the World Peace Council and the Women's International Democratic Federation, the Cuban delegates, as far as I know, never voted in favor of Chinese resolutions or abstained. When Castro was offered an agreement on the sale of sugar, he did not, as we know, have any objections to condemning the factionalist activities of the Chinese or to approving the moves of the Soviet Communist Party that were aimed at restoring the unity of the world Communist movement. In spite of all this Castro's position in relation to the conflict between the Chinese and the Soviets led to certain confusions. This was because from August 1963 Cuba failed to reproduce the documents involved in the dispute and pretended that no dispute existed. Cuba's relations with Albania remained unchanged, as did those with Yugoslavia, and Castro kept disregarding Khrushchev's frantic maneuvers to arrange an international conference that would condemn the Chinese.

Castro, both because of his background and his own nature, has always been essentially alien to a polemic in which ideological and pragmatic political motives are equally mingled and which is expressed in ideological terms. Hence he has always looked on the Sino-Soviet polemic, and still does, as just one more conflict that can be exploited in accordance with his own interests — which are to preserve his authority in Cuba and to extend it as he sees fit and not in accordance with any declarations of the Chinese and the Soviets. But with this in mind we still believe that his conduct

[80] On July 7 *The New York Times* published the official rejection by the U.S. Department of State, and on July 26 the OAS agreed to order its members to break off diplomatic, commercial, and maritime relations with Cuba.

throughout the period we have been studying was decidedly "pro-Soviet."

It must be conceded, however, that the confusion concerning his position is quite understandable, given Castro's cunning willfulness and the relative autonomy he has been granted by both sides. The behavior of both the Chinese and the Soviets has, of course, an explanation. Until the Marcos Rodríguez trial Castro had always shown himself infinitely superior to the local Cuban Communists, who formed the principal lever by which the Soviets could hope to impose themselves on Cuba; the other means at their disposal — either diplomatic or economic — had to be used with a certain reserve, on pain of manifesting once more that relations within the socialist community were the same as or worse than in the "capitalist" world. Furthermore, I see no reason for the Soviets to doubt Castro's determination, both before and after the trial, to "disappear as a revolution, as a people, and even as an island" rather than endure and be reduced to insignificance. As for the Chinese, it seems extremely doubtful to me that Mao could ever have been convinced — as some observers have thought — that Castro was someone irresistibly drawn to his variety of revolutionary Marxism. It seems more likely that because they could not provide Castro with the economic, political, and military aid he needed, the Chinese contemplated his maneuvers with a certain benevolence. Finally, if they had condemned the Cuban leader as a "revisionist," whom would they have had left in Latin America?[81]

81 It is difficult to determine whether the presence of Ernesto Guevara, whose position coincided at a number of points with that of the Chinese, also had some influence on their good will. To this day it is still more difficult to determine whether the Argentine adopted this position in agreement with Castro — who needed someone to play this role — or because his current form of Marxism acutally did incline him in the direction of China.

CHAPTER NINE

CASTROISM OR COMMUNISM?

In the summer of 1964 the Castro regime still presented the same fundamental political features that had characterized it from the beginning. State power was based on the charismatic qualities of the leader who had created it, who ruled autocratically and through his most trusted followers, and who used it to conserve and if possible to extend this same power. However, since the crisis of October 1962 Castro has not had the successes needed to confirm his "exceptional powers or qualities."[1] Both his economic failures and external circumstances have increased his dependence on the Soviet Union. This dependency and the Marxist-Leninist ideology to which he had declared his adherence obligated him to organize a party whose leadership he would theoretically have to allow to participate in decision-making.

The purpose of this chapter is to describe the way in which these factors exerted pressure on Castro, with special emphasis on those that constitute the theme of our investigation; his solution to the problems created by such pressures; and the standing of the regime in the spring of 1966. Finally, it has been considered pertinent to formulate some observations on the character of the political system established in Cuba as a consequence of such a haphazard evolution.

The Fall of Khrushchev

Repeated statements by Cuban political figures confirmed that Castro's main objective after late 1963 — to arrive at a *modus vivendi* with the United States — remained unchanged until the fall of Khrushchev. In July 1964, for example, Carlos Rafael Rodríguez quoted Fidel Castro's interview with Richard Eder,

[1] Max Weber, *The Theory of Social and Economic Organization* (New York: Free Press of Glencoe, 1964), pp. 358 ff.

214

referred to in the preceding chapter, and concluded by pointing out that Cuba was preparing herself "especially for peace."[2] A little later Raúl Castro went further than his brother by saying of the famous five conditions of October 1962, "perhaps we might agree in dropping them."[3] In August, Blas Roca applied himself to the most difficult point: the conflict between the need for friendship with "imperialism" and the revolutionary "duties" of the Cubans toward the peoples of the hemisphere. These peoples, according to Roca, should understand that Cuba had to "comply" with certain international norms, and they should content themselves with the "moral support" and "sympathy" offered them by the Cubans within the boundaries of these norms.[4]

Finally, in October, at the conference of nonaligned countries in Cairo, the Cuban President was very clear about the position of his government. Cuba, Dorticós affirmed, is not a "member of any military bloc"; her conflict with the United States "does not stem from the tendencies of a cold war"; she constitutes a "nonaligned" state; and she subscribes to the principles of peaceful coexistence.[5] In this period the Cuban position had become so reasonable that the press had no difficulty in reproducing the results of the conference, at which Washington was "earnestly" solicited, always in the most civil language, to enter into negotiations with Cuba about the evacuation of the naval base at Guantánamo.[6]

From Cairo, Dorticós went to Moscow on the invitation of the Soviet government. He announced his intention of exchanging opinions with "the chief of the Soviet government, our friend Nikita Khrushchev."[7] It is amusing to picture the surprise of the Cuban President when he found out that "Cuba's great friend" had become an "unperson" some hours before.[8]

[2] *Revolución,* July 18, 1964.
[3] *The New York Times,* July 22, 1964. These words do not appear in the Spanish version (*Revolución,* July 25, 1964).
[4] *Cuba Socialista,* August 1964.
[5] *Revolución,* October 12, 1964.
[6] *Bohemia,* October 23, 1964.
[7] *Revolución,* October 15, 1964. Before going to Moscow Dorticós went to Algeria, where he confirmed that Cuba wanted "honorable negotiations" with the United States (*ibid.,* October 14, 1964). Ben Bella for his part said that "the moment has come for the U.S. to start a dialogue with Cuba (*The New York Times,* October 14, 1964).
[8] *Revolución,* October 15, 1964. According to the communiqué of the Central Committee of the CPSU, *Pravda,* October 16, 1964 (*CDSP,* Vol. XVI, No. 40 [October 28, 1964]), Khrushchev was deposed on October 14, that is, the day of Dorticós' arrival in Moscow.

Castro did not comment publicly on Khrushchev's fall, and the Cuban press confined itself to reproducing the Soviet explanation.[9] But it was soon seen that the change of government in the Soviet Union necessitated a revision of Cuba's foreign policy line, although the communiqué released about Dorticós' visit did not contain anything really new.[10]

As in the previous succession crisis, the first act of Khrushchev's heirs was to proclaim a return to Leninist orthodoxy: the Communist Party as the "guiding and leading force of Soviet society," and the principle of collective leadership.[11] Later they devoted themselves to the task of amending the work of the deposed Premier. What interests us here is their attempt to reach what William E. Griffith has called a "pragmatic armistice"[12] with the Chinese, that is, an end to public polemics and a show of re-establishing international Communist unity in exchange for friendly gestures and economic concessions. Since this plan required a delay in Khrushchev's long and tortuous maneuver to achieve some type of arrangement with the United States, its effects were bound to be felt in Cuba. That Castro understood this was demonstrated by the fact that as soon as Dorticós returned, Castro called for C. L. Sulzberger, who had been waiting for about two years for a visa to enter Cuba.[13] While he gave his guest a new version of how the installation of the rockets had come about, he also made use of

[9] To C. L. Sulzberger (*The New York Times*, November 14, 1964), Castro said "this is an internal problem for the Soviet Union." But, he added, "The change can have positive results for the Socialist camp, although as a person I had a great liking and respect for Khrushchev." This interview was not reprinted in Cuba. *Revolución*, October 16, 1964, reprinted the communiqué of the Central Committee of the CPSU without any comment. But it seems that "a largely Cuban official audience" applauded Khrushchev's image at the movies (*The New York Times*, November 8, 1964); and in *Bohemia*, October 23, 1964, Segundo Casáliz, one of Castro's accomplices in the trial against Marcos Rodríguez, wrote: "I like Nikita Khrushchev and I have always liked him very much."

[10] *Cuba Socialista*, November 1964. The communiqué reaffirmed the policy of peaceful coexistence, expressed Soviet support for Fidel's five conditions, "seriously" warned the United States on Vietnam, and emphasized the necessity for "using every effort" to produce the unity of the Communist movement.

[11] "Unshakeable Leninist General Line of the CPSU," *Pravda*, October 17, 1964 (*CDSP*, Vol. XVI, No. 40 [October 28, 1964]).

[12] William E. Griffith, *Sino-Soviet Relations, 1964–1965* (Cambridge, Mass.: The M.I.T. Press, 1967), p. 60.

[13] "But my visa took two years," Sulzberger said to Castro (*The New York Times*, November 2, 1964).

the facilities of *The New York Times* to begin erasing the tracks of his Khrushchevite past. His "conciliatory mood" of July, he said, assumed "an improvement in relations between Washington and Moscow," but "one must be realistic. . . ." He did not expect the re-establishment of relations for "many years." And he wanted to make it clear that his offer to Eder should be considered "within a world framework," that is, once "relations between all Socialist countries and the U.S.A. improve."[14]

That was not the only indication of the change that was taking place. Neither his brother Raúl, nor Dorticós, nor Rodríguez, nor Roca, nor any other leader spoke again of an arrangement with the United States. Guevara, who had always been against this policy,[15] now found it opportune to dispel any suspicion of a split in the leadership by proclaiming that Castro alone was "the man capable of leading Cuba."[16] And Fidel in successive speeches emphasized those themes he knew were agreeable to the Soviet leadership: the essential role of the party as a vanguard of the revolution, the forthcoming elaboration of "our socialist constitution," and the need to raise the levels of production and technology.[17]

But neither Brezhnev nor Kosygin seemed to be satisfied with this. Their initial conversations with the Chinese had not met with success. The friendly and dependent parties were now requested to support the Soviets by applying pressure on the Chinese. Castro, for his part, since the end of the year was approaching, urgently needed to conclude economic agreements with the Soviets for the following year. Already on November 24, 1964 the CPSU was able to inform the Chinese Communist Party that Cuba was among the nineteen members in favor of convening the drafting committee in charge of preparing an international Communist conference.[18] Around that same date, Havana was the site of a conference of Latin American

[14] The interview was published in *ibid.*, November 2, 4, 7, and 8, 1964. The words in the text appeared in the November 4 edition.

[15] "This is a fight to death . . . ," said Che, referring to the United States (*Revolución*, July 20, 1964); "our principal task: to fight against imperialism everywhere with all the arms that we have. . . ." (*ibid.*, July 25, 1964); see also *ibid.*, August 17, 1964.

[16] *Ibid.*, October 23, 1964.

[17] Speeches of Castro in *ibid.*, October 22, 26, and 31, 1964; also November 14 and 21, 1964.

[18] The text of the letter from the CPSU to the CCP was published in *Peking Review*, Vol. VIII, No. 13 (March 26, 1965), pp. 21–22. See also Griffith, *Sino-Soviet Relations, 1964–1965, op. cit.*, pp. 79–83.

Communist parties. The communiqué issued after the conference demonstrates the meeting's pro-Soviet tendencies.[19]

Notwithstanding these contributions to the Soviet cause, the only things that arrived from the Soviets on the sixth anniversary of the revolutionary triumph were greetings and declarations of support.[20] As an indication of how badly things were going, the military parade was reduced to half its usual size, in order "to economize" as Castro explained. Moreover, in the same speech, Fidel speculated on the possibility that if the fuel reserves — furnished by the Russians — were reduced, the last reserves would be kept for use by the armed forces and the urban population would be evacuated to the rural zones.[21] A few days later Castro revealed a military secret: "The day and night interceptors . . . and the missiles are in the hands of Cuban technicians!" The "decision" to use them rested solely therefore in his hands.[22] In view of Soviet precautions in Vietnam to avoid an open clash with the Americans, no great perspicacity is needed to realize whom these warlike words were addressed to.

On February 15 it was announced that Castro had taken the place of Carlos Rafael Rodríguez as president of INRA. This was the bulwark from which Rodríguez, protected by the Soviets, had resisted Guevara's efforts to extend to the whole economy the principles he had established in the enterprises under the command

[19] I call this "a pro-Soviet event" because, although the meeting agreed to "help actively" "the fighters" in Venezuela, Guatemala, and elsewhere, it did not recommend to others to follow their lead, nor did it say anything about the "violent road." The meeting also demanded "an immediate end to the polemic" between the Chinese and the Soviets, called for the unconditional unity of the international Communist movement, and condemned "every fractional activity" within the parties. It seems that the meeting had another purpose: to reconcile Castro with the "old" leaders of Latin American communism. Following the meeting some of them began to eulogize the Cuban revolution as "the supreme achievement to date in the anti-imperialist struggle of the Latin American peoples" (A. Ferrari, J. M. Fortuny, P. Motta Lima, and L. Ferreto, "The Cuban Revolution and the Anti-Imperialist Struggle of the Latin American Peoples," *World Marxist Review*, Vol. 8, No. 1 [January 1965], p. 32). See also E. Judisi, "The Revolutionary Process in Latin America," *ibid.*, Vol. 8, No. 2 (February 1965). Text of the communiqué in *Revolución*, January 19, 1965. See also the commentary of the *World Marxist Review*, Vol. 8, No. 3 (March 1965) on the communiqué.

[20] Soviet greeting in *Revolución*, January 2, 1965. The Chinese greeting appeared side by side with the Soviet message on the front page — another sign of the tension between Castro and the Soviet Union.

[21] *Ibid.*, January 4, 1965.

[22] *Ibid.*, January 22, 1965.

of the Ministry of Industries.[23] As we shall soon see, this substitution did not mean that Guevara's point of view had triumphed. The policy of INRA did not change and was now secure from criticism by Guevara because Castro himself accepted responsibility for it.

Two days later a contract of payments for five years and the commercial protocol for 1965 were signed in Moscow.[24] According to the latter — we know nothing about the former — the exchange of goods would increase 12 per cent over 1964 and Cuba would receive credit for 167 million dollars to cover the deficit. It may seem nonsensical to establish a relation between the removal of Rodríguez and the new commercial agreements. Nevertheless, if one looks closely, a connection between the two events can be established.

Even after learning from the Soviet letter of November 24, 1964 that the CPSU had secured Cuba's vote, the Chinese maintained their unchanging benevolence toward Castro's maneuvers. On December 31 a protocol was signed to broaden commercial relations between Cuba and China;[25] and the Chinese press, when referring to Latin America, never forgot to mention "the heroic Cuban people" who "under the leadership of Premier Castro" wage a "tit-for-tat struggle against U.S. imperialism."[26]

On February 3, 1965, a delegation from the PURS, headed by Guevara, arrived in Peking.[27] We do not know what they talked about. But considering the time that had elapsed since the last visit of such a high-level Cuban delegation to China,[28] and considering that the forthcoming meeting of the drafting committee had been announced in *Pravda* on December 12, it is permissible to assume that Guevara's mission was to explain that the Cuban decision to participate in this meeting was part of the price Castro would have to pay for the commercial treaty with the Russians that was signed some days later.

After this and after Cuba's participation in the Moscow "con-

23 For this conflict see Chapter 8 of this work.
24 *Revolución*, February 18, 1965.
25 *Ibid.*, January 5, 1965.
26 "Latin America Marches On," *Peking Review*, Vol. VIII, No. 3 (January 15, 1965).
27 According to *Peking Review*, Vol. VIII, No. 7 (February 12, 1965), the visit was made in response to an invitation of the Central Committee of the CCP. The Cuban delegation consisted of Guevara, Aragonés, and Cienfuegos.
28 Dorticós visited Peking in October 1961. Neither Fidel nor his brother Raúl have been in China at the time of this writing.

sultative" meeting in March, called "schismatic" by the Chinese, relations between Mao and Castro naturally could not be the same. Peking was not very severe.[29] The Albanians, however, called the event "a pro-imperialist meeting," its participants "revisionists" and "experienced conspirators";[30] and two months later, when Mao personally condemned the U.S. intervention in Santo Domingo, he ignored "the heroic Cuban people under the leadership of Premier Castro."[31]

By that time, May 1965, the Chinese leader may have had additional reasons for omitting any mention of Cuba and Castro. On March 13 Fidel made a speech condemning the divisions in the "socialist camp," disassociating "our people" from "such discord and such Byzantine battles," and warning that in Cuba only "our Party" would make propaganda.[32] Today we know, because Castro himself has told us, that this was a warning to the Chinese.[33] Even at that time, seeing this speech reproduced in the Soviet press and knowing that his works had been banned from Cuban bookstores, Mao must have understood what "Byzantinisms" Castro was referring to.[34] From all of the preceding it might be concluded that by the spring of 1965 Castro had been reduced to a Soviet satellite. But with Fidel things are not always so simple. Under the pressure of circumstances Castro had retreated step by step before the So-

[29] The Cuban delegation to the March Moscow meeting was formed by Raúl Castro, his wife Vilma Espín, and O. Cienfuegos. I have not been able to find in the Cuban press any commentary about the meeting. The communiqué was published in *Revolución*, March 10, 1965. *Peking Review*, Vol. VIII, No. 13 (March 26, 1965), published the Chinese reaction to the meeting under the title "A Comment on the March Moscow Meeting":

> The 19 units in attendance were rent by contradictions and disunity. Some of them wholeheartedly supported Khruschev's revisionism and splittism; some did so half-heartedly; others, for reasons they might find it awkward to divulge, had to attend under orders to serve as a claque at the show; and still others may have temporarily fallen into the trap from naivete. (p. 7)

We do not know in which of these four groups the Chinese included the Cubans — perhaps in the third.

[30] "The Splitting Revisionist March 1 Meeting — A Great Plot Against Marxism-Leninism and International Communism," *Zëri i Popullit*, March 18, 1966; excerpts in *Peking Review*, Vol. VIII, No. 15 (April 9, 1965), pp. 18–21, at p. 18.

[31] See *ibid.*, Vo. VIII, No. 20 (May 14, 1965), p. 60.

[32] Castro's speech of March 13, 1965 is quoted from a pamphlet received from Cuba.

[33] *Granma*, February 6, 1966.

[34] *Revolución*, March 19, 1965, reported that *Pravda* had dedicated "nearly a whole page" to Castro's speech. Paul Hoffman noticed the disappearance of Mao's works from Cuban bookstores (*The New York Times*, May 2, 1965).

viets, but at the same time he completed the liquidation of their best friends in Cuba, the PSP, thus reaffirming his control over the only thing he had left, his little island. On November 19, 1964 it was announced that Joaquín Ordoqui had been relieved of all his positions in the administration and in the party.[35] On December 9 the attempted suicide of Minister of Labor Augusto Martínez Sánchez was announced.[36] We already know what happened to Carlos Rafael Rodríguez in February. Finally, affected perhaps by the fate of his two most loyal lieutenants, Escalante and Ordoqui, the old pilot of the PSP, Blas Roca, developed a strange malady: "His head wobbled minutely but regularly, and even though he rested his hands on a table in front of him, these, too, exhibited the tremor."[37]

On the external front things did not remain quiet. In December Guevara went to Africa. Untiring as ever and resolved not to give up the struggle, Castro trusted Guevara to seek there the support the Latin Americans had denied him.

The Conflict with Guevara

In the preceding chapter, finished in March 1965, we referred to Guevara's disagreements with Castro's policy since late 1963; and, with the caution imposed by the scantiness of information, we pointed to the necessity of waiting for new developments before deciding whether these disagreements were authentic. Today there is no longer any ground for doubting the sincerity of the revolutionary hero who has disappeared.

[35] The resolution adopted by the National Directorate of the PURS was "unanimous." It stated that the suspension was originated by the need to "investigate his [Ordoqui's] political behavior from 1957 until the present." It promised "restitution" if the results of the investigation were favorable. Ordoqui has not yet been reappointed. According to some reports he is in jail. The name of his wife, Edith García Buchaca, another ex-leader of the PSP, has also disappeared from the Cuban press.

[36] As far as I know, Martínez Sánchez was never a member of the PSP. Nevertheless he was one of the most pliable collaborators of the Communists. Martínex Sánchez did not die but has not been heard from since. His name did not appear among the members the Central Committee of the PCC founded in October 1965. He was replaced as Minister of Labor by Basilio Rodríguez, a young Fidelista.

[37] Edwin Tetlow, *Eye on Cuba* (New York: Harcourt, Brace and World, 1966), p. 52. Although this work contains innumerable errors, it seems unlikely to me that Mr. Tetlow could have invented such a meticulous description of Roca's illness. *The New York Times*, August 16, 1966, also reports the illness and Roca's subsequent operation without specifying their nature.

According to Castro, Guevara voluntarily left the island on April 1, 1965 because "other lands of the world" claimed his "modest efforts."[38] However, at the same time that Che is being placed in the pantheon of the revolutionary heroes — together with Camilo Cienfuegos who disappeared just as mysteriously — he is being presented as a symbol of "petit-bourgeois conceptions," an impertinent romantic, incapable of adapting himself to the iron-clad conditions imposed by the "construction of socialism."[39] It is not our task to investigate Guevara's fate or to salvage his authentic image for posterity. But since his eclipse is undoubtedly relevant to the theme of this book, we must consider the significance of his disappearance in relation to our inquiry.

This is not the place to trace the differences between the two leaders. It is enough to say that these differences had existed since the Sierra times and that they came to a head as early as May 1959, when Guevara was sent out of the country.[40] When he returned and found that Fidel was carrying out agrarian reform, the promised industrialization, and was challenging "imperialism" by promoting Latin American revolution, he identified himself with the regime, became one of the most assiduous collaborators of the Prime Minister, and participated in the general enthusiasm, apparently believing that a socialist "paradise" was around the corner.

This identification lasted for several years. But the results of the October crisis must have awakened new doubts in Guevara. It turned out that the rockets, in which he had believed just as had the rest of the revolutionaries, were at the service of Soviet interests, not of world revolution. The "socialist international division of labor" once more turned the project of industrialization into a dream. The Soviets demanded that Cuba abandon economic principles without which, in Guevara's opinion, socialism would never be achieved. Finally, Khrushchev insisted on the postponement of

[38] Guevara's letter, undated but according to Fidel signed on April 1, 1965, was read by Castro in his speech presenting the new Central Committee of the PCC (*Verde Olivo*, October 10, 1965).

[39] For the inclusion of Guevara in the revolutionary mausoleum see *ibid.*, October 31, 1965, dedicated to commemorate the disappearance of Camilo Cienfuegos. The photographs of Guevara and Cienfuegos are displayed side by side in this copy, suggesting the irrevocable disappearance of both. For Guevara's image as an incurable romantic see Sol Arguedas, "¿Donde está el Che?" [Where is Che?] *Cuadernos Americanos*, Vol. CXLVI, No. 3 (May–June, 1966). Of course the article does not give any answer. Also see François Fejtö, "Notas sobre Cuba" [Notes on Cuba], *Mundo Nuevo*, Vol. I, No. 1 (July 1966).

[40] See Chapter 2 of this work.

the revolutionary plans for the continent; and still worse, Castro adapted himself to this policy, trying to "blackmail imperialism," to "play" with it, using "marked cards," according to Che's own words.[41]

His visit to Moscow in October 1964 must have deepened Guevara's doubts; it is impossible to read the cutting criticism he afterward made about economic relations between socialist countries without seeing in it a reflection of his discussions on Soviet-Cuban economic relations during this stay.[42]

The following events remove any remaining doubts about the effects of that trip on Che. Within the first ten days of December he again left Cuba to participate in the sessions of the United Nations; from there he went to Africa and Asia, and was away for three months. On March 15, 1965 he returned to Havana; then nothing certain was heard about him until Castro read the famous farewell letter in October.

It would not be difficult to prove the falsehood of Castro's version of the split. But this is not the place to do it. Therefore we will describe only the facts relevant to our investigation — those that must have increased the disagreements between the two leaders to a degree where a break was inevitable.

First, when the bombing of North Vietnam began in February 1965, Castro demanded an energetic response from the socialist countries. On March 3 he felt so frustrated that he even complained of being so far away: "We are sorry not to be nearer to North Vietnam," he said, "to help her with all we have."[43] On April 28 the same "imperialists" who were bombing Vietnam landed in

41 "One cannot blackmail the North Americans. . . . We can talk to imperialism. . . . But we cannot talk trying to use 'marked cards.' . . . We cannot play with them. . . ." (*Revolución*, July 25, 1964).

42 Guevara went to Moscow this time with two military chiefs, Sergio del Valle and Guillermo García. In the conversations that took place the CPSU was represented by Kosygin, Brezhnev, Podgorny, and others. There was no communiqué. The Soviet press said only that both delegations had discussed "questions of the further development of relations between the CPSU and the PURS and of all-around cooperation between the Soviet Union and the Republic of Cuba." (*Pravda* and *Izvestiya*, November 19, 1964 [*CDSP*, Vol. XVI, No. 47 (December 16, 1964), p. 25].) For Guevara's critique of the economic relations between the socialist countries, see his speech before the Afro-Asian Economic Seminar in Algeria, February 22–27, 1965 (pamphlet published by the Cuban government, Ministry of Foreign Relations). See also "El socialismo y el hombre en Cuba" [Socialism and Man in Cuba], *Revolución*, April 13, 1965, that is, twelve days after Guevara had left Cuba, according to Castro.

43 *Revolución*, March 4, 1965.

Santo Domingo. Fortune was giving him a chance to show the Soviets and the Chinese how to comply with "proletarian internationalism." But he did nothing.[44]

What we know of Guevara permits us to assume that Fidel's passive attitude helped to increase the conflict between them. Castro's long-drawn-out explanations to justify his conduct at this time,[45] and his anger with Adolfo Gilly (who had pointed out that Castro's attitude increased the conflict) — like any Stalinist, Castro accused him of being a Trotskyite — are evidence in favor of our hypothesis. By giving April 1, a date before the Dominican events, as the date of Che's alleged farewell letter, Castro may well have been trying to refute what Gilly had alluded to, namely, that Santo Domingo was the final cause of the break with Guevara.[46]

Second, at the end of 1964 Africa was one of the few areas that offered certain immediate possibilities for revolution. This was where Che went, making the first preparations for the Tricontinental Conference held one year later in Havana. This revolutionary possibility was the only asset left to Guevara that would be appreciated by Castro as a factor in the juggling of forces — which for him is the essence of politics. But on June 20 Ben Bella was deposed. Since the Algerian leader was the man on whom the Cubans had pinned their hopes for an African revolution, his downfall meant that Guevara was now politically bankrupt.

It is difficult to imagine a more bothersome event for Castro than the fall of the Algerian leader. It ruined the hope of finding in Africa compensation for the reverses in Latin America. Moreover, the overthrow of the charismatic Algerian by his army might well awaken dangerous inclinations in the strong army created by Castro.

---

[44] The Cuban government of course denounced the American invasion before the United Nations (*ibid.*, April 30, 1965). But Castro did not help Santo Domingo "with all we have." In his speeches of May 1 (*Bohemia*, May 7, 1965) and May 18 (*Verde Olivo*, May 30, 1965), Castro lamented "the painful events," trying to justify his inaction, first, by "the limitations of our resources" and, later, because the "Constitutionalists" in Santo Domingo had remained isolated.

[45] In his speech to the Tricontinental Conference (*Cuba Socialista*, February 1966).

[46] Castro himself read a paragraph of Gilly's article about this connection in his speech before the Tricontinental Conference mentioned in the preceding note. *Revolución* on May 28, 1965 published the introduction to a Cuban book on geology, written by "the Minister of Industry and member of the National Directorate of the PURS, Major Ernesto Guevara." If, as according to Castro, Guevara left Cuba on April 1, why did the press refer to him by these titles two months later?

Fidel reacted to the misfortune with a speech that is one of his masterpieces — although he could not hide altogether his preoccupation with the effects of the coup on his armed forces — and he instituted various security measures.[47] But he was aware that this was not enough to protect him from the dangerous turn of events.

Third, to understand the decision Castro made, it is necessary to take into account other earlier events. The Cuban delegation to the March "consultative" meeting in Moscow was headed by the Minister of the Armed Forces, his brother Raúl, who stayed in the Soviet Union and then in other East European countries for more than a month. Both before and after his return reciprocal visits of high Soviet, Czechoslovak, and Cuban military officials took place.[48] The results were so positive that Fidel could announce he had "numerous and modern war equipment . . . received in due time and for free from the U.S.S.R. . . ."[49] And in September a new agreement of technical and economic aid was signed in Moscow, which, according to the announcement, assured the production of 10 million tons of sugar in 1970.[50]

Now we can understand Castro's decision. The situation was characterized by increasing American aggressiveness in Vietnam, an inadequate Chinese and Soviet response, the decline of the revolutionary movement in Latin America, and the disastrous

[47] This speech, which is fundamental for understanding Castro's concern about the military, was published in *Revolución*, June 28, 1965. See also Arguedas, *op. cit.* The author, a friend of the Castro regime, wrote that Fidel Castro "more than anyone else learned the lesson of the recent Algerian events." According to Arguedas the disappearance of Guevara was a *coup d'état* by Castro against himself, the victim of which was Che, the Cuban equivalent of Ben Bella. Although I do not agree with the analogy, this interpretation seems to reveal the importance for Castro's decisions of the coup against Ben Bella. By "security measures" I mean the order of the Minister of the Armed Forces (FAR) (*Revolución*, August 13, 1965) demanding that all civilians, including the reserve units and the militias, return the weapons they possessed; also the plans to "unite the children to the FAR," and the "reunions between the people in uniform and the organized people," that is, the FAR and the Defense Committees, about all of which there is information in *Verde Olivo*, September 12, November 7 and 21, and December 12, 1965.

[48] Czechoslovak military delegation to Cuba led by the Minister of Defense, General Bohumír Lomský (*Revolución*, March 31, 1965); Cuban military delegation to Moscow headed by the Chief of the General Staff, Sergio del Valle Jiménez (*ibid.*, May 7, 1965); visit to Cuba by the marshal of the Soviet air force, E. Y. Savitsky (*ibid.*, July 16, 1965); Cuban military delegation to Czechoslovakia headed by the Chief of the Artillery Pedro Miret (*ibid.*, July 18, 1965).

[49] *Ibid.*, May 15, 1965.

[50] *Ibid.*, September 7, 1965.

decline in the price of sugar;[51] the only consoling feature was the economic and military aid of the Soviet Union. Consequently it was advisable to tighten the bonds with Moscow, reject the economic principles put forth by Guevara, adapt to Soviet foreign policy, and grant the party a certain share in the governing of the state. Ben Bella's sad experience must have helped Castro to overcome to some extent his dislike for this institution, because there are no military coups in Communist states, and the liquidation of the "old" Communist hard core offered him some guarantee that the new "apparatus" would not be too serious an obstacle to his personal power.

The data we have firmly supports the preceding interpretation. In his speeches of July 24 and 26, 1965, published in *Cuba Socialista* under the meaningful title of "Criteria of Our Revolution,"[52] Castro defined the principles that were to govern the economy, explained the role of the party, and analyzed the revolutionary situation in terms that confirm our interpretation. Contrary to the usual practice, the PURS took responsibility for the July 26 celebration.[53] In August the formation of the party organization in the Ministry of the Interior was initiated.[54] In late September, after two years, the party also began to organize within the Western Army.[55] And on October 3 Fidel announced the birth of the Communist Party of Cuba. Finally, an article by Carlos Rafael Rodríguez appeared in the *World Marxist Review,* rectifying the history of the revolution. The decisive participation of peasants in the guerrilla movement — a thesis of Guevara's — had been sheer imagination.[56] Since this article must have been cleared with Castro before publication, it constitutes one more example of the way in which the events of this period are linked with the Guevara affair.

There is no convincing evidence that Che found any support for

---

[51] In August the price of sugar was 1.73 cents per pound, the lowest in twenty-four years, according to *The New York Times,* August 18, 1965.

[52] *Cuba Socialista,* September 1965.

[53] *Verde Olivo,* July 4, 1965.

[54] *Revolución,* August 30, 1965. The minister himself, Ramiro Valdés, inaugurated the building of the party in his department. This decision is very important for two reasons: first, Valdés has been a veteran Fidelista since 1953; second, the Cuban secret police, the Department of State Security, has been part of this ministry and thus under the authority of Valdés.

[55] *Verde Olivo,* September 26, 1965.

[56] *World Marxist Review,* Vol. 8, No. 10 (October 1965). This article was reproduced in *Cuba Socialista,* January 1966.

his position.[57] This is explainable: Once his revolutionary sincerity had been proved, his loneliness was understandable within the context of a revolution in which it is most difficult to distinguish between the man of convictions and the faker.

The New Apparat

The July 26 Movement, a tiny group of heroic youths, founded in 1954, which never possessed a formal organization, faded into oblivion in 1960. The ORI, created the following year, disappeared in the same way at the beginning of 1963 to give way to the PURS. In October 1965 the Communist Party of Cuba (PCC) replaced the PURS. But this time the event was publicized extensively. This publicity, the debate about draft statutes, the adoption by the PCC of the organizational forms characteristic of Communist party organization, and the growing tendency (with some exceptions that we shall discuss) to separate state administration from the party organization — all reveal that after six years the political system of a Communist country was for the first time being introduced formally in Cuba. But as we shall see later in this chapter, and as is shown by Castro's words at the inauguration of the PCC, it would be hasty to assume that a complete identity with the systems of the Soviet bloc countries was intended. In introducing the new Central Committee, Castro reiterated his intention to develop "our path . . . our ideas . . . our methods . . . our system."[58] And from that moment on he began to preach a new heresy by maintaining "that communism must be constructed parallel to socialism"[59] — in opposition to the well-known Soviet doctrine that one can think of the former only on finishing the latter.

It is instructive to make comparisons between the National Directorate of the ORI and the PURS and the Central Committee of the new PCC. The former consisted of twenty-five members:

[57] One of the most difficult questions to explain is the relationship between the Castro regime and the students at the University of Havana. The frequent change of deans (Inclán, Marinello, Mier, and now Vilaseca), the fact that the first nucleus of the PURS was founded only in mid-1965 (*Revolución*, June 15, 1965), and Fidel's frequent visits to the university — all give grounds for suspecting there are difficulties. I have, however, been unable to find any connection betwen these difficulties and the points of view maintained by Guevara.

[58] *Cuba Socialista*, November 1965.

[59] *Granma*, October 4, 1965.

the latter has one hundred. In the National Directorate the military comprised 40 per cent: in the Central Committee it has increased to 69 per cent;[60] but the labor representation has decreased from 8 per cent to 3 per cent. The participation of "old Communists" has also decreased considerably, from 40 per cent to 18 per cent. Although only one civilian leader of the July 26 Movement, Hart, was a member of the National Directorate, now there are three: Hart himself, Marcelo Fernández, and Faustino Pérez.[61]

As has been said, the PCC follows the model of Communist organization, and thus we must assume that its decisive organs are the Politburo — which the ORI and the PURS lacked — and the Secretariat. In the former, consisting of eight members, there is no "old Communist"; and in the Secretariat there are the familiar names of Roca and Carlos Rafael Rodríguez. Of the eight members of the Politburo only two are civilians: Dorticós and Hart. The rest are military men.[62] And with the exception of Dorticós, all come from the July 26 Movement or from the Rebel Army. The members of the Secretariat, besides Roca and Rodríguez, are the Castro brothers, Dorticós, and Faure Chomón, a member of the Revolutionary Student Directorate. Only Castro, the Premier; his brother Raúl, Minister of the FAR; Dorticós, the President; and Ramiro Valdés, Minister of the Interior, occupy positions in the state administration and in the Politburo of the party. But while the first three are also members of the Secretariat, with Fidel as Secretary-General, Valdés is not. Of the remaining members of the Politburo, Hart is organization secretary; Sergio del Valle is a member of the military commission; and García and Almeida are

60 The names of the members of the Central Committee were published in *Cuba Socialista,* November 1965. Every name is preceded by the abbreviation "comp" (compañero) or "Cmdte" (Major). The percentages have been computed according to these designations. But we know that in Cuba some majors are only honorary, that is, they do not command army forces at all (for example, Guevara and Faure Chomón). This means that the 69 per cent for military men in the Central Committee mentioned in the text is merely an approximation.

61 When the National Directorate of the ORI was founded in March 1962 Fernández and Pérez were not in the government, probably because they disagreed with Castro's "Communist line." After the removal of Aníbal Escalante, they were given high positions in the government, and they now appear in the Central Committee.

62 Here we find new difficulties. Since December 1965 (*Verde Olivo,* December 26, 1965) del Valle has not been mentioned as chief of the general staff; and since February 1966 (*ibid.,* February 20, 1966) neither has García appeared as chief of the Western Army. We cannot ascertain if these changes are definite, that is, whether from now on they will function only as members of the Politburo.

probably there because Castro considers their votes even more certain than those of the others.

The preceding breakdown gives us an approximate idea of the political power structure in Cuba after October 1965. The "maximum leader," Premier, Commander-in-Chief,[63] member of the Central Committee and Politburo, and Secretary-General, Fidel Castro, is still the decisive factor in the political equation. Immediately next to him is his brother Raúl. But Dorticós has climbed adroitly in the hierarchy of power and is now at the same level as Raúl; Ramiro Valdés ranks a step below both of them. Fidelistas such as Raúl and Valdés are in the majority in the Politburo and the Central Committee, although some of them — for instance, William Gálvez, Universo Sánchez, and René Rodriguez[64]—do not belong to either of these bodies. Fidelistas also hold the most important commands in the army. But new names are emerging. The guerrilla leaders' lack of education and the increasing complexity of military tasks may account for such changes. Nevertheless one cannot disregard the possibility that some of them may be "Raúlistas."[65] Lastly, if our thesis is correct that the party was established both

[63] I do not know the legal sources of this designation. But the truth is that everybody in Cuba calls Fidel "Commander-in-Chief." For example, *Revolución*, July 25, 1964, appeared with the following slogan on the front page: "Para lo que sea y como sea, Comandante en Jefe, ¡Ordene!" [At every moment and in every place, Commander-in-Chief, at your orders!].

[64] Ameijeiras, once a member of the Central Committee, was deprived of his office in March, accused of "irresponsible conduct" manifested by his close relationship with "antisocial elements, idle and corrupt people" (*Granma*, March 17, 1966). Among these "elements" was Rolando Cubelas, a major in the guerrillas of the Revolutionary Student Directorate, who had been accused and condemned a few days before for planning an attempt to assassinate Fidel.

[65] The author is preparing a monograph in which, based on abundant biographical material, he attempts to establish the characteristics of the Fidelistas. The term "Raúlista" is used in referring to the variety of Fidelistas especially associated with Fidel's brother, Raúl. The younger Castro is the Minister of the Armed Forces and also the president of the commission of the Central Committee of the PCC for the armed forces. The relationship between the two brothers is not easy. Until now, after some strain, Raúl has always ended by yielding to Fidel's will. Probably in the future he will do the same. But Juana, the sister who has devoted herself entirely to preaching anti-Fidelism in the United States and in Latin America with funds from unknown sources, demonstrates that this is a very strange family. There are some indications that Raúl's influence in the armed forces is increasing. We cannot substantiate this point at present. On the other hand, the Cuban press (*Granma*, March 24 and 27) twice in March 1967 referred to Juan Almeida as Minister of the Armed Forces. And there has not been any official announcement of the whereabouts of Raúl. These later occurrences may indicate that the situation has altered considerably since 1966, but it is too early to know what these indications mean.

to please the Soviets and as a counterweight to the increasing influence of the armed forces, then the presence of such a large
number of military men in the Central Committee may indicate
a certain weakness on Castro's part. One cannot, however, entirely
discount the possibility that Castro himself put them there precisely
with the object of manipulating one "machine" against the other.

In summary, since 1962 the leader has not been able to reassert
his charismatic qualities through new successes, and the form in
which he wields his power has begun to change, adopting a structure
that cannot yet be determined with certainty.

A final observation about Roca's humiliating fate. He is not in the
Politburo; he is in the Secretariat[66] but has lost the editorship of
Hoy, which has been merged with *Revolución* into the official organ
Granma. Moreover, at the ceremony at which the editorship of *Hoy*
was handed over, Fidel made him the victim of one of his gestures
of exquisite cruelty. He praised Rocca for his "humility," implying
that because of this he had "earned the right to live many
years . . ."[67] — obviously to distinguish him from Aníbal Escalante
and Ordoqui, who because they were not "humble" went, one into
exile and the other to jail. We do not know if, while Roca was
listening to Fidel, his head "wobbled minutely but regularly."

The First Tricontinental Conference

The disappearance of Che and the creation of the PCC were
followed by new tokens of Soviet friendship. In October Raúl
Castro and other important military leaders went to Moscow to
sign an agreement "of economic and technical collaboration."[68]
Fidel's speeches give an indication of the contents of this agreement.
In November he acknowledged Soviet aid "in essential matters"; in
December he alluded to "the extraordinary help . . . in arms"
received from the same source; and in January 1966 he justified the
absence of new arms at the anniversary parade by saying, "but there
is something that cannot be seen and that is many more arms."[69]
Finally, in early February 1966 the annual commercial protocol was

[66] He is also the president of the constitutional commission of the PCC, but it
is doubtful that his commission has anything to do in Cuba today.

[67] *Granma,* October 4, 1965.

[68] *Bohemia,* December 3, 1965.

[69] Speeches of November 7, 1965 (*ibid.,* November 12, 1965); December 2,
1965 (*ibid.,* December 10, 1965); and January 2, 1966 (*ibid.,* January 10, 1966).

signed without any mishap.[70] Such help, in proportions large enough to satisfy Fidel, is another expression of the policy finally adopted by the Soviet leaders. First, they had believed it possible to obtain Chinese collaboration in hiding the cracks in the international Communist movement without at the same time antagonizing the United States. Then, when this attempt failed, they tried to rebuff Mao's attempt to obtain control of the movement by simulating a move to the left. But in the meantime the United States had gone over to the offensive, and the Soviet leaders lacked the courage either to stop bluffing or to adjust themselves to the new reality. They have remained in the same place, believing they could satisfy the Soviet consumers, help North Vietnam, counter the Maoist challenge, and, on top of that, avoid a confrontation with the United States. As we have seen, this has not been entirely bad for Castro. It has enabled him to give valuable assistance to the Soviets, for instance, through the January 1966 Tricontinental Conference in Havana, while at the same time taking care of his own interests. In February 1963, during one of his worst crises with the Soviets, Castro suggested to the Afro-Asian People's Solidarity Organization that Cuba should be the site of a conference of the three continents. But once he had solved his difficulties with Khrushchev, he forgot about the invitation.[71] We have already seen that in early 1965 the project was revived, but this time with the support of the Soviets,[72] who saw in it an opportunity to demonstrate that they were an Asian power — which is denied by the Chinese — and to reduce the influence of Mao in the "third world." In May, the proposal to hold the meeting was approved in Ghana. And in September, in Cairo, the program and the date were set and a preparatory committee was created — the six Latin American members of which would decide which organizations should be invited in the hemisphere.[73]

In view of the acute Sino-Soviet rivalry, everything seemed to indicate that Havana would be the scene of a frontal clash that

[70] *Granma*, February 12, 1966.

[71] See Chapter 7 of this work.

[72] The Chinese have said, with reason, "For quite a long time, the Khrushchev revisionists had tried to hinder the convening of the Tricontinental Conference. . . . But in the past year they suddenly changed their attitude. . . ." (NCNA, Havana, January 17, 1966 [SCMP 3623, January 25, 1966, p. 34].)

[73] Bulletin published by the chairmanship of the International Preparatory Committee of the First Solidarity Conference of the Peoples of Africa, Asia, and Latin America and the Cuban National Committee, Havana, October 15, 1965.

might well break up the conference. But although there were frequent skirmishes, as we know from Soviet references and ample Chinese information, Castro's skill prevailed in assuring the completion of the program as planned and enabled him to chalk up new successes.[74] The maneuver by which Castro pushed the Chinese onto the defensive began the day before the conference opened.

As the event drew near, Peking recovered some of its cordiality. On December 31 Mao and Liu Shao-ch'i affirmed that "no force can undermine this friendship."[75] But on January 2, 1966 Castro informed his people that "for reasons beyond our control" the already scarce ration of rice — a staple element in the Cuban diet — had to be cut in half; he explained that the "reasons" consisted of a Chinese decision to offer only 135,000 tons of rice for 1966 as against 250,000 tons in 1965.[76]

It is impossible to follow all the intricacies of the polemic that began that day between Castro and the Peking government, as it is also impossible to attempt to analyze the conference, whose resolutions alone cover more than one hundred pages.[77] We shall confine ourselves, therefore, to a consideration of the influence of these events on Castro's policy as it presented itself in the spring of 1966.

First, once the conference was over, twenty-seven Latin American delegations resolved to create the Latin American Solidarity Organization (Organización Latinoamericana de Solidaridad — OLAS), with headquarters in Havana and directed by a committee of representatives of Brazil, Cuba, Colombia, British Guiana, Guatemala, Mexico, Peru, Uruguay, and Venezuela. The OLAS had the

[74] See the interview with Rashidov in *Pravda*, January 26, 1966 (*CDSP*, Vol. XVIII, No. 4 [February 16, 1966]), and the more explicit Chinese information in "NCNA Correspondent on Havana Tricontinental Conference," SCMP 3623, January 26, 1966, p. 34. See also the *Jen-min Jih-pao* editorial of January 18, 1966, "No One Can Stem the Tide of Anti-Imperialist Revolutionary Struggle of Asian, African, and Latin American Peoples" (SCMP 3622, January 24, 1966, pp. 22–25).

[75] The message, mentioning "profound friendship" and sending "warm greetings," in SCMP 3610, January 5, 1966, pp. 36–37.

[76] Castro's speech of January 2, 1966 in *Bohemia*, January 10, 1966.

[77] The resolutions were published in *Cuba Socialista*, February 1966. About the conference see "The Tricontinental Conference and After," by the editors of *Monthly Review*, Vol. 17, No. 11 (April 1966), and also the article by Adolfo Gilly in *ibid.;* François Fejtö, "Trois continents et une île," *Preuves*, No. 181 (March 1966); J. M. Fortuny, A. Delgado, M. Salibi, "The Tri-continental Conference," *World Marxist Review*, Vol. 9, No. 3 (March 1966); Lionel Soto, "First Conference of the Peoples of Three Continents," *ibid.*, Vol. 9, No. 4 (April 1966); and D. Bruce Jackson, "Whose Men in Havana?" *Problems of Communism*, Vol. XV, No. 3 (May–June 1966).

functions, among others, of preparing a conference for 1967, of utilizing "all means possible" to support the liberation movements, and of displaying a "constant campaign" against "imperialism."[78] It must be pointed out that the organizations in the OLAS are "national committees" from each country. The composition of these committees has not been made known. But if, according to Fejtö, the Cubans were the ones who decided on the admission of rival Latin American delegations to the conference, they must have taken measures to protect themselves from being at the mercy of the traditional Communist parties of the hemisphere.[79] On the other hand, since the OLAS is so close to Fidel, it is unlikely to be regarded with any enthusiasm by the CPSU or by any of these Communist parties.[80]

Second, we know that the mention of Guevara set off ovations at the conference.[81] Fidel devoted a large part of his closing speech to a refutation of those accounts of Che's disappearance that did not agree with his own.[82] The publicity he gave to Yon Sosa, an obscure Guatemalan guerrilla leader whom he labeled a "Trotskyite," can be explained only in relation to this same matter.[83] And the Tri-

---

[78] Communiqué on the creation of the Latin American Solidarity Organization, *Cuba Socialista*, February 1966.

[79] François Fejtö, "Trois continents et une île," *op. cit.* Fejtö says that the Cuban choice was in general in favor of the most orthodox against "the Chinese" factions. But according to José Vazeilles, himself one of the Argentine delegates to the conference, in eight Latin American delegations the Communist party had no representation, and in three others it was in the minority (*Monthly Review*, Vol. 17, No. 13 [June 1966]).

[80] According to *Borba*, January 24, 1966 (reprinted in *Granma*, February 12, 1966), some Latin American Communist parties have "considerable reservations" about the conference and its tactics. It seems significant that two of the most influential parties in Latin America, those of Chile and Argentina, do not appear in the organizing committee of the OLAS. We now know, from Vazeilles, *op. cit.*, that the Argentine Communist Party, "together with the other traditional CP's," was opposed to the creation of the OLAS.

[81] Gilly, based on the reporter of *Le Monde*, who wrote about "public bursts of thunderous applause" (*Monthly Review*, Vol. 17, No. 11 [April 1966]).

[82] Speech at the closing of the conference (*Cuba Socialista*, February 1966). In this speech Castro added one more detail on Guevara's disappearance, which completely undermines belief in his numerous explanations of this event. He said: "Comrade Guevara joined us when we were in exile in Mexico, and always, from the very first day, clearly expressed the idea that when the struggle ended in Cuba, he had other duties in other places, and we always gave him our word that neither state interest, nor national interest, nor any circumstance would make us ask him to stay in our country. . . ." However, nobody had ever heard of this request or this promise.

[83] It seems that at the time Sosa was indeed a supporter of the (Trotskyite) Fourth International. But the point is that Fidel, in the best Stalinist tradition,

continental Conference's resolution on Guatemala, which omits the names both of Castro's protégé Turcios and of his rival Sosa, shows that the opinions of the Cuban leader are not automatically accepted.[84]

All this, in my opinion, helps to explain why after the conference Castro returned to a strong emphasis on his Latin American revolutionary mission. I am aware that the situation in Vietnam also prompted him to adopt such an attitude. But it seems to me that the Latin American revolutionaries' recent lack of confidence in him is what has impelled him to promise unconditional aid "to any revolutionary movement in any part of the world."[85] He knows that his image has been damaged by the mysterious disappearance of Che, and he is trying to erase the effects of this by using, once more, the style that gave him such great prestige among leftists in the years from 1959 to 1962.

Third, the polemic with the Chinese — during which Castro accused Peking of "contacting Cuban military officers," and China retorted that the Cuban Premier had entered the ranks of "the anti-China chorus"[86] — reached its climax in March 1966. Visibly

called Trotskyism "an instrument of imperialism and reaction" (*Cuba Socialista,* February 1966). Sosa answered by condemning Castro as a traitor "at the service of the Russo-Yankee alliance" (*La Nación* [Costa Rica] April 29, 1966).

[84] There are numerous indications that Castro has lost a great deal of his prestige and influence among the radical revolutionaries of the hemisphere. For example, two of his most faithful propagandists abroad, Sweezy and Huberman, have finally confessed that "even more than Fidel himself, Che has come to symbolize all that is best, all that is pure, all that is beloved in the Cuban Revolution. . . ." (*Monthly Review,* Vol. 17, No. 11 [April 1966].) And, which is really extraordinary, Turcios, the Guatemalan guerrilla fighter exalted by Fidel, when asked who his two favorite heroes were, answered: "Mao and Guevara." (*Saturday Evening Post,* June 18, 1966.)

[85] This promise was made in the closing speech of the conference (*Cuba Socialista,* February 1966). Similar promises and demands for revolutionary activity in Latin America appear in Castro's speeches of March 13, 1966 (*Verde Olivo,* March 20, 1966), April 20, 1966 (*Granma,* April 21, 1966), and May 1, 1966 (*Cuba Socialista,* June 1966).

[86] After Castro's speech of January 2, 1966 the following documents referred to the polemic with the Chinese: The Chinese answer, "Facts on Sino-Cuban Trade," *Jen-min Jih-pao,* January 10, 1966, and *Peking Review,* Vol. IX, No. 3 (January 14, 1966), pp. 21–23; declarations of the Cuban Ministry of Foreign Trade (*Granma,* January 12, 1966); second Chinese answer, "Further Remarks on the Sino-Cuban Trade Question," *Jen-min Jih-pao,* January 31, 1966, and *Peking Review,* Vol. IX, No. 6 (February 4, 1966), pp. 15–16; and the document signed by Castro as Prime Minister (*Granma,* February 6, 1966). In this document Fidel accused the representatives of the Chinese government in Cuba of "mass distribution" of propaganda material "among the officers of the armed forces," and of trying "to establish direct contact with Cuban officers." The Chinese answered on

angry because they had used only minor functionaries to answer him, Fidel turned all his verbal fury on the Chinese, calling Mao's ideological documents "lightweight," suggesting the creation of a "council of elders" for aged leaders to prevent them from "putting their whims into effect when senility has taken hold of them" — a clear reference to the advanced age of the Chinese leaders — and threatening to do to the diplomats of that nation the same thing "that we did to the American Embassy. . . ."[87] By the first of May there had still been no public Chinese reply. However, it is doubtful that a total break will take place. Chinese influence in Latin America is insignificant, so Fidel, by controlling the OLAS, has now become even more important to the Chinese. And because Castro cannot disregard his isolation, his conditions for reconciliation should not be too difficult to meet.

Fourth, the duration and the seriousness of the Sino-Soviet conflict have produced so many tendencies within the international Communist movement that it is now well-nigh impossible to pinpoint the diverse positions toward each and every problem. The following are some of the most essential: The Chinese condemn peaceful coexistence, accuse the Soviets of collusion with the United States in Vietnam, and in the countries of the "third world" expressly reject the thesis of the "socialist" revolution, insisting on the Maoist concept of the "new democratic revolution" and preaching violence as the correct path toward that revolution.[88] The Soviet position is far from clear. Moscow insists on peaceful coexistence, explaining on some occasions that this has nothing to do with relations between "the exploited and the exploiters," "the oppressors and the oppressed," saying at other times that it means to "fight against interference by the imperialists in the internal affairs of other countries" and then, when they think it convenient, deny-

---

February 22, 1966, saying that the distribution of propaganda material was "perfectly usual"; asking "why such a lack of confidence in one's own cadres and officers . . .?"; and reserving their right to give "a systematic reply." ("Editor's Note on Prime Minister Castro's Anti-Chinese Statement," *Jen-min Jih-pao,* February 22, 1966, and *Peking Review,* Vol. IX, No. 9 [February 25, 1966], pp. 13–14, quotations from p. 14.)

87 *Verde Olivo,* March 20, 1966.

88 Lin Piao, "Long Live the Victory of People's War!" *Jen-min Jih-pao,* September 2, 1965, and *Peking Review,* Vol. VIII, No. 36 (September 3, 1965), pp. 9–30. See also Commentator, "A Clumsy Forgery, A Foul Plot," *Jen-min Jih-pao,* October 28, 1965, and *Peking Review,* Vol. VIII, No. 45 (November 5, 1965), pp. 20–22: "We have at no time said that the present task of Africa is socialist revolution. This is not at all China's viewpoint and position." (*Ibid.,* p. 20.)

ing both meanings.[89] The Soviets also reaffirm their support to Vietnam, but they are very cautious with their aid and spread rumors about the difficulties made by the Chinese for the transport of materials to Ho Chi Minh. Finally, with respect to the underdeveloped countries, the Soviet government accepts the possibility that "some peoples have to seek their freedom with weapons in hands," but they restrict that solution to "the specific conditions,"[90] and seem interested not in new revolutions but in convincing the triumphant revolutionaries of the advantages of friendship with the Soviet Union. For this purpose, they have invented the so-called "noncapitalist path of development," a concept that is not very clearly defined. However, it authorizes a leadership of "revolutionary-democratic elements representing in the main the nonproletarian and semi-proletarian masses of working people"[91] and thus enables anyone who leads a revolution, even if he is not a Communist, to count on Soviet help.

In contrast to the viewpoints of the Soviets and the Chinese, Castro's position in regard to Vietnam is "to liquidate the criminal aggression with all available means and assuming the necessary risks."[92] On revolution he says: "in the present condition of Latin America, the true revolution leads, quickly, to socialism . . . ," and

[89] "At the same time, it is clear that there is not and cannot be any peaceful coexistence between oppressed peoples and their oppressors . . . or between imperialist aggressors and their victims." Rashidov, head of the Soviet delegation at the tricontinental conference, according to "Consolidate in Struggle for Common Goals!" (*Pravda*, January 8, 1966 [*CDSP*, Vol. XVIII, No. 1 (January 26, 1966), p. 7].) "To defend peaceful coexistence in our time means to fight against interference by the imperialist in the internal affairs of other countries. . . ." (Brezhnev's speech at the signing of the Treaty of Friendship Cooperation and Mutual Aid between the Union of Soviet Socialist Republics and the Mongolian People's Republic, *Pravda*, January 16, 1966 [*CDSP*, Vol. XVIII, No. 3 (February 9, 1966), pp. 4–7, at p. 6.], hereafter cited as Brezhnev's Mongolia speech.) "It is . . . well known that the Soviet Union invariably adheres to the principle of noninterference. . . ." (L. Kamynin, "A Costume Farce," *Izvestiya*, January 28, 1966 [*CDSP*, Vol. XVIII, No. 4 (February 16, 1966), p. 24].)

[90] Brezhnev's Mongolia speech.

[91] R. Ulyanovsky, "Socialism and the National Liberation Struggle," *Pravda*, April 15, 1966 (*CDSP*, Vol. XVIII, No. 15 [May 4, 1966]). On the subject of the "noncapitalist path of development," the following three articles are essential: Uri Ra'anan, "Moscow and the 'Third World,'" *Problems of Communism*, Vol. XIV, No. 1 (January–February 1965), and "Tactics in the 'Third World,'" *Survey*, No. 57 (October 1965); Richard Lowenthal, "Russia, the One-Party System, and the Third World," *ibid.*, No. 58 January 1966).

[92] Speech of the head of the Cuban delegation to the Twenty-Third Congress of the CPSU, Armando Hart (*Granma*, April 1, 1966). The importance of this speech can be gauged by the fact that it was reprinted in *Bohemia*, April 8, 1966, and *Verde Olivo*, April 10, 1966.

such a revolution "in all or almost all the countries . . . will assume the most violent forms."[93] Castro's characteristic contempt for ideology prevents him from being more precise about the nature of his proposed revolution. Finally, Castroism shuns peaceful co-existence, or insists that it is not applicable to the relations between "the exploiters and the exploited," "the oppressors and the oppressed."[94]

We have already given our opinion about the factors that influence Castro's present position, which may seem to be closer to that of the Chinese than to that of the Soviets, although, in reality, it combines elements of both views. Let us now add another recent and original feature of Castro's "doctrine" that may give some indication of Fidel's future maneuvers. In his speech of May 1, 1966 Castro repeated his heresy of the previous October — the parallel construction of socialism and communism — but he "humbly" added something else. He said that, in his opinion, complete communism "cannot be built in one country alone. . . ."[95] Since this is precisely the aspiration of the CPSU — or at least it was in Khrushchev's time — it would be interesting to know the reaction of the Soviet ideologists to this new jewel of Castroite "dialectics." This was not all he said on May 1. He criticized "the various imitative tendencies" of the preceding stages of the revolution and he called upon the people not to count on anyone "except ourselves" in case of aggression.[96] It seems obvious that these words announce a new period of tension in the already very turbulent relations between Castro and the Soviet Union.

The Character of the Regime

While studying and organizing the sources on which this book is based, the author became aware that they shed much light on the internal development of the Cuban regime. It thus became necessary to deal with this subject also, and the book would certainly be incomplete if we did not add some final thoughts about the nature of the political system established by Fidel Castro in Cuba.

[93] The same speech by Hart and Castro's speech of March 13, 1966 (*Verde Olivo*, March 20, 1966).
[94] See for example, E. Vázquez Candelas, "Coexistencia pacífica y liberación" [Peaceful Coexistence and Liberation], *Bohemia*, January 25, 1966.
[95] *Cuba Socialista*, June 1966.
[96] *Ibid.*

The essential characteristics of the Castro regime may be summed up as follows. It was the product of a revolutionary movement in which the PSP — the Communist party — participated only at a late stage and to a rather insignificant extent. From the summer of 1959 onward, the regime began to import, to an ever-increasing extent, the institutions proper to Communist countries. Finally, in October 1965, it formally created that organ essential to every Communist regime: the party of a "new type," although with the limitations already mentioned.

We must add that Cuba, after long delays, has finally been admitted to the Communist family, but also with certain reservations. It is not a member of the Warsaw Treaty and does not form part of the Council for Mutual Economic Aid (CMEA). And even today, in the Soviet greetings for May 1, the words used to salute Cuba are not the same as those used for the other members of the camp. East Germany, Rumania, and Czechoslovakia are "Socialist Republics"; the rest are "People's Republics"; and the nature of Castro's regime is not specified; there are merely "fraternal greetings to the heroic people of Cuba. . . ."[97]

We can, then, ask ourselves two questions. First, are the singularities of the Cuban political system important enough to continue calling it Castroite, as we have been doing throughout this work, or should we label it Communist? Second, are we perhaps witnessing the transition from one to the other, the disappearance of Castroism and the birth of communism in Cuba? As we know, Theodore Draper has also posed the question of the nature of the regime.[98] He is the most acute investigator of Castroism, but his solution is not entirely satisfactory to me. According to him, the regime "represents a tendency within the world Communist movement," "more extreme than any existing Communist tendency," a "particular case of cross-fertilization . . . of a Latin American revolutionary tradition and the European Communist tradition," that is, analogous to Leninism, "a cross-fertilization of the Russian revolutionary tradition and the European Marxist tradition."[99]

---

[97] *Pravda* and *Izvestiya*, April 17, 1966 (*CDSP*, Vol. XVIII, No. 15 [May 4, 1966]).

[98] We Cubans are indebted to Theodore Draper for the great effort and intelligence that he has devoted to the study of the Castroite phenomenon. The author is especially indebted for the fact mentioned in the Preface. It seems to me appropriate, therefore, to state here our gratefulness and admiration for Mr. Draper, who is a defender of true democracy not only in Cuba but also in Santo Domingo.

[99] Theodore Draper, *Castroism: Theory and Practice* (New York: Praeger, 1965), pp. 52, 55, and 88.

My first reservation is easy to understand. If this work tries to show anything it is that we are not facing an extremist but, on the contrary, a consummate opportunist, gifted, it is true, with the audacity and courage to act with the most exaggerated radicalism if this serves his purposes. Neither does the "cross-fertilization" pointed out by Draper seem very convincing to me. Leninism is indeed the product of such a "cross-fertilization." But how can this be said of Castroism, which to this day does not possess a single ideologist familiar with "the European Communist tradition"? This is the position that Guevara tried to fill in his last years — and we do not know where he is today. And this was probably Régis Debray's hidden intention in a penetrating article in which, after mentioning Castroism in the title, he develops Guevara's thesis.[100]

The preceding, however, is not fundamental. What primarily separates me from Draper is that he places no emphasis on the subject of the party, and for me this is essential. Any text on Communist political systems teaches us that the Communist party is the indispensable element in regimes of this kind. Ivo Lapenna has stated the problem posed by such systems as a question of "whether, with such a powerful party apparatus at its full disposal, the holder of political sovereignty really needs state and law at all."[101] It is the party, then, that interests us. This is "a political warfare organization" and as such is conspiratorial, quasi-military, authoritarian, and intimately bound to an ideology.[102] And its ideology, Marxism, offers the following peculiarity: Its purpose is simply to end human history and enter into "the golden age." As is easy to understand, not everybody is fit to perform this gigantic task. Near the end of his revolutionary career, Lenin said that one can speak of a genuine Communist party only when the party "consists of thoroughly conscious and devoted communists trained and steeled by the experience of stubborn revolutionary struggle. . . ."[103] This characterization is exact. Anybody can be a Castroite, a Peronist, or a Nasserite: It is necessary to obey the leader only a certain number of hours per day. But to be a Communist one must become a founding

---

[100] Régis Debray, "Le Castrisme: Le longe marche de l'Amerique Latine," *Les Temps Modernes*, Vol. 20, No. 224 (January 1965).

[101] Ivo Lapenna, "Party and State in the Programme," in Leonard Schapiro, ed., *The U.S.S.R. and the Future* (New York: Praeger, 1963).

[102] Robert C. Tucker, "On Revolutionary Mass-Movements," in Robert C. Tucker, ed., *The Soviet Political Mind* (New York: Praeger, 1963).

[103] V. I. Lenin, "Thesis on the Basic Tasks of the Communist International, Adopted by the Second Congress, 1920," in Jane Degras, ed., *The Communist International, 1919–1943*, Vol. I (London, 1956), pp. 113–127.

father of a future paradise, unfortunately a utopian realm. And having taken on such an enormous task, one must prepare oneself "full time," in the underground and in jail, in obedience and in command, and become "steeled" for the appointed moment to crush the millions of heads that stand between the present, "full of darkness," and the "luminous" future, and then for the long historical period during which one will have to resist the pressure of the constantly resurging past.

We do not know of any Communist state so far that is not under the control of a party organized according to Lenin's rules.[104] But in Cuba, as we know, the original Leninists have been reduced to insignificance. Only in October 1965 was the party of a "new type" created, but under the direction of Castroites, not Leninists. Can a genuine Communist party be organized when its members do not face jail or death but the enjoyment of positions in the government? How is it possible, in such circumstances, to distinguish between the opportunist and the true believer? Is there any guarantee that these "Communists," who in 1959 only wanted to be commanders and high officials, have really undergone a "conversion" and are now ready to resist the multiple temptations that are offered by the remnants of the "bourgeois" society even today?

[104] I am aware that neither Kosygin nor Brezhnev is a genuine Communist, according to my definition of the term. But, in the first place, they belong to the leading nucleus of a party organized and wrought according to the Leninist rules, and, moreover, a party that strives hard to preserve that tradition. In the second place, this is precisely the problem that every Communist party faces once it has firmly established itself in power: how to make Communists when the revolutionary environment has disappeared and there is need only for bureaucrats. Now it seems that the party schools and the control of education are not enough. Stalin tried to cover these deficiencies with the theory of the "encircled camp" of socialism surrounded and seized by the capitalist powers. Mao also seems to be beginning to feel this need. It is impossible to add anything further now on such a difficult question. I will mention only a few works and articles that I consider essential in order to have a clear idea of the problem: Richard Lowenthal, *World Communism: The Disintegration of a Secular Faith* (New York: Oxford University Press, 1964), and "The Logic of One-Party Rule," in Abraham Brumberg, ed., *Russia Under Khrushchev* (New York: Praeger, 1962); George Lichtheim, *Marxism: An Historical and Critical Study* (New York: Praeger, 1961), and "The Transmutation of a Doctrine," *Problems of Communism,* Vol. XIV, No. 4 (July–August 1966); Zbigniew K. Brzezinski, "The Nature of the Soviet System," in Zbigniew K. Brzezinski, *Ideology and Power in Soviet Politics* (New York: Praeger, 1962), and "The Soviet Political System: Transformation or Degeneration," *Problems of Communism,* Vol. XV, No. 1 (January–February 1966); Tucker, *op. cit.;* and H. Gordon Skilling, "Interest Groups and Communist Politics," *World Politics,* Vol. XVIII, No. 3 (April 1966). Needless to say, this bibliography is by no means exhaustive.

It is highly doubtful to me that the Cuban regime can legitimately be called Communist in the sense in which I interpret the word, that is, a state ruled by the leading nucleus of a party organized according to Leninist norms. We cannot rule out, however, the possibility that history may have a new experience in store for us. The isolation from the West imposed on Cuba by U.S. policy; her growing dependence, both economic and military, on the Soviet Union; the lack of alternatives for those who came out of obscurity with weapons in their hands and seem determined not to return to it — cannot all these elements create the necessary conditions for the appearance of a political system so similar to that of the Communist nations that it would be pointless to call it by a different name? This reservation explains the question mark that appears in the title of this chapter.

The practical value of the preceding considerations is obvious. A policy designed to face the *Communist* challenge should set itself only limited goals, such as the containment of Communist expansion, the relaxation of its most obvious rigidities, the stimulation of national differences between the members of the camp. It cannot aim at changing the basic character of the regime. But this is precisely what it is possible to hope for in Cuba if our analysis is correct. Besides geographic circumstances, the character of the ruling elite is also a factor. No one will doubt that if, instead of Castro and his followers of the July 26 Movement, "thoroughly conscious and devoted communists trained and steeled by the experience of stubborn revolutionary struggle" governed Cuba, one would probably have to give up that hope, too.

EPILOGUE

Evidence of Castro's dissatisfaction with the state of his relations with the Soviet Union mounted throughout 1966,[1] culminating in his speech of March 13, 1967. This time the explicit victim of his verbal fury was the Venezuelan Communist Party (PCV), but the text of the speech makes it plain that the Soviets too were a target for his hostility.

Castro called the PCV Directorate "rightist," "vacillating," and "defeatist"—three of the worst epithets in revolutionary jargon. He criticized the Soviets because they had permitted diplomatic contacts with Venezuela and had established trade relations with Colombia[2] despite the fact that guerrilla movements were operating in both countries. And so that there could be no doubt about the object of his attack, he stated in reference to the differences that had developed in Eastern Europe over West Germany's new Eastern policy,

. . . while some are condemned for restoring relations with Federal Germany, a crowd is running about in search of relations with oligarchies of the Leoni and Co. type. A position of principle must be held in Asia and also in Latin America.[3]

The extent of his dissatisfaction was revealed not only in these criticisms and accusations but also in his revelations about the internal disagreements within the Latin American Communist movement. Castro read a document he had received in June of 1966 from

[1] See Castro's speeches: *Verde Olivo*, August 7, 1966; *Bohemia*, September 2, 1966; *Granma*, October 2, 1966; *Granma*, January 3, 1967; also, *Granma's* editorial on the anniversary of the Russian Revolution, November 7, 1966, and the speech of the Cuban delegate at the Congress of the Communist Party of Bulgaria (*Granma*, November 17, 1966).

[2] Castro speech of March 13, 1967, in *Verde Olivo*, March 26, 1967. Earlier, in January, when *Granma* reported the Chilean-Soviet commercial agreement, it quoted Castro's point of view in expressing its disapproval of Soviet conduct (see *Le Monde*, February 14, 1967).

[3] Castro speech of March 13, 1967, *op. cit.*

242

Fabricio Ojeda, a Venezuelan guerrilla leader who was killed shortly after writing it. Ojeda informed Castro that both the Central Committee and the Political Bureau of the PCV had fallen into the hands of those who wanted to negotiate with Leoni's administration. Since the Political Bureau controlled the financial resources of the guerrillas, these groups were now threatened with complete termination of economic aid. Ojeda also claimed that the true purpose of the new "line" adopted by the PCV, and by implication other Latin American Communist parties, amounted to a suspension of the guerrilla challenge: the Communists proposed to turn instead to the use of persuasion and political methods. According to Ojeda, this was a new "twist" (*viraje*), that is, "the start of a new tactical phase, in which instead of combining every form of struggle, action by the guerrillas and the UTC [Tactical Combat Units] will be suspended. . . ."[4]

Castro justified his attacks and revelations on the grounds that he was forced to answer accusations made against him by the PCV.[5] But it would be naïve to believe his explanation. True, Castro's conflicts with the Venezuelan Party had been going on for some time.[6] It is also true that when, in March, Leoni indicated that he might go before the United Nations to charge Cuba with instigating violence in Venezuela, the PCV's statements on the subject must have provoked the wrath of the Cuban leader. But even in view of all

4 *Ibid.* Since the appearance of guerrilla movements in some Latin American countries the Communists have claimed to be in favor of both the peaceful and the violent way of revolution. I consider this position a ruse adopted to deflect the guerrilla challenge to the Communists. Ojeda spoke only of the PCV and made no mention of the Latin American Communist parties as a group. The latter have not specifically proposed "to turn instead to the use of persuasion and political methods" but are advocating both the peaceful and the violent way. Ojeda concluded that the PCV was "twisting" this line in order to reject the guerrilla, or violent, method. I am extending his conclusion to refer to the other Latin American Communist parties as well.

5 Dr. Julio Iribarren Borges, former social security director of Venezuela and brother of the Venezuelan Foreign Minister, Ignacio Iribarren Borges, was kidnapped in Caracas and found dead two days later. A representative of the Venezuelan Armed Forces of Liberation in Cuba, Elias Manuit Camero, ascribed this act to his organization (*Granma*, March 6, 1967). The PCV rejected the "revolting crime" and reproached *Granma* for printing such "absurdities." Castro's speech was in response to the many statements by the PCV.

6 *Le Monde* reported the polemics between the PCV and Castro on March 11, 17, 18, and 22, 1967. On March 18 *Le Monde* published the PCV's answer to Fidel in which they rejected his pretensions to leadership of the Latin American Communist movement. Douglas Bravo, a Venezuelan guerrilla leader supported by Fidel, was expelled from the PCV (Havana Radio, April 22, 1967).

this, it is doubtful that Castro's vehemence of the 13th would have been so aggressive if the Cuban-Soviet commercial treaty for 1967 had been satisfactory. That it was not satisfactory was demonstrated by the brevity of the Cuban announcement concerning it. The press mentioned the treaty only when it reported the return of the functionary who had signed it in Moscow.[7]

The foregoing are only a few of the indications of high tensions in Cuban-Soviet relations and, therefore, in the internal revolutionary process. It would seem, then, that those who observe a "growing accommodation" in such relations,[8] or "the settling down into middle-aged respectability"[9] of the revolution have, at the very least, been somewhat premature in their judgments.

Since the revolution has passed its eighth anniversary without Castro's power being seriously threatened, and since Cuba's economic and military dependence on the Soviet Union are obvious, why is it not possible to speak in terms of "accommodations" or "*embourgeoisements*"? One of the objectives of this book has been the attempt to answer this question. A brief reference to the actual situation may help to clarify the difficulties of attempting a definitive answer at this time.

The most extraordinary phenomenon of Cuba's present situation is the reappearance of "Guevarism,"[10] now embellished with more ideological pretensions, probably because Castro has had the help of the French Marxist Régis Debray.[11] Of course the regime does not call it "Guevarism." In Cuba it is referred to as "Our Path," and it is based not on the teachings of the missing Che Guevara but on the "profound revolutionary ideas expounded by Fidel: the simultaneous construction of socialism and communism."[12]

[7] *Granma*, February 3, 1967. The Soviet press, on the other hand, reported the commercial treaty in some detail (*Izvestiya*, February 4, 1967; *CDSP*, Vol. XIX, No. 5 [February 22, 1967], p. 27).

[8] Daniel Tretiak, *Cuba and the Soviet Union: The Growing Accommodation* (Santa Monica, Calif.: The Rand Corporation, RM-4935-PR, July 1966).

[9] "To Fidel with Fertilizer," *The Economist*, January 7, 1967.

[10] My reference to Guevarism has nothing to do with the publication in Cuba of a letter attributed to Guevara (Havana Radio, April 17, 1967). Claude Julien of *Le Monde*, who was then in Cuba, seems to accept the authenticity of the document (*AFP*, April 28, 1967). But neither the document nor Julien's opinion about its authenticity makes me doubt the interpretation of Che's disappearance that I have given in Chapter 9.

[11] "Interview with Régis Debray," *Granma*, February 1, 1967. I have not yet seen the last work by Debray, *Revolution in the Revolution*, published recently in Havana.

[12] Report by Lionel Soto to the XIV National Assembly of the Schools for Revolutionary Instruction, *Granma*, November 28, 1966. The slogan for this Assembly was "The most important thing is to develop our own path."

One cannot yet elaborate the program implicit in "Our Path," although certain things are clear: inside Cuba, it means opposition to the introduction of material incentives in the economy and the use of money as a means of exchange; it singles out "bureaucratism" as the worst enemy of the revolution and warns that if the Communist Party is unable to vanquish this enemy "the Party will end up by bureaucratizing itself." It recommends an infallible defense against "bureaucratism": "Fidel's style . . . of working on the ground farm by farm, analyzing each problem . . . orienting, discussing, talking . . ."[13]

In relation to world revolution, "Our Path" implies a new definition of communism. Being a Communist no longer depends on having Marxist-Leninist ideas or on being a militant in a party of that name. A Communist will have to be an armed revolutionary fighter, "and whoever is not a revolutionary fighter cannot be called a Communist."[14] The analogies between this position and Guevara's stance of 1965 are evident. The reappearance of this theme must have some significance. In the first place, both "Guevarism" and today's "Fidelism" are expressions of discontent with the Soviet Union and indicate the obduracy of the differences between the Cubans and the Soviets. There are many reasons for these differences, but the most important is the inability of the Soviet Union, whether deliberate or imposed by its politico-military weaknesses, either to guarantee to protect Cuba against the United States or to fulfill any such guarantee. As long as this situation remains unaltered, it is unrealistic to anticipate an easing of tensions.

Second, "Guevarism" had a strong ideological component. But "Fidelism"—as we know and as was confirmed by Guevara's sacrifice in 1965—places its emphasis on power. Therefore, its most bitter conflicts with the Soviets are on the questions of economic and military aid and especially on the question of how the Party functions in Cuba.[15] The Soviet Union has apparently decided to attempt

[13] About "Our Path," see *Granma*'s editorials, February 27, 28, and March 1, 4, 1967. The fight against "bureaucratism" is so acute that Castro characterized one article in *Granma* as "idiocies of our irresponsible bureaucracy" (*Granma*, February 24, 1967). This hard language had far-reaching repercussions. In March the Minister of the Interior Commerce fired his Vice-Ministers, cut the personnel of the department to 87 employees, and handed the building over to the Department of Education (*Verde Olivo*, March 12, 1967).

[14] Castro speech of March 13, 1967, *op. cit.*

[15] The regime's most important support comes from the Armed Forces. But here, too, the Soviets can exert their influence only through the Party. According to official sources, the building of the Party in the Armed Forces has been completed (*Granma*, December 29, 1966).

to limit Castro's power through the Party organization.[16] But the PCC still plays a secondary role in Cuba,[17] and the directing organs remain solidly in Castro's hands. However, given the might of the Soviet Union and the powerful role assigned to the Party in Communist ideology, Castro cannot afford to tolerate any move that would make the Party *apparat* stronger. Furthermore, up until now Castro's challenges to the Soviets have been excused. But his choosing to publicize the conflicts within the Latin American Communist movement (or creating the OLAS, or criticizing the establishment of Soviet commercial treaties with Latin American countries and the differences between Soviet policy in East Europe and Latin America, and so on) appears as a serious attempt to wrest Communist leadership in Latin America from the Soviets, thereby threatening the essential objectives of Soviet foreign policy.[18] It is difficult to see how the CPSU can continue to exempt Fidel from the obligations imposed on him by his dependency on the U.S.S.R. As we see, Castro has undertaken a new dispute with the Soviets under conditions even more difficult than those prevailing during earlier disputes. What forces can he depend upon other than his indomitable energy? It does not seem likely that he can rely on the Chinese. True, they agreed to augment the quota of rice for Cuba after the acute crisis of 1966;[19] but they did not re-establish their former cordial relationship with Castro. Possibly the internal difficulties created by the cultural revolution had something to do with this. But as Ernst Halperin has observed, the fundamental reason for this loss of cordiality is that in Latin America the Chinese "have concentrated their organizational effort on the small and sterile Communist parties . . . while neglecting the far more dynamic 'Castroist'

[16] The Soviets seldom mention Castro, but they never forget the PCC. See the report about the commercial treaty with Cuba in *Izvestiya*, February 4, 1967 (*CDSP*, Vol. XIX, No. 5 [February 22, 1967], p. 27), and the speech by A. N. Shelepin at the Cuban Embassy in Moscow, *Pravda*, January 3, 1967 (*CDSP*, Vol. XIX, No. 1 [January 25, 1967], p. 26).

[17] As far as I have been able to determine, the Central Committee has had no sessions or made any decisions since October 1965. We know of two resolutions issued by the Politburo—one naming Jorge Risquet Minister of Labor (*Granma*, January 24, 1967) and another suspending the publication of *Cuba Socialista* (February 1967).

[18] On their policy in Latin America, see Herbert S. Dinerstein, "Soviet Policy in Latin America," *American Political Science Review*, Vol. LXI, No. 1 (March 1967), pp. 80–90.

[19] Economic agreement with the Chinese (*Granma*, May 27, 1966). Castro told the journalist Georgie Anne Geyer, "The amount of rice China did not send was really very small" (*Miami Herald*, July 7, 1966).

groups."[20] The ridicule that Castro heaped on the Latin American "Stalinists" when he took power and declared himself "socialist" created a hostility that persisted as anti-Castroism even after the Latin Americans had turned pro-Chinese. This can be seen in the political resolutions taken at the First Congress of the Chilean Revolutionary Communist Party, which is pro-Chinese.[21]

Castro has attempted to form a Cuba–North Vietnam–North Korea axis to offset his isolation.[22] But the Vietnamese have demonstrated no enthusiasm for this idea in spite of the unshakable support Castro has given them.[23] As for the Koreans, after the gratitude they exhibited at the Kremlin when signing a new commercial treaty, it is doubtful that they would risk anything so valuable as Soviet support for the sake of cooperation with faraway Cuba.[24]

Outside of Cuba, then, Castro can count on only the Latin American guerrillas, the majority of whom reaffirmed their support of Castro after the March 13 speech.[25] But so far their influence is negligible. It is still too early as of this writing (May 1967) to tell if the recent flare-up of guerrilla activity in Bolivia—including the capture there of the Fidelista ideologist Régis Debray—or the capture by the Venezuelan government of Cuban officers who landed on the Venezuelan coast (later confirmed by Havana)[26] presage any serious intensification of guerrilla activity.

Inside Cuba, it is difficult to measure the degree of cohesion of the forces that support the regime. In February, *Cuba Socialista* announced the end of its publication. The suspension, decided upon by the Politburo, was explained by the necessity to await the de-

[20] Ernst Halperin, "Peking and the Latin American Communists," *China Quarterly*, No. 29 (January–March 1967), pp. 111–154, at p. 154.

[21] *Peking Review*, Vol. 9, No. 35 (August 26, 1966), pp. 24–26. In January 1967 the Chinese were still rejecting "the line of not relying on the masses but attempting to win an easy victory by roving guerrilla actions of a handful of people" (*Hsinhua Selected News Item*, Hong Kong, January 9, 1967).

[22] "Commentaries: A Transcendental Visit," *Cuba Socialista*, December 1966, commenting on the visit by Dorticós and Raúl Castro to Hanoi and Pyongyang. Also, "Interview with Régis Debray," *Granma*, February 1, 1967.

[23] Compare the communiqués on both visits in *Cuba Socialista*, December 1966.

[24] *Izvestiya*, March 4, 1967 (*CDSP*, Vol. XIX, No. 9 [March 22, 1967], pp. 15–16).

[25] Support by the National Liberation Army of Colombia (*Granma*, March 30, 1967); by the National Liberation Army of Peru (Havana Radio, April 1, 1967); and by Cesar Montes, the leader of the Guatemalan guerrillas (*Granma*, April 3, 1967).

[26] *The New York Times*, May 19, 1967.

cisions of the Party's First Congress on "theoretical, strategic, and tactical problems of the revolutionary movement in the world and on various problems of the construction of socialism and communism." This could indicate the existence of internal rifts. It would seem that the "old" Communists, even after so many defeats, have not abated their opposition to Castro.[27] But the fact is that in the case of *Cuba Socialista* the "old" Communists lost one of the few propaganda media in which they retained some influence.

I have no evidence that the remaining Fidelistas object to the current position of their leader. Raúl Castro may be a possible exception, but it is still too early to determine the real meaning of the several contradictory statements about him.[28] As to the others of the faithful, in view of their political origins one cannot assume that they will falter in a conflict with the Soviets. On the other hand, this does not imply that I believe they are as totally loyal as they were during the victorious years. The leader's mistakes since 1963 and the inevitable exhaustion caused by more than ten years of continuous fighting may have produced in some of them a growing concern about their future. Unfortunately, it is difficult to see where they can turn for advice or help.

These pages must go to print when the historic drama of the Cuban Revolution has not reached its conclusion, and possibly when it is approaching one of its most exciting episodes. "The world of politics," Almond and Powell have written, "has never waited

[27] Although the influence of the "old" Communists is negligible, they do not seem, at least, to support Castro's views. For example, Carlos Rafael Rodríguez, after declaring, "The present position of Cuba is to give absolute preference to moral incentives in production," added, in response to a direct question, "Perfect unanimity neither can nor does exist" (*Marcha*, December 9, 1966, as reported in the *Monthly Review*, Vol. 18, No. 9 [February 1967], pp. 5–6). He also said that this position was adopted by "Fidel, Dorticós, and Che." Dorticós, then, is continuing to ascend in the hierarchy. Bernheim wrote, and I agree with him: "It is just possible that Moscow is trying to restrict Castro's influence . . . and to shift more responsibility to President Dorticós." Roger Bernheim, "Cuba," *Swiss Review of World Affairs*, Vol. XVI, No. 7 (October 1966), pp. 12–17, and No. 8 (November 1966), pp. 9–12.

[28] *Granma*, March 24, 1967, mentioned the Vice-Minister, Juan Almeida, as Minister of the Armed Forces ad interim without any explanation about Raúl Castro. At this writing, the whereabouts of Raúl are not known. *Le Monde* reported, on March 25, 1967, that he was in the Soviet Union taking military courses. But two days later *Granma* reported that Raúl was harvesting sugarcane with his brother. Then, on March 29, *Le Monde* said that Raúl had departed for Moscow two days earlier "according to a very credible source." To date, there has been no official statement on the subject.

for the observer to finish his quiet contemplation."[29] The observer, then, must take the risk of being confounded by future events not only because of his obvious personal limitations but because of the intrinsic nature of contemporary affairs.

[29] G. A. Almond and G. B. Powell, Jr., *Comparative Politics: A Developmental Approach* (Boston: Little Brown, 1966).

INDEX